D0071710

Figure 3.3. Tannenbaum's Who, What, and How of Giftedness

Who?	What?	How?	Examples
Producer of	Thoughts	Creatively	Novelists, artists, composers
	Thoughts	Proficiently	Mathematicians, computer programmers, editors
Producer of	Tangibles	Creatively	Inventors, architects, design engineers
	Tangibles	Proficiently	Diamond cutters, machinists, art forgers
Performer of	Staged Artistry	Creatively	Musicians, conductors, dancers, poetry readers, and actors who "breathe life" into the works of others
	Staged Artistry	Proficiently	Musicians, conductors, dancers, and the like who faithfully translate and reproduce the works of others
Performer of	Human Services	Creatively	Innovative teachers, political leaders, and researchers in medicine, education, and the social sciences
	Human Services	Proficiently	Successful teachers, physicians, and administrators who follow guidelines and procedures faithfully and successfully

The first question focuses on *who*: Is the gifted person a producer or a performer? The second question asks *what* is produced or performed: Does the gifted person produce thoughts or tangibles, or perform on-stage artistry or human services? The third question asks *how* persons demonstrate their giftedness: Are they creative or highly proficient? Examples of gifted professionals in each of the eight areas helps clarify Tannenbaum's model of giftedness.

Also, Tannenbaum emphasizes five factors that aid eventual giftedness and success: (1) high general intelligence, (2) strong special abilities, (3) supportive non-intellectual traits (e.g., personality, motivation), (4) supportive and challenging circumstance (e.g., family and school environments), and (5) chance, which he calls "the smile of good fortune at critical periods of life."[12]

Regarding chance, Tannenbaum often cites Atkinson, who argued that all human behavior and accomplishment can be ascribed to "two crucial rolls of the dice over which no individual exerts any personal control: the accidents of birth and background. One roll of the dice determines an individual's heredity; the other his formative environment."[13] As easy examples, children have no control over their genetics, socio-economic level, the parenting practices used on them, or the availability of G/T programs or other fortunate opportunities.

General Gifts and Specific Talents: François Gagné

François Gagné's Differentiated Model of Giftedness and Talent emphasizes a distinction between *gifts* versus *talents*.[14]

In Gagné's view, *giftedness* refers to innate, untrained, and spontaneously expressed natural abilities, also called *aptitudes* or *gifts*. He identifies four types of gifts: *intellectual* (e.g., reasoning ability, judgment, accumulated knowledge, memory), *creative* (e.g., imagination, inventiveness, originality in art), *socioaffective* (e.g., empathy, tact, social perceptiveness), and *sensorimotor* (e.g., coordination, endurance). To qualify for a G/T program, at least one gift (aptitude) should place a student in the top 10% of his or her peers.

Talents, however, are learned capabilities—systematically developed abilities and skills. Seven fields or categories of talents include academics, technology, business, sports, the arts, social action (e.g., public office), and leisure (e.g., games). To qualify for a G/T program, at least one field of learned ability, skill, or knowledge should place a student in the top 10% of peers who have been active in the same field or fields.

Intrapersonal and environmental *catalysts* help learned talents emerge from innate gifts. Intrapersonal catalysts that aid talent development include motivation (e.g., needs, interests, values), volition (e.g., will-power, effort, persistence), self-management (e.g., work habits, initiative, concentration), personality (e.g., temperament, self-awareness, self-esteem, adaptability), and physical qualities (e.g., health, physical characteristics, handicaps).

Environmental catalysts that aid talent development include one's milieu (e.g., family, social and cultural settings), important persons (e.g., parents, teachers, mentors, peers), provisions (e.g., available programs, activities, services), and events (e.g., awards, encounters, accidents).

Like Tannenbaum, Gagné emphasized another important catalyst that determines success and recognition: *chance*. He also cites Atkinson's popular quote.[15]

Conclusions

You have just reviewed leading definitions and theories of *gifted and talented*. You may be most comfortable with the personal definition with which you started, perhaps adjusted slightly by your local school policies and school district's selection procedures.

Legal Problems

Legal difficulties in gifted education center on the following 10 issues and their sometimes arguable resolutions.[16]

(1) *Providing gifted programs or suitable instruction (free of charge).* "The federal Constitution does not provide a right to an education, much less a right to a gifted education."[17] Pennsylvania, New York, and Connecticut courts ruled that non-disabled students are entitled to a free public education, not an individualized or gifted education program. Further, gifted students are not recognized as "exceptional children" with a right to an individualized education. Failure to provide gifted programs is not discrimination.

More positively, Ohio's highest court "ordered a complete overhaul of the funding system," partly because: (1) gifted students in Ohio are under-identified, and (2) "state funding...for gifted education is inadequate," especially in smaller, poorer districts.[18] The Pennsylvania Supreme Court demanded that a district individualize (i.e., accelerate) gifted students (e.g., in reading and math), as well as provide a more general enrichment program, in accord with the important *Centennial School District v. Pennsylvania Department of Education*, which requires an "appropriate" education for gifted students. However, because of obvious costs, a Pennsylvania court would not authorize "individual tutors or exclusive individual programs outside or beyond the district's existing regular...curricular offerings."[19]

(2) *District policies on early school admission to kindergarten or first grade.* Importantly, state decisions traditionally defer to local school district policies on most issues—and districts have wide discretion. In an absolutely bizarre Wisconsin case, a precocious four-year-old was denied admission to kindergarten—because the district had no special programs for gifted students. (Now wait a minute. If....) In a similar Texas case—and despite state

gifted legislation—a school district denied admission of a bright five-year-old to first grade because district policy required children to be six. (And who cares if the child's mental age was six, seven, or 10?)

Regarding early admission, a New York court would not "substitute the judgment of a justly proud parent for that of experienced educators."[20] Curiously, the court also suggested that the district's policies might be reviewed and revised.

(3) *Eligibility and identification procedures.* In one unsuccessful case, a student who failed to reach the 130 IQ criterion set by the state of Pennsylvania was judged by the court to be fairly excluded, because "the testing procedure is rationally related to the objective of identifying gifted students."[21] (Note that the girl might have had other strong gifts and/or a paltry IQ of 129½.) Conceded the unhelpful judge, "This is not to say that one may not question the wisdom of…policies [that] have a deleterious effect upon students who are not deemed gifted."[22]

(4) *College instructors, private tutors, private schools.* Despite an IEP (Individualized Education Plan) that recommended a gifted student take courses at Geneva College in Beaver Falls, Pennsylvania, a court concluded that the district was not obligated to pay for tuition and transportation. Another Pennsylvania court, citing the landmark *Centennial* "appropriate education" decision (item 1, above), similarly ruled that districts are not obligated to pay for "college level instruction, private tutoring, and/or education beyond the curriculum offerings of the District."[23]

Also in Pennsylvania, and despite *Centennial*, a district was not required to pay for a private school nor an out-of-state school placement for a gifted student. (Gosh, what a surprise!)

In a New York Vietnam-era case, and during a financial crisis, a court denied a group of parents the right to free transportation to private schools for their gifted children. But the sympathetic judge also lamented that "Congressional committees don't bat an eyelash [at the pitiful federal funding for the gifted] while pouring untold billions…into the Indochina rathole."[24]

The parents felt slightly better.

(5) *Under-representation and racial balance in programs for gifted students.*
An on-going—and unresolved—difficulty in gifted programs is
equal representation of racial and ethnic minority students. To
make selection more fair, court desegregation orders have forced
school districts to use an assortment of identification strategies—
for example, a variety of standardized and non-standardized
assessments; grades; interviews; and teacher, parent, peer, and self
nominations.[25] In 1991, Florida allowed school districts to vary
from the state-mandated 130 IQ criterion for gifted programs.
So Hillsborough county lowered its IQ requirement to 115 and
allowed programs to also consider academic achievement and
even personality (presumably interest and motivation).

Incidentally, Susanne Richert achieved racial balance by creating
local norms for *each* subgroup of students for *each* data source,
stating that high performance on "any one source should be sufficient to include a student in a program."[26]

The current legal resolution is a non-resolution. According to
Zirkel, the courts have decided that the defendant school districts have achieved Fourteenth Amendment requirements of
desegregated status based on their "good-faith, affirmative efforts
in the admissions process."[27] Further, even the Office of Civil
Rights concluded that racial under-representation does not violate the equal protection statements in the Civil Rights Act.

As a no-win complication, districts face the "risk of reverse discrimination suits if they move too far to resolve the
under-representation issue."[28] Agreed Karnes and Marquardt,
"School districts need to make certain that when they institute
measures to increase minority participation, the procedures are
academically sound and can withstand a [reverse discrimination]
legal challenge" from irritated, middle-class, White parents of
excluded children.[29]

Meanwhile, minorities remain underrepresented.

(6) *Individualization of instruction for gifted students who have a disability.*
Happily, individualized instruction—including advanced instruction— for gifted students with a disability is mandated by
the Individuals with Disabilities Education Act. It's a terrific IDEA.
However, such "double-labeled" or "twice-exceptional" students

continue to be underrepresented in G/T programs. Says Zirkel, hearing officer decisions sometimes have supported district claims that particular students with disabilities did *not* meet eligibility criteria for their G/T programs. For example, in Pennsylvania, a federal court would not order an evaluation of giftedness for a learning disabled child "because the evidence was insufficient to trigger the identification process under the then applicable state regulations."[30]

Zirkel named this a "stingy trend."

(7) *Eligibility of home-schooled children to participate in public school gifted programs.* Remarkably, home schooling has never led to court cases or even due process hearings.[31] Nonetheless, there are ongoing issues, apparently debated—with or without success—between parents and local school or district officials:

- If a school has a gifted program, can the home-schooled gifted child attend that program?

- Is the child entitled to *any* instructional assistance from the G/T teacher?

- If a district provides transportation to gifted programs, is a home-schooled child entitled to both the transportation and participation?

- If the local or state budget includes funds for G/T program materials and equipment, is the home-schooled child entitled to a prorated share?

- Can the home-schooled child participate in field experiences or other extracurricular G/T activities sponsored by the school district?

(8) *Legal status of teacher certification in gifted education.* Karnes and Marquardt describe two cases in which G/T certification meant job security. The West Virginia Court of Appeals reversed the (curious) decision of a school district to hire a person with no G/T certification and no G/T teaching experience (probably somebody's friend) and forced the district to hire the certified and experienced G/T teacher who had applied for the same G/T teaching job. Also in West Virginia, a court awarded a G/T

teaching position to an inexperienced teacher with G/T certification. She replaced a just-hired and experienced teacher of the gifted who did not have the G/T certification.

In Pennsylvania, which did not require G/T certification, a teacher of the gifted was retained while more senior teachers lost their jobs. The gifted teacher had done a good job, and the district superintendent concluded that removing her was "educationally unsound." But the Pennsylvania supreme court—after seven years of litigation—ruled that the G/T teacher must be replaced by a teacher with more seniority.

The reverse happened in a similar Pennsylvania case. The low-seniority but experienced gifted teacher held certification as a "program specialist." With pending staff reductions, a more senior person wanted the G/T job. The court used the "program specialist" certification to justify retaining the experienced teacher of the gifted.

(9) *Tort liability.* Field trips, summer programs, and transportation present opportunities for severe injury or even death. Note that a child's gifted status is unimportant in such disputes. Karnes and Marquardt describe several seemingly simple circumstances that led to death or severe injury.[32] Two gifted children drowned at a field trip to a beach. A TV set fell from its wheeled cart and killed a seven-year-old gifted girl who was retrieving it from a storeroom. Four children were severely burned by chemicals while making sparklers in a lab experiment; one set of parents won an eight million dollar settlement.

One court case debated *when* the school district's responsibility began. An 11-year-old girl was instructed to be at an elementary school at 6:55 A.M. to await transportation to another elementary school for a special arts program for the gifted. One morning, she was attacked and raped. The Florida Court of Appeals ruled that the district had a "general duty of care."

(10) *Fraud and misrepresentation by private schools that claim to offer special services for gifted students.* According to Karnes and Marquardt in 2003, a 1985 court case was not yet settled(!). A private school had advertised that its teachers were certified in gifted education, its programs were individualized, and its curriculum was designed

for gifted students. Many parents disagreed and filed charges against the school's owner.

As a guide, Karnes and Marquardt recommend that parents ask these types questions about the gifted offerings of a private or even public school: Do students in gifted programs actually receive differentiated instruction? If a state requires gifted certification, are all teachers in the gifted program certified? They also recommend comparing written and oral claims to the services actually offered.

Handling Disputes

If parents of gifted students have problems with their local school or district, gifted education legal experts Karnes and Marquardt recommend that parents first register their complaint via (1) informal discussions with school and school district personnel.[33] If unsuccessful, they might progress to more time-consuming and expensive (2) informal mediation at the state level (available in 21 states; consult your state board of education); (3) due process hearings (available in 26 states), which includes presenting the complaint at a meeting, which can include school personnel and lawyers, before a hearing review officer, who alone makes a decision based on that state's laws; (4) state court; and perhaps even (5) federal court. Pursuing the last two options will require lots of money and several years.

Zirkel pessimistically noted that gifted students receive little or no legal help from either state or federal sources[34]—that is, unless they are both gifted *and* have a disability (Individual with Disabilities Education Act) or are both gifted *and* a member of a racial/ethnic minority (Office of Civil Rights).

State and Federal Financial Assistance and Legislation

Regarding funding, there is an Office of Gifted and Talented in the U.S. Department of Education. However, it does not fund city or state G/T programs. The federal *Jacob K. Javits Gifted and Talented Students Education Act* of 1988 largely supports G/T research and national leadership activities, such as that conducted by Renzulli's NRCG/T.

By 2002, a slight majority of states (32 of 52, but not the District of Columbia and Puerto Rico) had passed legislation on behalf of the gifted regarding school services—which does not necessarily reflect actual practice at the school level. A slight majority of states (not the same states, but still 32 of 52) dispersed at least some funds to district or school gifted programs.[35]

Is there a legal right for a *non*-disabled gifted student to have an enriched and/or accelerated education appropriate to the students' needs? In many states, no. Certainly not under federal law. State laws usually evolve around the definition and identification of gifted and talented students. Only a few states specify the types of services that are—or should be—provided to gifted students (e.g., creativity and other thinking skills; library, computer, and other research skills; advanced curricula).

As a final exposure to reality, Russo, Harris, and Ford astutely observed that "supporters see gifted education as a *right*, the unaffected see it as a *privilege*, and opponents see it as *superfluous*."[36]

Summary

- There are no universally accepted theories or definitions of *gifted and talented*. The formal definition accepted by a state, district, or school will guide selection procedures, influence the content of the program, and perhaps discriminate against subgroups of gifted students.

- Students selected—and labeled—as gifted will experience improved self-esteem and motivation. Students not selected may miss valuable opportunities and suffer reduced self-esteem.

- No accepted term differentiates students who barely meet admission criteria from extraordinarily brilliant or talented students.

- Instead of *gifted and talented*, some G/T leaders prefer the terms *able learner* or *potentially gifted* or refer to *gifted behaviors*, not *gifted students*.

- The influential five-part federal definition includes general intellectual ability, ability in a specific academic area, creativity, artistic ability, and leadership capability.

- Joseph Renzulli's National Research Center on the Gifted and Talented researches central G/T problems and topics. His three-ring model emphasizes high creativity, high motivation, and at least above-average ability—which are characteristics of creatively productive people.

- Both Howard Gardner and Robert Sternberg warn against the short-sightedness of viewing intelligence as a single IQ number. Gardner's multiple-intelligence theory proposes eight types of intelligence: linguistic, logical-mathematical, spatial, musical, bodily-kinesthetic, interpersonal, intrapersonal, and naturalist.

- Sternberg's theory of successful intelligence includes analytic (academic ability), synthetic (creativity), and practical (applying analytic and synthetic abilities) giftedness.

- Taylor's multiple-talent totem pole concept illustrates that most students can be at least above-average in one or more talent areas. His totem poles emphasize the difficulty of defining giftedness.

- Tannenbaum's model of giftedness includes the eight categories created by *who, what,* and *how* questions. A person may be a producer of thoughts or tangibles (creatively or proficiently), or a performer of staged artistry or human services (creatively or proficiently). Tannenbaum noted five factors that aid success: high intelligence, strong special abilities, supportive traits (e.g., motivation), supportive and challenging circumstances, and chance—which includes heredity and early environment.

- Gagné differentiated between innate natural gifts (four types) versus learned talents (seven types). Intrapersonal catalysts (e.g., motivation, self-management skills, personality) and environmental catalysts (persons, available programs/activities, events) aid talent development. Like Tannenbaum, Gagné noted the role of chance in high-level success.

- Legal problems have centered on these 10 issues:

  1. A right to gifted programs or suitable instruction (free of charge)

  2. Early admission to kindergarten or first grade

  3. Eligibility and identification procedures

  4. Free college, private tutors, or private schools

  5. Minority under-representation

  6. Under-representation of students with disabilities

7. Eligibility of home-schooled students to participate in public school gifted programs

8. Legal status of teacher certification in gifted education

9. Tort liability

10. Misrepresentation by private schools that claim to offer services for the gifted

- Disputes should be pursued at the school level, then proceed, in order, to mediation at the state level, due process hearings, state court, then perhaps federal court.

- The Office of Gifted and Talented funds national research and leadership activities, not city or state G/T programs.

- Thirty-two states have passed legislation on behalf of the gifted. A slightly different 32 states provide some funds to district or school programs.

- Gifted students without a disability are not promised federal educational help. State laws evolve around definition and identification procedures.

4
Identification of Gifted and Talented Students

An explicit definition of giftedness is keystone for the
development of programs for the gifted...because of the
close link that must exist between the definition
and the identification system.

~ John F. Feldhusen and Fathi A. Jarwan

[*Scene*: *Laboratory of Dr. Frankenstein. The Frankenstein monster is strapped to his table as Kool-Aid® bubbles mysteriously over Bunsen burners. Dr. Frankenstein is discussing the giftedness of his creation with assistant Igor.*]

Dr. Frankenstein: Well, Igor, he looks great! Those insightful eyes! That brilliant intellect! He's ready for Paramount Pictures® anytime!

Igor (hesitantly): I don't know, boss. He's got eyes, but I think I'd worry about his intelligence!

Dr. Frankenstein: What's this? A hint of doubt? Very well, my skeptical friend, we'll evaluate just how brilliant and gifted he is!

Igor: But how will you evaluate his giftedness? I mean, there are intelligence tests, achievement tests, creativity tests, nominations...

Dr. Frankenstein: We'll start with nominations. Take a memo: "I, Dr. Frankenstein, hereby nominate Monster as brilliantly gifted!" Now the intelligence tests. Monster, let's begin with math ability. What's 20 times 40? And what's 2 times 9?

Monster: EEGHUNH!! EEGHUNH!!

Dr. Frankenstein: Excellent! Excellent, Monster! Did you hear that, Igor? First he said 800 and then 18! Absolutely brilliant! Now, Monster, let's evaluate your knowledge of geography and world history. In what country would you find pyramids?

Monster: EEGHUNH!! EEGHUNH!!

Dr. Frankenstein: Excellent again, my brilliant fellow! Egypt, of course! Now what do you say, Igor?

Igor: But boss, I don't think he...

Dr. Frankenstein: No excuses, Igor. Now, Monster, let's evaluate your knowledge of American sayings. What must you do before you can walk?

Monster (beginning to grin): GROWWL!! GROWWL!!

Dr. Frankenstein: Crawl! Of course. A genius answer! And now, Monster, just one more. A test of your knowledge of world problems. What problems do London, Paris, and Washington D.C. have in common?

Monster (grinning from electrode to electrode): GROWWL!! GROWWL!!

Dr. Frankenstein: I rest my case, Igor! Another ingenious answer! Traffic crawls in all three cities!

Igor: But boss, he's just...

Dr. Frankenstein: I'm surprised at you Igor. A better man would admit he's wrong! I'm calling Paramount Studios right away! He can shuffle and growl with the best of them!

Igor (shaking his head): If you say so boss....

Identifying gifted students is, predictably, a can of worms. Two informed opinions are: (1) there may be as many identification strategies as there are programs, and (2) the ideal identification system has yet to be developed.

There are disagreements over both definitions of giftedness and selection criteria, which, when you think about it, mean about the same thing. The two most common selection methods, usually used together, are: (1) teacher recommendations, often with parent input, based on characteristics and behaviors of bright, fast-learning children; and (2) achievement and IQ scores. An IQ criterion is often a minimum IQ number (usually 125 or 130) or a fixed percentage of top IQ students (usually with minimums set at the 95th or 98th percentile, or even the 90th percentile).

Some enlightened programs select students with artistic, poetic/creative writing, or musical gifts, or even outstanding independent projects. Such students may or may not fit the "characteristics" and "achievement and IQ" criteria.

The U.S. Office [Department] of Education Definition

Many teachers of the gifted have taken one or more college courses in gifted education and are familiar with the federal definition quoted in Chapter 3. Such teachers will—or at least should—pay attention to all five categories of the U.S.O.E. definition: general intellectual ability, specific academic talent, creativity, leadership, and artistic talent (visual or performing arts). As we will see later, the Gifted Evaluation Scale was created specifically to help teachers identify capable students in the five U.S.O.E. categories.[1]

Multiple Criteria

Using several criteria to identify gifted students is logical, fair, and defensible. The multiple-criteria approach helps solve the long-standing problem of far too few minority and poor students being selected for gifted programs. Such students are likely to be missed when selection criteria are based strictly on IQ scores, grades, and achievement test scores.

In addition to ability and achievement scores, a good multi-factor screening procedure might include:[2]

- Nominations by teachers, parents, psychologists, counselors, and/ or peers.

- Teacher reports of each student's intellectual, social, and emotional functioning.

- Information about each student's motivation and preferred learning style(s).

- Information about each student's self-reported interests, values, attitudes toward school, and extracurricular activities.

- Parents' support for their child's participation.

A hypothetical danger is that using lots of criteria could lead to nominating everybody in the classroom, all of whom have some strength somewhere. Of course, an identification procedure that uses multiple criteria must be sufficiently restrictive to maintain program quality.

As one example, the state of Georgia originally had defined *giftedness* as surpassing a fixed IQ score. In 1994, influenced by Joseph

Renzulli, Georgia passed a bill requiring multiple-criteria identification. Teachers had proven that they could identify gifted children from every economic and cultural background by evaluating abilities, traits, and behaviors that reflect giftedness. The now-revised law in Georgia (HB 1768) includes meeting criteria in any three of four areas: (1) *mental ability*—intellectual ability above the 96th percentile; (2) *achievement*—a standardized achievement test score above the 90th percentile for the whole battery, or just math, or just reading, or a superior student product or performance; (3) *creativity*—a score above the 90th percentile on a creativity test or a creative characteristics inventory, or a superior evaluation of a creative student product or performance; and (4) *motivation*—as indicated by a GPA above 3.5, or a score above the 90th percentile on a motivation scale, or motivation ratings above the 90th percentile on a student product or performance.

Fortunately, some intelligent, creative, and enthusiastic children who did not meet the formal state criteria were admitted anyway by sensible and enthusiastic G/T staff, including school administrators.

Incidentally, note that a *multiple-criteria* ("either-or") strategy for identifying gifted students must not be a *multiple-hurdle* ("both-and") approach if a school district wants to reasonably include different kinds of gifted children. One Southwest elementary school required an IQ score of 130 (top 2.28%) *and* a standardized achievement test score above the 95th percentile; the two, when combined, constitute a formidable barrier. The achievement test criteria could be replaced instead by demonstrations of outstanding creativity (as defined in state regulations) or outstanding critical thinking or problem-solving ability (also as defined in state regulations).

Gifted program directors and administrators also should consider the following identification recommendations and issues:

1. Adopt a clear and broadly-defined definition of *giftedness*—one that assumes the use of multiple criteria and multiple varieties of giftedness.

2. Use separate and suitable evaluation procedures (tests, ratings, nominations, portfolios) for different areas of giftedness. Be sure that all procedures are reliable and valid.[3]

3. Base identification on gifted students' educational needs, not fixed program quotas.

4. Understand that giftedness can appear in different shapes and forms in different cultural or socio-economic groups.

5. Include *authentic assessments*—that is, examples of student work.

6. Include evaluations of student creativity and problem solving.

7. Focus on *including* students, not *excluding* them. A program that serves 15 or 20% of students, rather that 3 to 5%, would be considered inclusive. A greater variety of gifts and talents will be considered. More students will benefit from the program. Fewer parents will complain of their child's exclusion. Some G/T scholars refer to inclusive selection procedures as "casting a wide net."[4]

8. Continue over time to identify additional gifted students. There need not be a fixed identification deadline.

9. Continue to evaluate your identification procedures.

10. Some programs use a quota system to assure representation of poor and minority students, which also assures equal representation and fair treatment, along with avoiding charges of elitism and violating civil rights.

11. Identification information will help to better understand gifted students.

12. Identification information should help guide instruction—for example, with students who have specific talents or strong specific interests.

Intelligence Tests

Stanford-Binet Intelligence Scale

In Chapter 1, we briefly mentioned the *Stanford-Binet Intelligence Scale* and related its IQ scores to the normal distribution. Every school psychologist is trained to administer and interpret the Stanford-Binet and other IQ tests.

In 1986, the *Stanford-Binet Intelligence Scale, Form L-M* was revised and renormed, producing the *Stanford-Binet Intelligence Scale-Fourth Edition*. One advantage of the newer Fourth Edition is that it produces four *standard age scores* (consider them IQ scores) in the areas of *verbal reasoning, quantitative reasoning, visual/abstract reasoning,* and *short-term memory,* along with the overall IQ score.

73

However, the newer Stanford-Binet Fourth Edition brings with it two new disadvantages for evaluating the intelligence of gifted students. First, the upper limit of this newer test is around IQ 160. The rare child who might have scored IQ 170, 180, or 200+ on Form L-M obviously cannot do so on the S-B Fourth Edition. The older Form L-M essentially had no upper limit.

On the other hand, measuring such lofty IQ scores was not particularly reliable; a few chance errors dramatically lowered a person's final IQ score. Perhaps more important, even if sky-high IQ scores remained available, such IQs are now considered much less important than a student's reasoning ability, work habits, short-term memory (STM), and response to intervention (RTI).[5]

A second important difficulty is that Fourth Edition IQ scores average about 13.5 points *lower* than the earlier Form L-M.[6] Sometimes *much* lower. Research on the problem described three children who scored IQ 160, 160, and 144 on the older Form L-M. On the newer Fourth Edition, their respective IQ scores were 110, 121, and 112. At least two of these children—maybe all three of them—would not have met the minimum IQ criterion for many G/T programs.

It's obviously a lot more difficult to obtain a gifted score when evaluated with the *Stanford-Binet Intelligence Scale-Fourth Edition.*

Wechsler Intelligence Scale for Children (WISC)

With the *Wechsler Intelligence Scale for Children-Fourth Edition* (WISC-IV), scores on 10 specific tests combine to supply four subscale scores plus one Full Scale IQ score. If you remember your ability testing in school, you probably will recall (with a smile) the content of some of the tests. Specifically, *Verbal Comprehension* is evaluated with subtests titled Similarities, Vocabulary, and Comprehension. *Perceptual Reasoning* is measured by the subtests Block Design, Picture Concepts, and Matrix Reasoning. *Working Memory* includes Digit Span and Letter-Number Sequencing. *Processing Speed* is composed of Coding and Symbol Search.

The WISC-IV shows exactly the same two problems as the Stanford-Binet Fourth Edition. First, the highest possible IQ score on the WISC-IV is only about 155, which is considerably lower than the earlier WISC-Revised. Second, average IQ scores on the new WISC-IV run about five points lower than on the WISC-R. At higher levels—where bright children score—WISC-IV scores run eight or nine points lower than on the earlier WISC-R.

Tests that produce lower IQ scores—both the Stanford-Binet Fourth Edition and the WISC-IV—could underestimate a gifted child's need for accelerated school work, and perhaps exclude the child from a G/T program.

Group Intelligence Tests

Group intelligence tests are routinely administered in many schools. It's easy for the G/T committee to check the office file to find the school's highest IQ kids. Some prominent group intelligence tests, mentioned in Chapter 1, are the *Cognitive Abilities Test, Henmon-Nelson Test of Mental Ability, Kaufman Brief Intelligence Test, Kuhlman-Anderson Intelligence Tests, Otis-Lennon School Ability Test, School and College Ability Test,* and the *SRA Primary Mental Abilities Test.*

Despite their problems, the individually-administered Stanford-Binet and WISC tests are superior. Consider these weaknesses of group intelligence tests:

- Top scores are about IQ 135 or 140.

- Group tests are less reliable and less valid—in short, less accurate.

- They mainly evaluate verbal abilities; they favor good readers and discriminate against children who are non-verbally gifted (e.g., in math, art, creativity).

- At young ages (through about second grade), they favor students from homes with higher exposure to language (books, magazines, reading, conversation).

- They are likely to discriminate against students who speak a foreign language, an American minority dialect, or have a deficiency in English.[7]

- They are likely to discriminate against minority students and low socio-economic status students.

- They are likely to discriminate against students with language, speech, or hearing problems.[8]

- Unmotivated children are likely to produce low and inaccurate scores.

- Group tests were constructed for children in the *middle* section of the bell curve. At the top level, a few chance errors will dramatically lower a bright student's IQ score.

- With group tests, speed is an important factor, which is not true of the Stanford-Binet or WISC.

- Scores may be affected by many other factors, such as family stresses, slight illness, how well the students slept the night before, springtime allergies (which may require medication), room temperature, classroom noises or interruptions, or even what students ate for breakfast.

Two comments. First, an advantage of all intelligence tests—individual and group—is that they can identify the quietly invisible underachieving students whose classroom work and grades give no hint of their actual, unused intellectual capability. Second, a too-strong emphasis on IQ scores will risk missing students with other genuine gifts and talents—for example, in music, art, or creativity.

An Intelligence Continuum: Ruf's Five Categories

As we noted, the newest *Stanford-Binet Intelligence Scale-Fourth Edition* tops out at about IQ 160. The ceiling of the *Wechsler Intelligence Scale for Children-IV* is 155. And both tests produce lower IQ scores than their predecessors. Then how do we measure—that is, estimate—the IQs of persons who could score at higher levels? Maybe 180 or 200?

Deborah Ruf's solution takes the form of five levels of giftedness—with IQ scores measured by our modern, low-ceiling tests.[9] Each level includes: (1) the percentile range on standardized ability tests (whatever scores were available), (2) IQ test score range, and (3) the likely proportion of such students in the population. To help interpretation, note that test publishers and Ruf categorize high-scoring students—from low to high—as *Superior, Gifted,* or *Advanced.*

Level One Gifted

- Students who score in the 90th to 98th percentile on standardized tests
- Superior to moderately gifted on intelligence tests (approximate IQ score range 120-129)
- About the top one-third to one-fourth of students in a mixed-ability class
- Descriptive designation: *Moderately Gifted* (IQ 120-124) to *Gifted* (IQ 125-129)

Level Two Gifted

- Students who score in the 98th to 99th percentile on standardized tests
- Gifted, highly gifted, or very advanced on IQ tests (approximate IQ score range 130-135)
- About one to three students in a mixed-ability class
- Descriptive designation: *Highly Gifted*

Level Three Gifted

- Students in the 98th to 99th percentile on standardized tests
- Highly gifted, exceptionally gifted, or very advanced on IQ tests (approximate IQ score range 136-140)
- About one or two students per grade level (but more in high socio-economic areas)
- Descriptive designation: *Exceptionally Gifted*

Level Four Gifted

- Mainly 99th percentile on standardized tests
- Exceptionally to profoundly gifted or highly advanced on IQ tests (approximate IQ score range 141+)
- About one or two students across two grade levels (but two or three per grade level in high socio-economic areas)
- Descriptive designation: *Exceptionally to Profoundly Gifted*

Level Five Gifted

- Mainly 99th percentile on standardized tests
- Exceptionally to profoundly gifted or highly advanced on IQ tests (approximate IQ score range 141+)
- Nationally, about one per 250,000 students (more in metropolitan areas)
- A uniformly high intellectual profile, plus a strong inner drive to learn across domains
- Descriptive designation: *Exceptionally to Profoundly Gifted*

Ruf's five-category solution addresses the problem of dealing with today's ceilings of the Stanford-Binet, Wechsler, and group tests. It also includes the critical "strong drive to learn" at Level Five. But it remains based mostly on ability tests and IQ scores and ignores aesthetic gifts.

As a final thought, Ruf reminds us that teachers, administrators, and even school psychologists and school counselors typically have little or no experience interpreting test data for extremely bright children, nor addressing their educational needs. A common result is that such students spend their days receiving the same (boring, repetitive) instruction as their age-mates. Because so little serious thinking is required, they soon learn to underachieve. Ruf's "free, or at least inexpensive" solution is partial or full acceleration—moving students to higher grades for some or all of their school subjects—at least when higher grades are available in the same building. She also recommends careful selection of the most appropriate schools.

Nationally Standardized Achievement Tests

Most American schools routinely administer nationally standardized achievement tests every few years. Scores from these will quickly identify—or confirm a teacher's impression of—high talent in specific academic areas—for example, math, science, reading, or social studies. In Chapter 1, we listed the main tests: the *Metropolitan Achievement Tests, Iowa Tests of Basic Skills, Stanford Achievement Tests, SRA Achievement Series, California Test of Basic Skills,* and *Sequential Tests of Educational Progress* (STEP).

As an example, the *Metropolitan Achievement Test* (MAT) evaluates the five disciplines of *reading* (word recognition, vocabulary, reading comprehension), *math* (math concepts and problem solving, math procedures), *language* (listening, prewriting, composing, editing, spelling), *science* (research skills), and *social studies* (geography, history, culture, political science, economics). The MAT also evaluates thinking skills, including critical thinking. It usually is administered to grades 3, 5, 6, 7, and 9.

As mentioned briefly in Chapter 1, there is one critical advantage of using nationally standardized tests for identifying gifted students, compared with using teacher-made tests. In a small town or depressed section of a large city, a child who consistently scores high on teacher-made tests may quickly be judged as gifted. Perhaps the slightly-above-average student simply appears gifted in comparison with classmates. Vice versa, in an elementary or secondary school near, say, the University of California-Berkeley. Every child in the class might perform at the same level on the teachers' tests. Is no child in the Berkeley school gifted?

In both cases, a nationally standardized test will compare every student with other kids the same age across the country. The percentile rankings show exactly the achievement level of each student relative to others the same age. In such a national comparison, perhaps the bright child in the depressed area *does* surpass 90 or even 99% of other students nationwide. And perhaps every kid in the Berkeley class also falls in the top 90 to 99% in achievement.

In fact, some schools with uniformly bright kids don't bother with special programs for the gifted. The regular curriculum already is tailored to bright, fast-learning students. However, such schools—and indeed all schools—should watch for any highly gifted student who simply is "off the charts."[10]

As a final caution, both the nationally standardized tests described above and teacher-made tests will suffer from the ceiling effect described earlier. The only way to identify the exceptionally or profoundly gifted child *capable* of scoring at the 99.999[th] percentile on a formal test is with parent, teacher, and counselor judgment regarding, as mentioned earlier, short-term memory and reasoning ability, work habits at school, and receptiveness to educational interventions.

Creativity Tests

A student's creative ability may or may not be visible to the teacher. Creativity tests can help confirm a teacher's observations of high creativity or help identify students whose creative talent is not visible.

There are two kinds of creativity tests. First are *divergent thinking tests* that ask a person to think of lots of ideas for a verbal problem (e.g., "How many uses can you list for a cardboard box?") or to add details to an incomplete drawing (imagine a bent-up piece of string) to make it meaningful or interesting. The best known are the *Torrance Tests of Creative Thinking*, which include both verbal (*Thinking Creatively with Words*) and figural (drawing; *Thinking Creatively with Pictures*) subtests.[11] Both subtests are scored for *fluency* (number of ideas), *flexibility* (number of categories of ideas), and *originality* (uniqueness of ideas). The figural test also is scored for *elaboration*.

In 1984, Torrance and Ball developed a scoring system for the figural tests that measures 18 characteristics of creativeness. In addition to *fluency, originality,* and *elaboration,* the streamlined scoring evaluates *humor* (in the title or the drawings), *fantasy, abstractness of the titles, expressiveness of the titles, expression of feelings or emotions, storytelling articulateness, richness of imagery, colorfulness of imagery, movement or action, combining lines* (Form A) *or circles* (Form B), *combining two or more figures, unusual visual perspective, internal visual perspective, extending or breaking boundaries,* and *resistance to premature closure.*

The second type of creativity test is *personality inventories,* which try to measure these kinds of traits and characteristics of creative people: *high originality, good sense of humor, confidence and independence, high motivation, risk-taking tendencies, artistic interests, open-mindedness,* and *good intuition.* Four published creative personality inventories are PRIDE (pre-school), GIFT (elementary school), and GIFFI I (middle school) and GIFFI II (high school).[12] GIFFI I and GIFFI II were inspired by the relatively good but unpublished college-level *How Do You Think?* (HDYT) creativity inventory.[13]

Creativity expert Jane Piirto claims that there is *no* correlation between scores on creativity tests—perhaps divergent thinking tests, such as listing unusual uses for a cardboard box—and later real-world creative productivity.[14] However, most innovators share such creative personality traits as confidence, independence, good intuition, high motivation, risk-taking tendencies, and openness to new ideas, which can be evaluated with creativity inventories.

A difficulty is that creativity is complicated (surprise!). We have creative teachers, inventors, artists, actors, scientists, business entrepreneurs, and politicians. We also have creative children who write poetry, invent games, design posters, explore history and science topics on their own, teach themselves to juggle or perform magic, or create innovative ways to stop littering, smoking, drug use, and traffic accidents.

Creative people do have many thinking and personality traits in common.[15] But it's impossible to create one test that accurately evaluates all varieties of creative capability.

Our two-part guideline is that, first, a child who produces a *very high* creativity test score probably is above average in creative ability and experience. Second, *low* scores can be misleading. A child's creativeness may simply be different than the "creativity" measured by listing clever uses for a paperclip or by rating oneself (or being rated) on umpteen traits of a creative person.[16] Generally, schools do not use formal creativity tests.

Teacher Nominations

Teacher nomination is the most common procedure for selecting students for gifted programs. Day after day, a teacher watches the same bright students complete their work quickly and accurately and respond intelligently to questions. A teacher also may examine students' past academic records, IQ scores, previous teachers' comments, school psychologist referrals, truancy or home problems, and whatever else is on file for every student.

Teacher nominations can be quite informal, perhaps based on the principal's surprise announcement that "Our new Astronaut program for gifted and talented students will be launched October 15! Please select two or three students you think have the right stuff!" Or the selection procedure can be very formal, using a prepared nomination form resembling the one in Table 4.1, which essentially asks the teacher to: (1) report grades in specific areas, (2) explain why the student should be in the program, and (3) explain each nominee's strengths in various areas of possible giftedness. Generally, teacher nominations improve when teachers are familiar with traits and characteristics of giftedness, such as those described in Chapter 2 (e.g., Table 2.1).

Teachers also should be well-acquainted with students before being asked to nominate them. If it helps, a teacher can create five-point rating scales to evaluate such traits as general academic ability, ability in specific subject areas, ability to interact with others, leadership, creativity, motivation, or other traits and abilities deemed important.

There are several potential biases in teacher nominations. The first is the well-documented tendency to nominate "teacher pleasers"— middle-class children who smile, cooperate, dress well, complete all work neatly and on time, have no disability, do not come from a sub-cultural group, and never make faces or mumble insults. Teachers also might overlook or deliberately ignore highly intelligent underachievers, bright but disruptive students, and unconventional (perhaps nuisance) creative students.

Interestingly, teachers tend to *not* over-identify gifted students; perhaps they fear such selection errors could make them look incompetent.[17] The result is to not recommend students they believe are borderline gifted.

Coordinators of gifted programs, sometimes called *resource teachers*, typically have taken one or two college courses in gifted education and sometimes have a master's degree. They help plan gifted programs, they might present enrichment (e.g., creativity, thinking skills) activities in the regular classroom to all students, and they might travel from school to school to teach small groups of gifted students in pullout programs. Siegle and Powell also found that, compared with regular teachers, the more confident G/T coordinators tend to be more generous in the number of students they rate as "gifted." They worry less about making selection errors, believing that it is better to be inclusive than exclusive.[18]

Table 4.1: Sample Teacher Nomination Form

Date _____ Nominating Teacher _____ Grade _____

Student Name _____

Grades for Current Year (Average):

    Arithmetic _____   Language _____

    Science _____   Social Studies _____

    Other _____   (Specify Area _____)

Why do you believe that this student should participate in our Astronaut program for gifted and talented students?

_____

_____

_____

In addition to the above, please explain any areas of unusually strong interest that you have observed, for example, in math, science, art, music, reading/literature, history (including pre-history), social studies, community concerns, social welfare, hobbies, or politics. _____

_____

_____

★ ★ ★ ★ ★ ★ ★ ★ ★

For Gifted Committee Use Only

Intelligence (IQ) Score(s) _____ Name of Test(s) _____

Standardized Achievement Scores (national percentiles).

    Name of Test _____

    Reading ___ Math ___ Language ___ Science ___ Social Studies ___

    Other _____ (Specify _____) Decision: _____

Gifted Evaluation Scale

The five-part U.S. Office [Department] of Education definition of *giftedness* appeared in Chapter 3 and again at the beginning of this chapter. The *Gifted Evaluation Scale* created by McCarney and Anderson is a 48-item inventory, said to require 15 minutes to complete, that allows teachers who are familiar with students to rate them in each of the five U.S.O.E. categories.[19] is High ratings, of course, will lead a teacher to nominate a student as gifted.[20]

Scales for Rating the Behavioral Characteristics of Superior Students

Joseph Renzulli and colleagues prepared the brief but excellent *Scales for Rating the Behavioral Characteristics of Superior Students* for use by teachers or others (e.g., parents).[21] The main four rating scales evaluate characteristics of learning, motivation, creativity, and leadership. The scales can be used as presented, or they can guide the construction of an original district G/T identification form.

As a brief summary, the *Learning Characteristics Scale* allows teachers to rate students on advanced vocabulary, large storehouse of information, quick mastery and recall, rapid insight into cause–effect, ready grasp of underlying principles, keen and alert observations, whether or not they read a great deal, and understanding of complicated material. The *Motivational Characteristics Scale* allows a teacher to rate the extent to which a student becomes absorbed in topics or problems, is easily bored with routine tasks, needs little external motivation, strives toward perfection, works independently, is interested in adult problems, is self-assertive, organizes and brings structure, and is concerned with right and wrong. The *Creativity Characteristics Scale* evaluates a student's curiosity, ability to generate a large number of ideas, ability to be uninhibited in expressing opinions, risk-taking, playfulness and fantasy, sense of humor, awareness of impulses, sensitivity to beauty, nonconformity, and ability to criticize constructively. Finally, the *Leadership Characteristics Scale* evaluates how much a student is responsible, is self-confident with children and adults, is well-liked, is cooperative, expresses him- or herself well, adapts to new situations, enjoys other people, tends to dominate, participates in social activities, and excels in athletics.

Parent Nominations

Parents have information that only they know—that their child could speak in sentences at age two, could read at age four, and by five composed music, painted creatively, drew the solar system, and displayed extraordinary curiosity for his or her age, perhaps asking why oranges only grow in Florida and California or why Israelis and Palestinians so often fight.

However, as a routine selection procedure—and despite their likely value—parent nominations are rarely used to select students for gifted programs. Therefore, if parents are convinced that their first or second grader has strong gifts, talents, and/or interests, they should discuss possible testing and evaluation with the child's teacher and share their behavioral information about the child. A sample parent nomination form appears in Table 4.2.

Table 4.2. Sample Parent Nomination Form, Elementary Level

Student Name _____ School _____ Grade _____

Parent Name _____

Address _____

Compared with other children your child's age, please circle a number that best describes your child's characteristics. "1" = "Low"; "3" = "Average"; "5" = "High."

Thinks rapidly.	1 2 3 4 5
Has a large vocabulary.	1 2 3 4 5
Learned to read before kindergarten.	1 2 3 4 5
Has a long span of attention.	1 2 3 4 5
Is aware of what's going on.	1 2 3 4 5
Learned self-care—dressing, eating—early.	1 2 3 4 5
Acts more "grown up."	1 2 3 4 5
Associates with older children.	1 2 3 4 5
Tends to be a leader.	1 2 3 4 5
Is easily bored.	1 2 3 4 5
Is open-minded regarding new ideas, others' views.	1 2 3 4 5
Is motivated, persistent, energetic, adventurous.	1 2 3 4 5
Has original activities and interests.	1 2 3 4 5
Is intuitive, perceptive; sees relationships.	1 2 3 4 5
Has a good sense of humor.	1 2 3 4 5
Is curious—often asks "why?"	1 2 3 4 5
Is independent, self-confident.	1 2 3 4 5
Is artistic.	1 2 3 4 5
Likes to try new things, even if they fail.	1 2 3 4 5
Needs some "alone time."	1 2 3 4 5
Has good muscle coordination.	1 2 3 4 5

Self Nominations

Teachers are not always aware of every student's interests and abilities. With a self-nomination form, students can report their artistic, poetic, and scientific interests, as well as their other creative activities, hobbies, and experiences. A sample self-nomination form appears in Table 4.3.

Table 4.3. Sample Self-Nomination Form

Name _____ Grade _____ Teacher _____

Place an "X" next to any of the areas in which you believe you have special ability or talent.

Tell why you believe you have this special ability or talent.

1. ____ General School Ability
   Explain:_____

2. ____ Science
   Explain:_____

3. ____ Math
   Explain:_____

4. ____ Reading
   Explain:_____

5. ____ Language Arts
   Explain:_____

6. ____ Social Studies
   Explain:_____

7. ____ Music
   Explain:_____

8. ____ Art
   Explain:_____

9. ____ Dance
   Explain:_____

10. ____ Drama
    Explain:_____

11. ____ Creativity
    Explain:_____

12. ____ Leadership
    Explain:_____

Do you have other abilities, talents, or hobbies? What are they? Please explain.

_____

_____

Peer Nominations

Children often have been in class together for years. They know who's who. They know which kids are unusually intelligent; who is talented in science, art, or dance; and who has creative ideas and does creative things. The also know who is bright and talented among students likely to be overlooked—for example, minority and culturally different students and students with a disability.

A peer nomination form can be *direct* or *disguised*. An example of a direct nomination form appears in Table 4.4. Note that students are given permission to nominate themselves, and they can write the same name more than once. They also might be warned not to just list their friends or children who are simply popular.

Table 4.4. Example of a Peer-Nomination Form

Read the questions. Then write the name of a student in this class who fits the description. You may write your own name. You may write a name more than once.

In this class:

1. Who is the smartest? _____

2. Who is second smartest? _____

3. Who finishes his or her work first? _____

4. Who is the best reader? _____

5. Who is the best writer? _____

6. Who is the best at math? _____

7. Who might become a scientist? _____

8. Who is best at solving problems? _____

9. Who has good judgment? _____

10. Who has lots of interests? _____

11. Who has a good imagination? _____

12. Who has the best ideas for games and class activities? _____

13. Who could invent the most things to do with a pile of junk? _____

14. If you needed help with schoolwork or homework, who would you ask? _____

15. Who spends extra time working on a project and likes to do a good job? _____

As another example of a direct approach, a teacher can announce, "Let's pretend we're going to form some committees. We need to select one person to lead each committee. The first is a math committee. Write down the name of a person who would be a good leader for a math committee." And so forth for language arts, science, art, social studies, and perhaps other areas.

With students above the lowest grades, a simple and direct nomination form might read:

I think _____ *should be in the gifted program because:* _____

_____

With a disguised approach, a teacher might ask students, "Imagine a space ship just landed in the school yard. It's filled with friendly aliens—and they're coming to visit our class!"

Who is likely to ask the aliens the most unusual questions?

_____

Who will probably remember the most details about their visit?

_____

Or a teacher can ask students to imagine that they are stranded on a small island. Students can nominate who is the best *leader* (organizer, gets others to do things), *inventor* (invents, discovers), *fixer* (makes things better), *judge* (settles arguments), and *entertainer* (tells jokes, acts).[22]

Identification Matrices

Perhaps the best known identification matrix is the *Baldwin Identification Matrix*—designed by Alexinia Baldwin—to improve the selection of gifted minority students.[23] The matrix includes the six main categories of *Cognitive, Creative Products, Creative Process, Motivation, Psychosocial* (e.g., leadership), and *Psychomotor.* Information is combined into a single total score.

Included in each category are tests and rating information of the types we have described. For example, the *Cognitive* category includes a Stanford-Binet IQ score, a *Stanford Achievement Tests* reading score, a math score, and a rating on the Renzulli *Learning Characteristics Scale.* The *Creative Products* category includes ratings on, for example, art products and musical performances. The *Creative Process* category includes a rating on the Renzulli *Creativity Characteristics Scale* and scores on the *Torrance Tests of Creative Thinking.* The *Psychosocial* category includes, for example, a rating on the Renzulli *Leadership Characteristics Scale* and the results of peer nominations.

As a warning, any G/T selection procedure—including the *Baldwin Identification Matrix*—that combines test scores and ratings into a single composite number creates a serious, simple, built-in problem. A student strongly talented in just one area, perhaps even two, will be passed over. If the Baldwin Matrix is used more flexibly, of course, it presents a nice summary of intellectual, creative, motivational, social, and even psycho-motor abilities on which to base a selection decision.

Project APOGEE: Susanne Richert

Susanne Richert is extraordinarily conscious of discrimination by gifted programs against cultural minority and other disadvantaged groups.[24] Her landmark *National Report on Identification* identified these groups as badly underrepresented in gifted programs: students who (1) are poor, (2) are from a different culture, (3) have minimal English profi-ciency, (4) are male (when evaluating verbal ability below fifth grade), (5) are female (when identifying math ability), (6) are creatively gifted, (7) are academic underachievers, (8) are physically handicapped, or (9) have a learning disability.[25]

Cultural minority groups in Richert's project APOGEE (Academic Programs for the Gifted with Excellence and Equity) included African American, Hispanic, Indian (from India), American Indian, White, Lim-ited English Proficient, and other groups, all of which varied according to the particular school district.[26]

Project APOGEE involved intensive training of classroom teachers mainly to individualize instruction according to students' interests, abili-ties, academic needs and achievement levels. The gifted students might be homogeneously grouped, as in pullout programs or separate classes, or they might be "mainstreamed" in regular heterogeneous classes.

Richert's strategy for selecting gifted students began with creating local (school) norms for *each data source, each minority group,* and *each gender.* Her data sources—approved by the Office of Civil Rights—included: (1) available test scores, (2) teacher nominations (grades K-11), (3) parent nominations (grades K-3), and (4) self nominations (grades 6-11).

Self nominations were subtle; students were invited to visit APOGEE program options, then to apply to programs in which they were interested. The strategy helped locate gifted underachievers who would never, ever nominate themselves as gifted.

The unique and impressively successful identification step was *renorming*. Students first were separated by minority group. Then they were rank-ordered based on their highest score for each data source (test scores, teacher nominations, parent nominations, self nominations). If the average scores of males and females differed by more than 15%, males' and females' scores were rank ordered separately. Then an equal percentage of the highest scoring students in each category were identified for the G/T program. The procedure guaranteed equal representation of every minority group and both genders. Parents of minority students became program supporters.

Talent Pool Identification Plan: Joseph Renzulli

The thoughtful five-step identification plan of Renzulli and Reis aims at selecting 15 to 20% of students for a gifted program.[27] As noted in Chapter 1, such a generous percentage gives more students the opportunity to participate in gifted education, along with reducing complaints from parents of excluded children.

In Step 1, *Test Score Nominations*, students who score above the 92nd percentile on a standardized intelligence and/or achievement test are admitted—without further evaluation. About half of the students in the program will be selected with this step.

In Step 2, *Teacher Nominations*, teachers nominate students—other than those selected in Step 1—who show other "worthy" characteristics—for example, high creativity, high motivation, unusual talents or interests, or specific areas of high performance (or potential).

Step 3, *Alternate Pathways*, includes parent nominations, peer nominations, self nominations, product (e.g., art, science) evaluations, creativity test results, and any other information that might be important to a school screening committee. The screening committee is likely to examine school records and previous IQ and achievement test scores, as well as to interview teachers, students, and/or parents. Admission to the G/T program may be on a trial basis.

Step 4, *Special Nominations*, "Safety Valve No. 1," is designed to avoid biases of current teachers. The names of all students nominated are circulated to teachers of previous years, who may add names to the list of nominees. Also, the G/T resource teacher who conducts enrichment activities in the regular classroom may wish to nominate students who appear creative, bright, or have unusual strengths.

Step 5 is *Action Information Nominations*, "Safety Valve No. 2." Renzulli's *Schoolwide Enrichment Model*, described in Chapter 9, includes "Action Information Messages." Typically, these are used by students in the talent pool (G/T program) to describe an independent project or problem (e.g., scientific, historical, social, artistic, literary) that they are eager to pursue. The nice part is that students not in the talent pool also can fill out an Action Information Message and, after review by the G/T screening committee, may be included in the talent pool to work on their exciting projects.

Summary

- There is little agreement on an ideal identification system.

- Two common methods use teacher recommendations and achievement and IQ information. Some programs examine, for example, artistic or poetic gifts.

- Teachers should attend to the five categories of the federal definition: general intellectual ability, specific academic talent, creativity, leadership, and artistic talent.

  A list of recommendations for identification includes:

  - A broad definition of giftedness.

  - Separate reliable and valid procedures for evaluating different areas of giftedness.

  - Selection based on student needs, not quotas.

  - Awareness that giftedness takes different forms in different student subgroups.

  - Authentic assessments—student products or performances.

  - Tasks that elicit creativity and problem solving.

  - A focus on including (not excluding) students.

  - Continuing over time to identify additional gifted students.

  - Continuous evaluation of selection procedures.

  - Systems to assure representation of poor and minority students.

- Using identification information to both understand students and guide instruction.

- Using multiple criteria reduces the problem of selecting too few minority and poor students, who may show lower IQ and achievement scores and grades. Multiple criteria will include nominations by teachers and others; intellectual, social, and emotional functioning; student motivation and learning style; student interests, values, school attitudes, and outside activities; and parent support.

- Compared with the newer Stanford-Binet Fourth Edition, IQ scores on the earlier Stanford-Binet Form L-M are substantially higher. Also, Form L-M had no upper limit, but the newer version has a significant ceiling effect. Similarly, compared with the newer *Wechsler Intelligence Scale for Children-IV,* the older WISC-R IQ scores are higher.

- Extremely high IQ scores now are generally deemed less important than reasoning ability, work habits, short-term memory, and other factors.

- Group IQ tests usually are routinely administered but have problems: top scores on group IQ tests are lower than for individual IQ tests; group tests are less reliable and valid; they mainly evaluate verbal abilities; low socio-economic status, immigrant, minority, and unmotivated children may score low; scores at high levels are unstable; and scores are affected by factors such as family stresses, illness, noises, or interruptions.

- Any intelligence test can help identify gifted underachievers. However, a too-strong emphasis on IQ may exclude students with other gifts and talents (e.g., in art, creativity, computers).

- In view of lower IQ test ceilings, Ruf created five categories of giftedness based on percentile scores on standardized ability tests, IQ scores, and the likely number of students in each category. She also looked at developmental milestones and inner drive.

- Ruf recommended partial or full acceleration to reduce bright students' boredom.

- Standardized achievement tests, such as the *Metropolitan Achievement Test* and the *Iowa Test of Basic Skills,* allow (percentile-ranking) comparisons with a national sample of students. There may be a ceiling effect.

- The original *Torrance Tests of Creative Thinking* evaluated four divergent thinking abilities: fluency, flexibility, originality, and elaboration. The scoring was later extended to 18 abilities. Creative personality inventories evaluate such character traits as originality, humor, confidence, motivation, risk-taking, artistic interests, open-mindedness, and intuition.

- Because of complexity, creativity test validity is mediocre. A very high creativity score promises above-average creativity, but a low score easily may be inaccurate.

- Teacher nomination may be informal or may formally use a prepared nomination form. Nominations improve if teachers rate students on specific characteristics of giftedness.

- Biases include nominating "teacher pleasers" and overlooking gifted underachievers, disruptive or problem students, and creative students.

- Trained G/T coordinators (resource teachers) typically have taken college courses or even have a master's degree in gifted education. They help plan programs and present enrichment activities. They tend to nominate more students as gifted than do regular teachers.

- To select gifted students, teachers may use McCarney and Anderson's *Gifted Evaluation Scale,* which is based on the five U.S.O.E. categories.

- Teachers also may use Renzulli's *Scales for Rating Behavioral Characteristics of Superior Students.* The four main rating scales evaluate learning, motivation, creativity, and leadership.

- Although parents are aware of their child's early—and current—gifts and talents, parent nominations are rarely used.

- Self nominations permit students to report their artistic and scientific interests, hobbies, and other creative activities.

- Peer nominations can be direct: "Who's the smartest (best reader, best scientist, most imaginative) kid in class?" Or they may be disguised: "If you were stranded on an island, who would be the best leader (inventor, judge, entertainer)?"

- The *Baldwin Identification Matrix* assembles information in the categories of cognitive, creative products, creative process, motivation, psychosocial, and psychomotor. While the single total score could miss students gifted in just one or two areas, the form summarizes helpful selection information.

- Richert's Project APOGEE, a teacher training project, selects gifted students (with test scores, teacher and parent nominations, and self nominations) who are poor, minority, speak poor English, underachieve, or are otherwise under-represented. Her renorming strategy involved creating local norms for each minority group, each source of data, and sometimes each gender. Teachers are taught to individualize instruction for the gifted students, who might be grouped (e.g., in pullout programs) or mainstreamed.

Renzulli's Talent Pool Identification Plan includes five steps of: (1) Test Score Nominations, (2) Teacher Nominations, (3) Alternate Pathways (e.g., parent, self, and peer nominations; product evaluations; creativity, motivation, interest, and talent information), (4) Special Nominations from previous teachers or the resource teacher, and (5) nominations based on Action Information Messages.

5
Acceleration

In the ordinary elementary school situation,
children of IQ 140 waste half their time.
Those of 170 IQ waste practically all their time.

~ Leta Hollingworth

[*Scene*: Donald Letterperson's Late Show. His guest is a charming 11-year-old gifted girl, Sally Cerebrum from Panguitch, Utah. Letterperson steps toward her, leans down, and gives her a peck on the cheek. She wiggles into the chair, her feet dangling.]

Donald Letterperson (enthusiastically): Hello Sally! I'm so happy you could join us tonight! Are you a little nervous about being on national television?

Sally Cerebrum (smiling): Not really. You know, I'm on TV a lot! How come you wear white socks with a double-breasted suit? Nobody does that!

Letterperson (grinning widely): That's true. That's why I do it! Now, Sally, it says in my notes that you've read the complete works of Shakespeare. Is that true?

Sally: Yes, but I wish people wouldn't keep bringing that up! I finished Shakespeare when I was eight. It took me nearly a month! I was such a slow reader then!

Letterperson: Wow! I'm impressed! I imagine you've been accelerated a few grades. What grade are you in now?

Sally: Yes, I kinda' was grade-skipped a lot. You know, maybe two or three grades at a time. Right now I'm a junior.

Letterperson: A junior! That's remarkable! Eleven years old and you're a junior at Panguitch High School! Didn't you missing anything by

95

accelerating so fast? What about math? English? Geography? History and social studies?

Sally (smiling): I skimmed the text books. Actually, I'm a junior at the University of Southern Utah in St. George. I'll graduate in another semester.

Letterperson (startled): Goodness, a junior in college!

Sally: I'm studying particle physics. Did you know that by studying electrons, muons, and leons, we can figure out the origin of the universe? I just wrote a paper that I called "Big Bang: Before and Before That!"

Letterperson: I'm dazzled! We have lots of Leons (ha ha) on our staff! But tell me, exactly what did happen before the Big Bang?

Sally: Well, my theory is that space, time, and all the matter in the universe were condensed into a tiny nuclear cabbage.

Letterperson: Gosh, I didn't know that! But what happened to your childhood, Sally? Didn't you miss playing with children your own age?

Sally: Oh, not at all! I had a wonderful childhood—you know, when I was young. At 12 months, I played dolls with the other kids. It wasn't easy because I could barely walk! When I was three, I rode my bike and played checkers, you know, with the other kids.

Letterperson: Now that you're older, do you play chess?

Sally: Oh, I learned chess when I was four!

Letterperson: Really?

Sally (tilting her head with sarcastic smile): You know, Mr. Letterperson, you're awfully nice. But…well…did you drop out of elementary school?

Acceleration, Enrichment, and Grouping

Three terms that you will encounter in gifted education are *acceleration*, *enrichment*, and *grouping*. This chapter concerns *acceleration*, Chapter 6 covers *enrichment*, and Chapter 7 deals with *grouping*. Of course, the three are related in perhaps obvious ways. For example, students may be grouped in part-time or full-time gifted classes for accelerated work in math or languages, or for greater depth—enrichment—in history or social studies.

One-room schoolhouses often used a combination of acceleration and grouping. It simply was easier and more practical to group and teach kids of the same ability level with little worry about differences in chronological age.

In larger school districts before about 1978, there were virtually no acceleration programs. The reason? A misguided fear that placing gifted students with kids who are older and bigger would upset the bright kids' social and emotional development.[1] There also were attitudes that teachers should focus their efforts on struggling students because "gifted kids can get it on their own" and because the bright kids could help teach slower learners—as unpaid teacher aides, of course.

We mentioned in Chapter 1 that America's *No Child Left Behind Act* damages acceleration and enrichment activities for gifted kids. The educational focus is on disadvantaged students—students who are economically impoverished, members of racial and ethnic groups, physically disabled, or have limited English ability. The Act requires that all school children meet minimum educational standards, as confirmed by competency tests usually administered every two or three years.[2]

The standard complaint is this: most children—both average and gifted—are left behind when teachers and principals are threatened that even their weakest students *must* meet minimal levels of academic competency.

We described some cases of accelerated students in Chapter 1. As the label suggests, *acceleration* refers to moving a gifted child through academic content at a faster pace. This implies allowing younger students to study curriculum usually assigned to older students. *Enrichment* is exposing gifted students to richer, more varied educational experiences that supply greater breadth and depth than the usual classroom offerings. Acceleration and enrichment both accommodate the educational needs and abilities of gifted students. Both can help develop creative thinking and other high-level thinking skills.

In practice, the terms *acceleration* and *enrichment* often are used ambiguously and sometimes incorrectly. Any enrichment experience will of course involve new topics, more depth, or both—which is accelerated content compared with the regular curriculum. And so many teachers refer to *any* type of non-standard activities or procedures for gifted students as "acceleration."

To simplify the distinction, *acceleration* refers to any strategy that results in advanced curriculum placement or credit. *Enrichment* refers to any other educational adjustment for gifted students—that is, any other teaching strategies that go beyond standard grade-level work but do not result in advanced placement or credit.[3]

Grouping procedures are ways to bring gifted students together. Grouping usually aids both these students' academic and social-emotional development. Acceleration and enrichment often, though not always, involve grouping gifted students.

Is Acceleration Effective?

Based on decades of experience at the Belin-Blank International Center for Gifted Education and Talent Development at the University of Iowa, Nicholas Colangelo nicely summarized the problems and proven benefits of the acceleration issue.[4] Critics claim—incorrectly—that acceleration damages students educationally, psychologically, and/or socially. Specific misguided charges are that accelerating bright students: (1) leads to gaps in knowledge; (2) causes social/emotional maladjustment from placing them with older students, with awful long-term effects; (3) hurries and pressures children; (4) is unfair to other children "because all second-grade children belong in second grade!"; or (5) is unnecessary because non-acceleration does no harm.

Karen Rogers adds additional parental concerns about grade acceleration: (1) a child's self-esteem may become lower if the new, older classmates act like the accelerated child is weird; and (2) because school work is no longer easy, a bright student may lower his or her academic self-perception.[5]

Said Colangelo, opponents to accelerating bright students are unaware of acceleration research—or simply dismiss it. Also, hostility toward acceleration may stem from the personal preferences or political biases ("We're all equal") of superintendents, principals, or teachers.

As for research, Rogers surveyed the results of 314(!) studies of accelerating students at all grade levels and found positive and statistically significant academic effects for most types of acceleration.[6] She also concluded that *no acceleration option damaged psychological health, social adjustment, academic self-esteem, or academic achievement.*

Colangelo has stated that acceleration helps gifted students academically without short-changing them socially or emotionally.[7] He quoted acceleration enthusiast Julian Stanley: "We should help students learn *only* what they do not already know."[8] At the very least, emphasized Colangelo, *all* profoundly gifted students (e.g., those with IQs of 150+)

absolutely need acceleration. We have lost generations of bright students who were ready but were not accelerated. He listed these considerations: Is the student socially and emotionally, as well as intellectually, ready to be accelerated? Which type of acceleration is most suitable? What can we do to ensure that acceleration will work for this student?

Many aptitudes are important for both the selection and success of bright kids who are accelerated.[9] Aptitudes that predict successful acceleration include the ability to comprehend instructions; knowledge, skills, and reasoning abilities within a particular symbol system (e.g., math, language); the ability to work alone; high interest; persistence; non-impulsiveness; and low anxiety. Acceleration decisions can be guided by tools such as the *Iowa Acceleration Scale*, which is used throughout the United States and in some other countries as well.[10]

Despite the highly supportive research, some inflexible districts do not permit grade skipping. They simply tell parents, "We don't believe in that."

Early Admission to Kindergarten or First Grade

Like all forms of acceleration, early admission to kindergarten or first grade matches the needs and abilities of the young child to the school system. Early admission helps accommodate the gifted child's enthusiasm, imagination, curiosity, and needs to observe and investigate.

As a warning, some educators worry that: (1) children admitted early cannot socialize well with older children—and so they will have few friends and be unhappy; (2) they will miss out on important childhood experiences; (3) the academic demands will cause stress—leading to rebelliousness, burnout, or maladjustment; (4) because of the academic competition, achievement will be poor; (5) they will not develop leadership skills; (6) they will become arrogant and conceited; and (7) some parents will push their children into early admission whether or not the children are ready.

In fact, there is occasional validity to this last point. In trying to smuggle her child into kindergarten, one parent used white-out and a copy machine to change her child's birth certificate. Another parent stole her doctor's stationery and forged a letter recommending that the child be admitted.[11]

Certainly, candidates for early admission to kindergarten or first grade must be carefully evaluated regarding cognitive, emotional, and social maturity and physical readiness. *If they are not ready, the young children may* indeed experience social and emotional problems. Given this qualification, research shows that the academic achievement of early entrants is *better* than that of their older classmates. Their academic superiority continues through high school, resulting in more academic awards and college admissions.

Gifted education leader John Feldhusen recommended the following criteria for early admission to kindergarten or first grade:[12]

- An IQ of 130 or more. However, if the average IQ level of an entire school (e.g., in a university community) is 120 or 125, the bright child may as well wait; the school's regular curriculum will be suitably challenging.

- At least average eye-hand coordination.

- Advanced reading comprehension and arithmetic reasoning.

- No serious adjustment (social, emotional) problems.

- The child's receiving teacher should favor early admission and be willing to help the child adjust. (However, if a child is truly ready, most initially negative teachers will change their attitude.)

- The child's family must value academic achievement over athletic success, since the undersized child may be less likely to become a soccer or baseball star.

Grade Skipping

One advantage of allowing a bright child to skip, say, the third grade is that no expensive school adjustments are required—no G/T teacher, no special class, and no special books, assignments, projects, or equipment. Just some paperwork. The educational cost to a school system actually is lower by moving the gifted child through the system ahead of schedule, though schools sometimes resist this because they lose a state reimbursement due to their having one less student (i.e., it lowers their "average daily attendance count").

Two strategies may be used in grade skipping. First, the acceleration can occur during an academic year.[13] For example, sometime during her second-grade school year, little Roberta might be moved to third grade for the rest of that academic year. Such a decision normally results from a conference that includes a parent, Roberta's second-grade teacher, the receiving third-grade teacher, the school principal, and a school counselor and/or school psychologist. In the second approach, a child may skip one entire grade. For example, after Roberta's completes second grade, she enters fourth grade the next fall. Again, the same folks hold a conference to discuss issues and potential problems.

Grade skipping, or "double promotion," usually happens in the lowest elementary grades, but sometimes in higher grades. It may be initiated by parents or teachers who observe that the child is one or two years ahead of everybody else, is bored with school, and perhaps is impatient with slower-thinking classmates. Some gifted children skip two or three grades (occasionally more) and enter college at age 15 or 16 (or even younger). This is often called *radical acceleration*.

One concern with grade skipping is missing critical skills. However, the child typically learns those skills independently or from a parent, and so the skills actually are not missing. Another concern is with social adjustment, since the child suddenly is placed in classes with older students. The research consensus is that gifted children normally are quite comfortable with intellectual peers—older students—and experience virtually no social-emotional problems.[14]

And consider the benefits. As shown in the research, accelerated students' motivation improves—they do not become lazy, which happens when non-accelerated bright students too easily sail through school. Their scholarship improves. Their self-esteem improves, because the school recognizes and accommodates their abilities.[15] They learn to study, since they suddenly are faced with material they do not already know. They aspire to higher-level careers. They attend more competitive colleges. They are able to complete their professional training earlier.[16]

Considerations for grade skipping resemble those for early admission to kindergarten or first grade: IQ over 130; skip one grade at a time; diagnose and remediate any skill gaps; the receiving teacher should be supportive; parents should value academics over sports; and the child should be mature, motivated, and in need of intellectual stimulation and challenge.

Subject Skipping

Subject skipping is *partial acceleration*, compared with the *full acceleration* of grade skipping. It involves studying particular subjects—especially sequential subjects like math and reading—with students in higher grades. Subject skipping therefore is suitable for students with special abilities in (usually) one area. It may begin in elementary school and continue though high school. It permits a child to remain with peers while joining a higher-level class for work in the student's area of special strength (such as math).

Continuity can be a problem. A child who completes a year of math at the next higher grade might find him- or herself repeating the same material the next year. Subject skipping obviously must be carefully planned for continuous, non-repetitive work.

Skipping single subjects sometimes is used to experiment with academic and social adjustment at a higher grade level. If academic and social-emotional adjustment is fine, a teacher may then recommend a full-grade acceleration.

Telescoped Programs

If enough capable students are available, a three-year math and algebra sequence in middle school might be condensed into two years. The same could be done in middle school science. Or a high school counselor might help an intelligent and energetic student condense a four-year high school program into three or three and a half years, for example, by cutting down on study hall and optional classes. The trade is more work in exchange for early graduation.

Hsu described the results of eight intensive three-week summer physics courses in Minnesota for 128 gifted students between 12 and 17 years old. Each physics class included eight to 19 students who took no other summer classes. The three-week courses were taught by lecture and demonstration and were equivalent to regular year-long high school courses or semester-long college courses. The result? "The average gains achieved by students in the intensive courses were comparable to those achieved by students in the ordinary-length courses."[17] Wow!

Credit by Examination

In junior or senior high school, a student talented in, usually, math or languages—stemming perhaps from summer study or foreign travel—often can "test out" of a course and receive full credit. Such a policy prevents repetition and boredom and encourages capable students to set goals and work toward them. To be fair, a candidate should receive a course outline so he or she can evaluate his or her own skills and concentrate study on material not yet mastered.

College credit also may be earned by examination with the College Level Examination Program (CLEP). CLEP exams are available in 30 subject areas, including math, English composition and literature, business, computer science, nursing, education, psychology, and foreign languages. Unfortunately, not all colleges accept CLEP credits. Before paying to register for CLEP exams, interested students must check to see if their chosen college will accept CLEP credits.

College Courses While in High School

There are three strategies available which allow high school students to take college courses. First, with the *dual enrollment* plan a high school student is excused for part of the day to take one or more courses at a local college. The credits normally can be transferred to a different college.

Second is the *Advanced Placement* (AP) program. Colangelo described the AP program as the best large scale option currently available for challenging the abilities of gifted high school students.[18] Many medium to large high schools offer college-level AP courses taught by an instructor who follows an AP course outline and who uses suggested and other teaching resources. AP courses and exams exist in several dozen subject areas—for example, English composition and literature, computer science, psychology, French, German, Spanish, Latin, music theory, American history, European history, art history, biology, economics, calculus, chemistry, and more. With AP classes, students might enter college with a year or even more of college credit.

The good news is that AP classes bring bright, high-achieving students together, and these students earn college credit The bad news is that AP classes sometimes require huge amounts of homework.

AP for non-gifted students? Some AP courses will accept any highly motivated student, including "C" and "D" students.[19] But the students are counseled about AP course difficulty. Also, highly motivated parents sometimes want their less-motivated children in AP courses; AP teachers normally will try to persuade them otherwise.

AP tests are given at high schools in early May of each year. Without taking the AP classes, anyone may prepare individually and take the AP tests.

The third strategy available for high schools students is *university correspondence courses*. These courses are offered by every major university, usually at the college freshman and sophomore level. They award college credit to high school students. They are available in most subjects, but not those requiring student-teacher interaction (e.g., speech) or laboratory work (e.g., chemistry, physics). The written exams are taken at the university offering the course, which may be hundreds of miles away.

Early College Admission

Some gifted high school students—and on very rare occasions, junior high school students—are permitted to enter college early as full-time students. As with all forms of acceleration, the goal is an appropriate educational challenge. Bright high school students can either accelerate their high school work and graduate early or simply leave high school early without graduating. For either option, a counselor—*seen regularly from the beginning of high school*—will: (1) help outline an accelerated program that permits early graduation, or (2) make sure that the intended college will admit capable students who do not graduate high school.

Muratori, Colangelo, and Assouline used interviews, observations, and student and parent surveys to explore the first semester academic, social, family, and other adjustments of 10 (six female, four male) early college entrants to The University of Iowa.[20] All skipped just one year of high school. Some students found leaving home quite easy, especially those who earlier had participated in academic camps, lived in college dorms, or lived in a foreign country. A few students—those who had never before lived away from home or who lost friends—described the experience as "hard" or "horrible." All students formed friendships on campus; nonetheless, three became homesick. Despite positive experiences at The University of Iowa, one intensely homesick girl returned to high school at the college semester break.

Living in residence halls aided these students' social adjustment. Further, they all appreciated the academic challenge—compared with the busywork and slow pace of high school, along with a few inept and rigid high school teachers. Their first-semester average college GPA was 3.18—which is higher than other University of Iowa first-year students.

Regarding their choice to enter college early, one student commented that if she had stayed in high school, "I probably would have gone insane!... I would have been really bored." Another jokingly said that she would have suffered "an emotional breakdown or something!" One student said that in his junior year, he became "lethargic and...apathetic about school.... It was the same routine every day."[21] However, four of the 10 students had mixed reactions about early college entrance, and two of these flatly regretted the choice. Problems included dislike of (arrogant, reclusive) professors, dislike of a dorm roommate, missing valuable high school experiences, and missing the hometown community. A strong network of college friendships vastly improved their satisfaction with college.

Residential High Schools

State-supported residential (live-in) high schools have appeared in just the past quarter century.[22] Most focus on subjects like math, science, and computers. Such schools accurately assume that regular high schools simply cannot provide enough math and science courses for students who zip through a school's offerings in one or two years.

As of 2003, there were 10 states with residential high schools. School names and Internet addresses appear in Table 5.1.

Table 5.1. Residential High Schools and Internet Addresses

School	Internet Address
Arkansas School for Math and Science in Hot Springs	www.asmsweb.com
Illinois Mathematics and Science Academy	www.imsa.edu
Indiana Academy for Science, Mathematics, and the Humanities	www.bsu.edu/academy
Louisiana School for Math, Science and the Arts	www.lsmsa.edu
Massachusetts Academy of Mathematics and Science	www.massacademy.org
Mississippi School for Math and Science	www.msms.k12.ms.us
Missouri Academy of Science, Mathematics, and Computing	www.nwmissouri.edu
North Carolina School of Science and Mathematics	www.ncssm.edu
South Carolina Governor's School for Science and Mathematics	www.gssm.k12.sc.us/gssm.pdf
Texas Academy of Mathematics and Science	www.tams.unt.edu

Curiously, despite the size of many western cities, there are no math/science residential high schools west of Texas.

The residential high schools in Illinois and Arkansas admit students beginning at grade 10; all others begin at grade 11. Student body populations range from under 100 to over 600. All residential high schools were created by state legislation and are supported by state funds. All include a racial and ethnic student body that matches the racial and ethnic composition of the particular state.

All but three are located on college campuses, which supply dormitories, cafeterias, recreational facilities, classrooms, and other academic resources, plus art, music, and theater opportunities. The Illinois school operates in a vacated high school. The North Carolina and Arkansas schools converted hospitals into classrooms, libraries, dorms, labs, and recreational areas. All three already had cafeterias.

Complaints and criticisms seem to follow any new educational plan. In the case of residential high schools, complaints include: (1) high schools lose their best students (the "brain drain" problem), (2) students leave home too early, (3) such elitist schools create arrogance, and (4) young people will be influenced by evil college students, all of whom are involved in drugs, sex, murder, terrorism, and jaywalking.

Charter School of Wilmington, Delaware[23]

The Charter School of Wilmington, Delaware, which opened in 1995, is an outstanding model for designing programs for gifted high school students. The focus is on college-preparatory math, science, and language arts. Students may specialize in discrete math, biotechnology, or forensics—hardly the typical high school merchandise. Median admissions test scores are about the 90th percentile. The school uses both acceleration and enrichment, as needed.

It's philosophy and core assumption? The curriculum will challenge all students. When bright students are concentrated in one school, they will motivate each other and compete for high levels of achievement.

On surveys, Charter's gifted students regularly and predictably praise the school. As one parent noted, her bright son tries to do well at Charter "because it's cool to be smart!" Principal Ronald Russo smiles, "The environment encourages students to higher achievement. I do not see boredom here."

Compare this description of Charter with the reported experiences of one public school student, who the authors safely assigned the fictional name "Chintan." In seventh grade, Chintan was permitted to take eighth-grade math—which still bored him. Peers teased him because of his advanced interests and abilities. Some were openly hostile, knocking books from his hands in the halls. On Charter's first orientation day, Chintan happily realized that he would fit in. He succeeded at the school's most challenging classes—for example, multivariable calculus and discrete math. And he became an outstanding scholarly role model, not a distressed target for bullies. One of Chintan's eventual projects was "replicating heart functions with nonlinear mathematics to predict and control the effect of a pacemaker and certain drugs on cardiac cells."[24] He also was selected for the U.S. Physics Olympiad team.

Charter boasts some elementary features of a sensible school for gifted students. It uses ability grouping based on entering math and reading tests. If students believe they already know the content of a course, they can test out and avoid the boredom and repetition. Charter hires only teachers who strongly believe in helping superior students learn at high levels.

Charter's reputation now attracts remarkably qualified teachers. For example, a teacher of Spanish holds a Ph.D. in science, and a biology teacher also is a chiropractor. Overall, the school sees itself as a proud and satisfied community of scholars.

International Baccalaureate Programs

Worldwide, there are 1,310 "authorized" International Baccalaureate (IB) programs in 110 countries. Exactly 1,000 are the highly selective two-year high school Diploma Programmes for students age 16 to 19. The rest are Middle Years Programs and Primary Years Programs, which are simply designed for younger students and are not prerequisites for the high school Diploma Programme. IB programs are highly selective, include advanced coursework and foreign languages, and expose students to international concerns and problems.

Students are selected by a committee of teachers, counselors, and administrators who examine academic performance, conduct, motivation, extracurricular activities, and a written statement from each applicant. Academically, all IB students are in the top 10%.

In the high school Diploma Programme, course offerings include two-year Higher Level (HL) courses and one-year Standard Level (SL) courses. The courses cover six areas: (1) *Language A1* (first language), which includes study of world literature; (2) *Second Language*; (3) *Individuals and Society* (e.g., business, geography, psychology, anthropology); (4) *Experimental Sciences* (e.g., biology, physics, environmental systems, design technology); (5) *Mathematics*; and (6) *Arts and Electives* (art, music, theater).

According to *Washington Post* writer Jay Mathews, we have a nasty course credit snag.[25] Most American colleges apparently will award college credit only for the two-year HL courses, but not for the one-year SL courses. This, despite the fact that they *do* award college credit for one-year AP courses, which actually could be easier. To earn college credit, many IB students must take AP exams in addition to their IB exams. One IB school administrator viewed each May as a "testing zoo" because his high school gave 532 IB exams and 961 AP exams—all during that one month!

Talent Search and Elementary Talent Search

In 1971, Julian Stanley began his *Study of Mathematically Precocious Youth* (SMPY) at Johns Hopkins University.[26] He assumed correctly that mathematically talented students are slowed down by math teachers who assume that all students must work at a lock-step rate. Using the *Scholastic Aptitude Test-Mathematics* (SAT-M), he identified seventh- and some eighth-grade students who scored above the 51st percentile—in comparison with college-bound high school juniors and seniors. The IQ scores of the seventh- and eighth-grade students ranged from 135 to 200.[27] These students took summer math classes at Johns Hopkins and mastered one or two years of high school algebra and geometry *in three weeks*. Said Stanley, they were working, not sleeping. Stanley also advised students of such acceleration options as: (1) attending college part time, (2) condensing two or more years of math into one, (3) earning college credit in the CLEP or AP programs, (4) skipping a grade, and/or (5) entering college early.

SMPY at Johns Hopkins currently conducts a national search for the "one in 10,000" students in two groups labeled the "700-800 SAT-Mathematics Before Age 13 Group" and the "630-800 SAT-Verbal Before Age 13 Group." Students in both groups are helped education-ally—for example, with scholarships for pre-college summer activities, particularly Talent Search (described below), and with newsletters describing how to accelerate their education. These rare kids also are studied.

University Talent Search programs are patterned after SMPY at Johns Hopkins. Extremely bright seventh-grade students are identified with the (newer) *Scholastic Aptitude Test-I* (SAT-I), which evaluates both math and verbal ability. As with SMPY, the main activity is summer courses, some of which carry AP credit. For example, one recent Talent Search program offered 14 courses: calculus (AP), computer science courses (AP), advanced language and composition (AP), laboratory science, economics, survey of social sciences, speech and debate, Greek, Latin, mythology, and others.

The unusual Talent Search program at Duke University offered 99(!) courses in science, math, and humanities to 2,300 students at six university campuses. "Learning excursions"—working with adult professionals—took groups of students to Costa Rica, England, Italy, Greece, or Germany.

Elementary Talent Search is relatively new. This summer program begins at grade two or three and extends through grade five or six; the specific grades vary with which university offers the program. Students become involved in independent learning and research projects, contests, mentorships, mini-classes, and other learning opportunities.

Universities in the U.S. and elsewhere that offer Talent Search and Elementary Talent Search programs are listed in Table 5.2.

Table 5.2. Talent Search and Elementary Talent Search Programs, Websites, and Grade Levels[28]

California State University, Sacramento, CA 95819.
  http://edweb.csus.edu/projects/ATS
  Elementary and middle school
Carnegie Mellon University, Pittsburgh, PA 15213.
  www.cmu.edu/outreach/c-mites
  Elementary school, grades 3 through 6
College of DuPage, Glen Ellyn, IL 60137.
  www.cod.edu/dept/teens/spring2002/talent_search.htm
  Elementary, middle, and high school, grades 5 through 10
Duke University, Durham, NC 27708.
  www.tip.duke.edu
  Upper elementary and middle school
Iowa State University, Ames, IA 50011.
  www.public.iastate.edu/~opptag_info/mainpage.htm
  Elementary and middle school, grades 2 through 9
Johns Hopkins University (CTY), Baltimore, MD 21218.
  www.jhu.edu/~gifted/index.html
  Elementary and middle school, grades 2 through 8
Northwestern University, Evanston, IL 60208.
  http://ctdnet.acns.nwu.edu
  Elementary and middle school, grades 3 through 8

University of Denver, Rocky Mountain Talent Search, Denver, CO 80208.
www.du.edu/education/ces/rmts.html
Elementary, middle, and high school, grades 5 through 9
University of Iowa (Belin-Blank Center), Iowa City, IA 52242.
www.uiowa.edu/~belinctr
Elementary and middle school, grades 3 through 9
University of Washington, Seattle, WA 98195.
http://depts.washington.edu/cscy
Elementary and middle school, grades 5 through 9
Utah Talent Search, Utah State Office of Education, Salt Lake City, UT 84114.
www.usoe.k12.ut.us/curr/g&t/talent
Middle and high school, grades 7 through 9
Western Carolina University, Cullowhee, NC 28723.
www.wcu.edu/talentsearch
Elementary, middle, and high school

* * * * *

University of Calgary, Calgary, Alberta, Canada T2N 1N4.
www.acs.ucalgary.ca/~gifteduc
Elementary school
Warwick University, Warwick, England.
www.warwick.ac.uk/gifted
Middle school, ages 11 to 16
Dublin City University, Dublin 9, Ireland.
www.dcu.ie/ctyi
Middle school, ages 12 to 16
University of New South Wales, Sydney 2052, Australia.
www.arts.unsw.edu.au/gerric
Elementary school

Summary

- *Acceleration* is any strategy that results in advanced placement or credit.

- *Enrichment* is exposing students to greater breadth and depth of subject material, but without awarding advanced placement or credit.

- *Grouping* is bringing gifted students together, at least part time, to aid both academic and social-emotional well-being. Acceleration and enrichment often require grouping.

- Despite accusations, research shows academic advantages of acceleration with no social or psychological damage. All students above IQ 150 need acceleration, as well as many in the 130 to 150 range.

- Early admission to kindergarten or first grade as a form of acceleration normally is successful if young children are screened regarding mental, emotional, social, and physical readiness. Considerations are an IQ above 130, average eye-hand coordination, advanced reading and arithmetic skills, no emotional or social problems, a supportive teacher, and a family that values achievement above athletics.

- Grade skipping is cost effective and leads to early college admission. Grade-skipped students usually are comfortable with intellectual peers. Considerations are similar to those for early admission to kindergarten or first grade.

- Subject skipping—partial acceleration—accommodates students with strong abilities in, for example, math, reading, or languages. Subject skipping must be well-planned to avoid repetition.

- Telescoping refers to condensing, for example, three years of math or science into two. One intensive three-week summer physics course was equivalent to a year-long high school course or semester-long college course.

- Credit by examination allows prepared students to "test out" of a middle or high school course and receive course credit. The College Level Examination Program (CLEP) awards college credit in 30 areas.

- Three high school strategies allow students to earn college credit. With dual enrollment, a capable student attends a local college part time. Advanced Placement (AP) courses carry college credit. Larger universities offer correspondence courses.

- Early college admission is possible by accelerating high school work and graduating early, or by leaving high school without graduating. Either way, the student should work with a counselor.

- Most of the 10 U.S. residential high schools focus on math and science and usually begin at grade 11. Most are on college campuses.

- The selective International Baccalaureate (IB) high school programs offer two-year Higher Level (HL) courses and one-year Standard Level (SL) courses in six academic areas. Most colleges award credit only for the HL courses.

- Based on Stanley's Study of Mathematically Precocious Youth, Talent Search programs use the SAT to select bright seventh-grade students for advanced summer courses, some of which carry AP credit. Students receive educational and career counseling. Elementary Talent Search programs typically cover grades 3 through 6.

6
Enrichment

*At age six, Joshua was a music student at Julliard. He
made his concerto debut playing Haydn's D-Major Piano
Concerto with the New York String Society. But this
didn't matter. In first grade, he had to spend hours with
the other children clapping the rhythm for quarter notes.*
~ Adapted from Jan and Bob Davidson
and Laura Vanderkam

[*Scene: Tavern on Hollywood Boulevard in Los Angeles. Dr. Malaprop is slop-
ping down his fourth mug of Splatz Red Ribbon beer when Sally Straightman
sits down beside him.*]

Sally Straightman: Say, aren't you the famous Dr. Malaprop? Can I
buy you a beer?

Dr. Malaprop: Why thanks! I'll have a Splatz Red Ribbon, and I appreciate the jester of good will!

Sally: Say, have you had any enriching experiences lately? Like traveling
to Panguitch, Utah?

Malaprop: Oh yes, definitely! My wife and I are both expired now, and
so we have lots of travails—London, Moscow, Panguitch, Paris, Anchor-
age…our journals just go on and on *ad mausoleum*. Just last week we
were strolling Shawn's-Easy-Way in Paris. We saw some very poor
people, so we gave each one a few cranks. We have a great affliction for
the poor. But we get tired of hotel signs that say "No Vagrancy."

Sally: You mean *vacancy*.

Malaprop: That's what I said.

Sally: What would you say are your most enriching experiences?

Malaprop: Travel is so impudent! I think we were most suppressed by Count Dracula's Castle in Pennsylvania. We were absolutely enameled by the whole place!

Sally: I see.

Malaprop: But you must always plan your travails with a clear porpoise. At Count Dracula's Castle, we planned to learn about Munsters!

Sally: Tell me about your porpoises. Is your fish bill high?

Malaprop (sneezes): Excuse me! I think I have a defection in my androids. Now, what was your question?

Sally: Never mind, Dr. Malaprop. But can I buy you another Splatz Red Ribbon? You're such a clone!

Process and Content Goals

Enrichment strategies have *content* and *process* goals. *Content* refers to the advanced and enriched subject matter itself. *Process* refers to the mental procedures of problem solving, creative thinking, scientific thinking, critical thinking, reasoning, planning, analyzing, evaluation, and many, many other thinking skills.[1]

One common—and often justified—criticism of enrichment activities for gifted students is "Wouldn't that be good for all students?" The answer often is "yes." For example, enrichment that is good for all students includes positive ethics and values, field trips, college and career information, and most or all of the thinking skills listed above.

Goals of enrichment suited especially for gifted and talented students include:

- Educational content and activities consistent with the gifted student's ability and educational needs—that is, challenging learning experiences not included in the regular classroom curriculum.

- High content complexity, including theories, generalizations, and applications.

- Inspiring high academic motivation, including high educational and career aspirations.

- Exposure to a variety of fields of study and careers.

- Stimulating gifted students' individual interests.

- Individual in-depth research involving student-selected content, which includes acquiring library and computer skills.

- Meeting educational, social, and psychological needs, including helping gifted students develop good self-concepts.

- Developing higher-level thinking skills (the process goals mentioned earlier).

- Maximizing learning and individual development and minimizing boredom and frustration.

Sandra Kaplan emphasized several important process goals and instructional strategies for teaching gifted students.[2] For example, teachers should help students develop: (1) *accountability*—that is, responsibility for their learning, achievement, and their lives; (2) *curiosity*, for example, by teaching them to ask good questions ("What's behind this decision?" "Who else had a motive?" "Was there a better way?"); (3) *perseverance*, which stems from understanding and appreciation, by teaching students to describe the effects of events (e.g., the circumstances between the North and the South before the Civil War), recognize value (including monetary, worldwide, and personal value), and understand longer sequences of events ("What came before?" "What was happening at the same time?"); (4) a *risk-taking* attitude, by encouraging students to not worry about making mistakes or being wrong; (5) a *thirst for knowledge*, which directly affects their learning capacity ("What happened in the 2004 presidential election?" "How can you check it out?"); (6) *active participation*; and (7) *inner reflectiveness* or *pondering* ("What's the point?" "What are we trying to do?").

School Projects and Activities

Library and Internet Research Projects

Library and Internet research projects typically begin with a question, which may change as the project evolves. For example, "What is the evidence for American Indian migration from Asia?," "Are there relationships and similarities among Greek, Roman, Nordic, and Aztec gods?," and "How does the FBI work?" It's important that a product or report be created and that this final outcome be presented to an audience—either the class or outside group(s).[3]

Creative Writing, Art, Drama

Creative writers can be coached in writing short stories or poems for publication. The G/T teacher, working with the student writer, can track down magazines and newspapers that publish student writing.

Possibilities in art and handicrafts are endless. The budding artist can explore drawing; painting with watercolors, oils, or acrylics; sculpting with clay, wood, or metal; silk-screening; batiking T-shirts; lettering; printing; weaving; ceramics and pottery; photography; designing and building exotic bird houses; and more.

Theater buffs can explore how plays are written—with plots that elicit suspense, conflicts, emotion, and drama—then write, direct, and perform in their own play.

Science Projects

With science projects, a teacher's usual role is "guide on the side"—helping the student clarify the problem and plan the project; directing the student to suitable Internet, library, or human resources; and helping locate needed equipment or other resources. Most elementary and middle schools have science fairs which display and reward student science projects. Further, many children's museums will exhibit high-quality student science projects.

Other Independent Projects

Creating a newspaper is a terrific project for a group of enthusiastic gifted students. The project will involve researching topics, interviewing people, taking photos, writing stories, and using a computer to design and print the newspaper.

One group of elementary students interviewed and photographed residents of a retirement home. They took notes about local and state history and about how to quilt, make candles, and be a blacksmith. Their respect and appreciation for the elderly went way, way up.

Most young people don't even think about building a better mouse trap, can opener, or pet door. The Invent America program rewards (what else?) exciting inventions submitted by young people. One thoughtful elementary student—tired of stumbling in the dark—used a can of luminous spray paint to create a Glow in the Dark Toilet Seat. His simple invention was later displayed at the Smithsonian Institution.

Nearly 200 ideas for enrichment activities and independent projects appear in Table 6.1.

Table 6.1. Sample of Topics for Enrichment Activities or Independent Projects[4]

Mathematics

Algebra	Math puzzles	Probability
Engineering	Measurement	Statistics
Geometry	Money management	

Science

Aeronautics	Ecology	Microscopes
Agriculture	Electronics	Mineralogy
Anatomy	Energy (solar, geothermal,	Natural resources
Animal behavior	tidal, wind)	Nuclear energy
Aquarium design	Evolution	Optics, optometry
Archeology	Fish, marine biology	Physics
Astronomy, space,	Forestry	Physiology
space travel	Fossils	Pollution
Biology, animals, birds,	Genetics	Prehistoric animals
insects	Geology	Reptiles
Botany	Health, nutrition	Robots
Brain science	Horticulture	Rocketry
Chemistry	Medicine	Scientists
Conservation, natural	Metals	Solar power
resources	Meteorology	Veterinary science
Diseases	Microbiology	
Drugs (abuse)		

Literature, Writing, Communication

Broadcasting	Mythology	Writing poetry, short
Classic literature	Public speaking	stories, mysteries,
Journalism	Speed reading	plays, editorials, "how
		to do it" essays

Computers and the Internet

Computer building	Stock market information	Word processing
Computer repair,	and operation, stock	Writing music on
Computer searches and	prices, stock trading	the computer
resources (e.g., maps,		
weather, history, travel		
finding persons,		
researching any topic)		

Visual and Performing Arts

Acting	Folk art	Pottery, ceramics
Architecture	Folk music	Print making
Art history	Graphics	Puppetry
Artists	Jewelry making	Radio shows
Ballet	Leather craft	Rug hooking
Batik	Macramé	Sculpture (clay, wood, metal)
Calligraphy	Movie making	Shakespeare
Candle making	Music composition	Silk screening
Cartooning	Music history	Slide show making
Costume design	Musical instruments	Soft sculpture

Visual and Performing Arts (continued)

Dance, choreography	Opera	Television
Designing (machines, toys, clothes, etc.)	Painting	Theater (dramatic production, acting techniques, set
Drawing	Pantomime	design, lighting, makeup,
Film making	Photography, cameras	literature, history)
	Political satire	

Language, Culture, Social Sciences

African American history	Folklore	Political cartoons
Alcoholism	Foreign languages	Politics, political science
Ancient China, Egypt,	Futuristic thinking	Population problems
England, Greece,	Geography	Prehistoric life
Germany, Rome, etc.	Geology	Presidents
Anthropology	Government (U.S., foreign)	Psychology, mental illness
Archaeology	Handicapped, the	Public opinion surveys
Careers	Historic persons	Religion
Children, child development	History (local, state, U.S.,	Sign language
Civil rights	Russian, military, etc.)	Social problems
Communism	Holidays	Sociology
Criminology, prisons	Map making	Travel
Cultures (modern, ancient, etc.)	Mayas, Aztecs, Incas	Voting, elections
Current events	Minority groups	Women's rights
Debate	Newspapers	
Divorce	Parapsychology, occult	
Elderly, problems of	Philosophy	
Famous people		

Economics, Business

Accounting	Careers	Law
Advertising	Economics (and models)	Stock market
Banking	Finance	Trucking, transportation
Business Ownership	Insurance	

Interests, Hobbies, Etc.

Bicycles	Football history	Running
Bridge	Gardening	Sailing
Chess	Horses	Stamps
Coins	Interior decorating	Test taking
College preparation	Magic	Trees
Creativity	Martial arts	Xylophones
FBI, Secret Service	Rugby	

Learning Centers

Learning centers are "tabletop" work stations for individual work and contain materials for educational enrichment. They may be in classrooms or the school instructional materials center. Commercial learning centers may be purchased, or innovative teachers can design and construct them. They virtually always include one or more computers. Learning centers are useful for gifted students who either are mainstreamed in regular classrooms, are to be used when these students finish work early, or are located in special G/T classrooms.

With or without computers and commercial computer programs, centers can teach history, geography, foreign languages, above-grade math, more advanced science, music appreciation, handicrafts, and other topics. Centers also can display, for example, science projects and student art.

Gifted and other students can self-select appealing learning centers, or a teacher and student together can outline attractive learning center goals.

Field Trips

Field trips present excellent opportunities to acquaint students with cultural, artistic, or scientific areas—or career options. Some big-city possibilities are museums, art galleries, manufacturing plants, a planetarium, insurance company, newspaper company, research laboratory, hospital, large hotel, bank, fire station, symphony rehearsal, or middle-eastern restaurant. An entire class, a small group of interested students, or a chaperoned individual student can take a field trip.

Gifted students should be prepared in advance with problems and questions to resolve. The teacher and guide should plan a stimulating program that is flexible enough to accommodate wide student interests and questions. Gifted students might later prepare reports or projects which will exercise and reflect their advanced thinking skills and knowledge.

Service Learning and Global Awareness

Students are taught politeness, concern for others, a sense of justice, and concern for the environment with the depth of coverage set by teacher interest and district guides. They also learn about other countries and cultures.

Today these areas are covered by the catch phrases *service learning* and *global awareness*. The two are related in that both are teaching goals that include a strong and international concern for others. For both, the intensity of classroom coverage and actual student involvement has increased dramatically, especially for gifted students.

At the 2004 National Association for Gifted Children (NAGC) conference in Salt Lake City, a remarkable number of presentations dealt with service learning and global awareness, particularly the latter. In fact, "Global Awareness" was one of 15 broad conference topics.

Service learning is promoted at our federal level. The first President George Bush created the *National and Community Service Act* of 1990, which led to the creation of the Commission on National and Community

Service.[5] President Bill Clinton in 1992 promoted the *National and Community Service Trust Act,* leading to the Corporation for National and Community Service.

Current service learning projects include helping others and solving actual community problems—for example, helping the elderly, cheering up hospitalized children, picking up street litter, reducing school theft and vandalism, or pestering the mayor to install traffic lights at dangerous intersections or reduce habitat (lakes, streams, woodlands, wetlands) destruction. One class helped remodel a small, dilapidated building that was a historically significant landmark.

By participating in service learning projects, young people become sensitized to community problems and acquire civic responsibility. They learn to care about the welfare and problems of others. They become inspired to take positive social action. They become conservationists, for example, after picking up trash from a streambed. Their self-assessment and philosophy of life changes. In short, they reach higher levels of moral development, self-actualization, responsibility, leadership, reflective judgment, and empathy for others. Service learning fosters new generations of caring, participatory citizens.[6] Small wonder that interest in service learning is sky high.

Alice Terry and Jann Bohnenberger emphasized that service learning projects inspire students to become catalysts for needed changes in their communities.[7] They also reminded us that: (1) Paul Torrance's Community Problem Solving program merged creative thinking with social action to solve real problems and needs in the community, (2) Harry Passow recommended curricula that sensitize students to major problems in our world, and (3) both Dabrowski and Roeper independently noted that highly creative and gifted individuals show greater empathy, sensitivity, moral responsibility, and sense of justice. Bohnenberger and Terry quoted Judith Ramaly of the National Science Foundation as stating, "I know of no better way to invoke the many facets of cognitive development, moral reasoning, and social responsibility than to engage students in service-learning opportunities."[8]

Terry described three levels of service learning. *Community Service* involves volunteer work, which raises awareness of community problems. *Community Exploration* includes, especially, participation in environmental education programs. *Community Action* includes both of the above, plus making a positive impact on one's community.[9]

In Terry's service learning research, 28 gifted students at Horton Middle School—"Horton's Helpers"—used the Creative Problem Solving model (Chapter 11) to identify community problems and select one problem to resolve. She concluded that—due to their service learning experiences—students showed an improved sense of accomplishment, greater respect for and from the community, a sense of pride, and better attitudes generally. They felt empowered to independently make decisions and take action. They also improved in academic, intellectual, personal, social, and creative development. Because of their outstanding service learning work, some students appeared on *The Phil Donahue Show,* and others were featured in *Reader's Digest.*

With the same mindset, Joseph Renzulli made eye-opening statements on the goals of gifted programs.[10] In addition to cultivating academic prowess and good study habits, gifted programs should promote *social capital.* That is, they should teach awareness and concern for the needs and problems of others. Gifted programs should incorporate socially relevant activities and training in leadership, which also includes a willingness to take social action. Renzulli's University of Connecticut project, Operation Houndstooth, focuses on developing optimism, moral courage, integrity, sensitivity to human concerns (empathy, altruism), and a sense of destiny, along with passion for a topic or discipline. Such virtues should replace self-interest and consumerism with a strong social conscience.

Similarly, global awareness—as the name suggests—educates students regarding diverse world cultures and the often severe problems of their people. The goal is not just increased knowledge, but increased empathy and concern—just as with other forms of service learning. From grades K through 12, global education promotes such aspects of self actualization as "empathy, profound relationships, identification with humanity, and devotion to a task or cause."[11] Many "globally gifted" students spontaneously show concerns about the world at large, as Ellen Fiedler has pointed out.[12] Other leaders in gifted education, such as Michele Kane and Annemarie Roeper, have also noted that some global-thinking gifted children see themselves as "citizens of the world."[13] However, realities such as war, poverty, starvation, injustice, environmental degradation, and worldwide health crises create feelings of helplessness and despair among some compassionate gifted students who wish to use their gifts to save the world.[14] Stephanie Tolan suggested that we must help these students adopt a more realistic and mentally healthy attitude of "serving the world" rather than wanting to save it, thus supporting their empathy and compassion more realistically.

At a less stressful level, Freeman and Williams' Project REACH (Respecting Ethnic And Cultural Heritage) put elementary students in direct contact with kids in other countries.[15] For example, in one project, second graders wrote about "One special day in my life," then shared their reflections on the Internet. In their "Drums, Dragons, and Dance" project, students learned about Chinese folklore. Worldwide communication likely was aided by the fact that in Freeman's elementary school, various kids spoke 15(!) different languages. Freeman and Williams emphasized that technology aids students' natural needs to "explore, reflect, communicate, dream, and celebrate."[16]

Saturday Programs

Some universities and gifted child organizations offer Saturday programs for gifted students. Saturday programs almost always take the form of mini-classes taught by university faculty, graduate students, or community experts—who are often parents of gifted students.

As one remarkable example, Purdue University's Super Saturday program recently included the following classes, all of which extended over nine Saturdays. For kindergarten and lower elementary students: Creative Thinking, Mime, Exploring Space, and Chinese. For intermediate elementary students: Art, French, Probability and Statistics, and Insects. For upper elementary students: TV Production, Computers, American Indian Culture, and Chemistry. For junior and senior high school students: Economics, Electrical Engineering, Computers, and Horses, plus Psychology, French, English Composition, and Political Science for college credit.

Goals of the one-hour workshops of the Gifted Child Society of Glen Rock, New Jersey, are to challenge the learning needs of gifted children and stimulate higher levels of thinking, problem solving, creativity, and leadership.[17] Their workshops for two-year-old(!) children taught movement, music, songs, rhythm instruments, and imagination. Their first- and second-grade children could learn about magic, oceanography, cartooning, computer LOGO, metal and clay design, rocketry, astronomy, drama, and "Blood and Guts Biology."

Summer Programs

The National Association for Gifted Children (NAGC) lists many summer programs on its website (www.nagc.org/summer/intro/html). These programs are listed separately for northeastern, mid-Atlantic, southern, midwestern, and western American states, in addition to an "International" category. The information includes Internet and e-mail addresses. Also, most cities offer summer programs open to all students. Teachers, counselors, and parents may capitalize on the NAGC-listed programs and city programs to supply valuable enrichment for bright, enthusiastic children.

Logan School for Creative Learning

As a stellar example, the Logan School for Creative Learning in Denver offers both a Creative Learning Camp and a Summer Musical Theater Workshop. The Creative Learning Camp includes a Discovery Group (ages 6-8) and an Explorer Group (ages 9-12). In 2004, the Discovery Group spotted birds, tracked animals, and were involved in arts (painting) and crafts (making jewelry). They also went bowling, swimming, and ice skating. The Explorer Group visited cliff dwellings at Colorado Springs and learned some anthropology at the Denver Museum of Natural History. They also went hiking, rock climbing, go-karting, bowling, and swimming, and they watched the Rockies Red Sox at Coors Field.

The 2004 Logan School Summer Musical Theater Workshop program was based on the story of "Weslandia," a civilization created by a boy that "has its own language, clothing, number system, agriculture, and games." Based on this story, students age six to eight created their own play with original songs, games, music, movement, and paper sets. For information, see http://theloganschool.org.

Governor's School Programs

Governor's Schools are state-supported summer residential programs for gifted high school students.[18] At least 32 states support at least 43 summer Governor's Schools, virtually all of which are held on college campuses. All Governor's Schools are highly selective. Twenty-four of the 43 charge nothing for tuition, rooms, or meals; the remaining 19 require students to pay some costs; and all require students to supply their own spending money.

The content of Governor's Schools summer programs usually evolves around: (1) math, science, and technology; (2) arts and entertainment; and (3) humanities and social sciences. Enthusiasm of both students and educators runs high. Said one student said, "For the first time in my life, I can really be me. I can talk about opera or heavy metal music and no one will think I'm weird!" Another reported, "Awesome!... This has been one of the best experiences of my life!"[19]

As an example, in Pennsylvania, a three-year pilot project for artistically talented high school students began in the late 1960s. Following its glowing success, the Pennsylvania Governor's School for the Arts began officially in 1973.[20] In the 1980s, the Pennsylvania Governor's School program expanded. At present, the five-week residential Governor's Schools of Excellence include summer programs titled *Agricultural Sciences* (environmental studies, genetic engineering, water quality, robotics), *The Arts* (visual arts, creative writing, dance, music, theater), *Global Entrepreneurship* (entrepreneurship around the world), *Health Care* (medical, social, psychology, professional issues), *Information Technology* (networks and telecommunications, systems analysis and design, software development, electronic commerce), *International Studies* (foreign languages, geography, history, economics, negotiations, cultures and societies), *The Sciences* (modern physics, organic chemistry, biotechnology, discrete mathematics), and *Teaching* (educational psychology, learning styles, social foundations of education, school design, teaching strategies).

Gifted students in grades 10 or 11 can apply for programs in Agricultural Sciences, The Arts, and Global Entrepreneurship. Only students in grade 11 can apply for the programs in Health Care, Information Technology, International Studies, The Sciences, and Teaching.

All of the Pennsylvania programs emphasize leadership development. For example, students are encouraged to become involved in service projects in their local communities and to share their talents and energies in their home schools.[21]

Governor's Schools are selective. Also, eligibility and application procedures vary between programs. The Pennsylvania program specifies that: (1) the student's family must reside full-time in Pennsylvania, (2) the student is in the appropriate grade for the particular program, (3) the student cannot apply to more than two programs, (4) the student has not previously attended a Pennsylvania Governor's School program, and (5) the student must intend to participate for the full 35 days. Room, board, tuition, and cost of instruction materials are paid by Pennsylvania.

Parents cover health care costs, transportation to the program, spending money, and a returnable deposit on keys, linen, and the dormitory. For further information, visit http://pgse.cis.drexel.edu.

College Programs

Many colleges offer summer programs for enthusiastic gifted students. We described Talent Search programs in Chapter 5.

As other examples, the Berkeley Academic Talent Development Program (ATDP) is a six-week program that accommodates about 1,000 students between ages 11 and 17. Students take just one course, spending only three to five hours per week in class. They may learn to write short stories or poetry; put on plays; write computer programs; speak Russian or Japanese; learn about chemistry, archaeology, or biology; or work with archeologists at digs or with marine biologists collecting samples.

Students work together in and out of classrooms, students and teachers telephone each other about coursework, and students meet with professionals in their mutual interest areas. Berkeley scientists, accomplished poets, and dance choreographers often visit classes.

The three-week, half-day College for Kids program at the University of Wisconsin-Madison accommodates 250 fifth graders from local gifted programs. Following their early morning gifted seminar, 27 or 28 teachers meet with their 25 "families" of about 10 children. They begin their morning with approximately one hour of practicing brainstorming, problem solving, analyzing, evaluating, and other thinking skills. To help self-understanding, they also consider the advantages and disadvantages of being gifted. Advantages always win.

The main College for Kids feature, which follows the one-hour opener, is two one-week workshops available in about 40 areas—for example, TV production, photography, dance, university history, chemistry, and the popular limnology, which includes boat excursions on adjacent Lake Mendota. After the workshops, the family groups visit, for example, the geology museum, the art museum, cows on the agriculture campus, the space science building, or a robot demonstration in the engineering department. The third week is for large group "extravaganzas"—for example, exploding physics demonstrations or slide shows about Belize narrated by an anthropologist who dug there.

Purdue University offers summer programs at four age levels. The Meteor program for grades 3 and 4 is a three-week day program that includes three one-week classes on, for example, Animation Studio, Artistic Math, and Phenomenal Physics. The residential Comet program for grades 5 and 6 also includes three one-week courses on, for example, Aquatic Underworld, Civil War Adventure, Architectural Geometry, and Web Page Design. The Star program for grades 7 and 8 includes two one-week residential sessions that teach, for example, Aeronautical Physics, Pre-Med, Advertising, Prehistoric Biology, Machines and Bridges, and Suspenseful Spanish. The Pulsar program for high school students is a two-week residential program that offers such courses as Entrepreneurship, Veterinary Medicine, Pop Art, Electrical Engineering, and "Movies and Mental Illness."

The Belin-Blank Center at the University of Iowa (UI) also hosts an assortment of summer courses and programs for young people. In 2006, for example, in their 12-day Challenges for Elementary Students (CHESS) program, students in grades 3 to 6 could take the course Writing Your World or Playing the Game of Chess at CHESS. Students in grades 4 to 6 could take Math Problem Solving, Photography, Computer Programming, or Chemistry: Gases and Solutions. Summer programs for students grades 6 to 8 included Junior Scholars Academy, Iowa Governor's Institute, and the Blank Summer Institute. For grades 9 to 11, summer programs included Asian and Pacific Studies Institute, Environmental Health Sciences Institute, and Foreign Language Summer Institute.

Camp Invention

Camp Invention is sponsored by the National Inventors Hall of Fame and the U.S. Patent Office. Many states offer this one-week summer program for middle-school students. In 2003, Wisconsin hosted 14 Camp Inventions around the state, usually held in middle schools.[22] The program promotes creative and inventive thinking and teamwork.

The 2003 Camp Invention focused on flight, in honor of the 100th anniversary of the Wright brothers' flight. At the July program in Waupun, Wisconsin, more than 70 students created spinning and flying devices with parts from dismantled appliances, VCRs, computer keyboards, telephones, record players, and more. "It's messy and noisy, with lots of creative thinking outside the box," laughed one Camp Invention teacher.

Kids also created non-flight inventions. "We asked them to think of things that bugged them or chores they didn't like," reported one teacher. Guided by attitudes of experimentation and fun, students invented automatic bed-makers, no-splash swimming goggles, and a combination-code door lock to keep siblings out of their bedrooms. "Who knows?" said another teacher, "the kids at Camp Invention today might become our future problem solvers of tomorrow!"

Study Abroad Programs

An expensive summer option is study abroad. Such programs normally include travel plus study of at least one country's language and culture. With study abroad *school-year* programs, a student lives with a family and attends a local school, where the student usually takes special foreign language classes. Kathleen Kardaras used spring break to take students to Europe, Mexico, or Canada to connect classroom instruction with international experiences by immersing students in another culture.[23]

Think global awareness.

Music, Language, Art, and Computer Camps

Many colleges offer summer programs variously called *clinics, institutes, retreats,* or *camps* that usually focus on art, drama, music, foreign languages, or computers. Such programs never claim to be for gifted students, but they will attract students with high interest or talent in an area.

Benefits of Saturday and Summer Programs

While all acceleration and enrichment plans are designed to help the academic and often social needs of gifted students, some specific benefits of both Saturday and summer programs held on college campuses include:[24]

- Gifted students are taught at a faster pace and at greater levels of complexity—which matches their abilities.

- The challenges help cure poor study habits and offset underachievement.

- The students cover topics not usually included in regular school classes.

- They sometimes conduct in-depth creative investigations, with opportunities to identify problems, plan and conduct research, and evaluate and present results—which strengthens creative thinking, problem solving, and other thinking skills.

- They interact and form friendships with other bright and talented students—mental peers.

- They come to better understand their own special talents and abilities.

- Despite some humbling effects of working with other capable students, self-esteem and self-concepts typically improve.

- They learn to take both academic and social risks.

- They learn about college life and to value higher education. Educational and career aspirations improve.

- High-level instructors are excellent professional models.

Mentorships

Mentorships for Secondary Students

When we hear the word *mentorship*, we typically think of an individual high-school student—gifted, average, or below average—who works with an adult professional probably once per week in an occupation of high interest to the student. Normally, the adult mentor becomes a role model, guide, teacher, and friend. The student learns the activities, responsibilities, benefits, problems, necessary training, and lifestyle that accompanies the specific business (profession, occupation, art) of the mentor. Perhaps incidentally, the student also notes the mentor's personality and enthusiasm for the occupation. The student usually receives high school credit and sometimes is paid by the professional.

Desirable mentors are interested in teaching young people. They provide enjoyable and challenging learning experiences that stimulate thinking and problem solving, and they help students see their own potential. Especially for gifted students, a good mentor should be an outstanding person in the community and a "creative producer of acknowledged reputation."[25]

Cox, Daniel, and Boston recommended that the teacher or counselor who establishes the high school mentorship should seek the best possible student-mentor match. Generally, the mentor and protogé (mentee, intern, apprentice) should be matched in gender, social class, ethnicity, background, and values. It follows that mentorships are especially valuable for students who are female, economically disadvantaged, minority, or underachieving—given that the mentor/professional has similar characteristics or background.

In one modification of the typical mentorship, college students—not working professionals—met with gifted high school students after

school and on weekends for 12 weeks.[26] The high school students benefited from being matched with college experts according to area of
interest—for example, archeology, geology, photography, marine science, drama, or French culture.

The Executive Assistant Program and the Performing Arts Program
in Dallas, Texas, seem to sit in the blurry intersection among
mentorships, apprenticeships, and internships. Participants are called
assistants. Students in the upper 20% of their class and who have "excellent
communication and computational skills...initiative and leadership...
maturity, dependability, and creativity" qualify to participate in a
business-oriented program (e.g., working with a vice-president at
Neiman Marcus) or in one of these art areas: dance, instrumental music,
voice, sculpture, or painting.[27] Uniquely, the program also includes the
"athletic arts" —for example, golf, tennis, gymnastics, and ice skating.

For one semester, students attend academic classes for half-days
and work with their executives, artists, or other "master teachers" for
the other half of the day. They attend seminars on Fridays. If they
prefer, they can work full time in their business or art area for the
semester.

Mentorships for Elementary Students

Mentorships sometimes are used with elementary students. The
duration of the mentorship varies from a one-time visit to regularly
scheduled meetings with a professional.

In one version, college students majoring in education served as
mentors for elementary students.[28] The mentors helped students
develop study skills, tutored them in difficult areas, assisted with composition and writing skills, taught library skills, helped with special projects,
helped explore new interest areas, and assisted with personal and social
problems. As always, the mentors were good role models.

In another version, groups of about six interested elementary students met—just once or more frequently—with a doctor, engineer,
lawyer, judge, professor, business owner, chef, TV weather announcer,
professional artist or dancer, or other professional.[29]

On-Line Mentors

With e-mail, students can communicate with professionals and experts anywhere in the world. Ursuline Academy, a women's college, recruited its own alumni to serve as mentors to female high school students in grades 9 to 12.[30] Back-and-forth weekly e-mails informed students about specific careers and the necessary coursework. The mentorships clearly motivated the students to take advanced courses and plan for college. Students and their sympathetic mentors also shared problems and solutions.

Two sources for on-line mentors are http://mentor.external.hp.com and, for international mentoring, www.telementor.org.

Future Problem Solving and Odyssey of the Mind

Although born in America, *Future Problem Solving* and *Odyssey of the Mind* are both international programs—competitions—that stretch students' thinking, imagination, and problem solving. Participants work together in teams, practicing over many months. Conveniently, the gifted students already may be meeting together in one of the grouping plans described in Chapter 7 (pullout programs, special classes, part-time special classes). Or they may meet after school.

Future Problem Solving

The Future Problem Solving (FPS) program is designed to help gifted children: (1) be more aware of the future, (2) think more creatively, (3) speak and write more persuasively, (4) learn teamwork and leadership skills, (5) learn the FPS seven-step problem-solving process, and (6) develop information-gathering and research skills.

Students register in one of three divisions for the year-long program: Junior (grades 4-6), Intermediate (7-9), or Senior (10-12). They receive five practice problems that are solved using this seven step FPS model:[31]

1. Research the topic.

2. Brainstorm problems related to the "fuzzy" situation.

3. Select one important underlying problem (there may be several).

4. Brainstorm solutions to the selected problem.

5. Select five criteria for evaluating the possible solutions.

6. Evaluate the 10 best solutions according to the criteria chosen; then select the single best solution.

7. Describe the best solution in written essay form with outcomes and consequences elaborated and explained.

Each year, the national FPS organization selects three problems to be used in formal state competitions. Past problems have dealt with garbage disposal, dropping out of school, poverty, crime, terrorism, water shortages, energy shortages, ethics in sports, new educational options, organ shortages, rainforest depletion, habitat destruction, and many others.

As completed, each problem is sent to the state FPS organization for evaluation and feedback to the student thinkers. The first two problems are for practice. Based on students' responses to the third problem, teams are selected for a state competition.

For the state competition, teams are given a topic in advance, and they research it. At the competition itself, the team is given a specific problem within that topic. Each team is sequestered in a room for two hours to create written problem statements and solutions following the seven steps. One winning state team per division competes in the International FPS Competition, always held in the U.S. Additional information is available at www.fpsp.org.

Odyssey of the Mind

Odyssey of the Mind (OM) is another international educational program that provides creative problem-solving opportunities for students from kindergarten through college. Children apply their creativity to solve problems over a broad range of topics, and then they bring their solutions to competitions on the local, state, and world level. OM assumes that the mind, not just the physical body, also can be strengthened with exercise.[32]

Four age divisions are: Division I, younger than 12 or in grades K-5; Division II, younger than 15 or in grades 6-8; Division III, grades 9-12; Division IV, college teams. The Internet site—http://odysseyofthemind.com—explains registration procedures and fees, current OM problems, practice problems, classroom activities, and updates and clarifications. It also elaborates on coaching, selecting team members, training, brainstorming, parent involvement, long-term problems (and how they are scored), style points (awarded for creative presentations), spontaneous problems (described later), competition rules, penalties for violating the rules, and lots more.

Teams are limited to seven players, just five of whom "can be on the playing field." Performance time is eight minutes. Expenses per problem are fixed and limited (usually $125), which encourages scrounging junkyards. Registration for the academic year 2004–2005 was $135.

Five long-term problems will require virtually the entire academic year to prepare. The 2004–2005 long-term problems included the following.

(1) *Stunt Mobiles.* The problem was for teams to design, build, and run two original Stunt Mobile vehicles that would travel from behind start lines and over five obstacle courses. The Stunt Mobiles operated on different power systems, and they overcame different obstacles to cross a finish line and break balloons. Divisions I, II, III, and IV.

(2) *In Your Dreams.* Teams created a performance that included a dream that, at different times, was cheerful, nonsensical, or nightmarish. The nightmare included a monster, designed and built by the team, that changed in appearance and performed various tasks, including two designed by the team. Parts of the dream included sounds. Divisions I, II, and III.

(3) *Get the Message?* Teams presented an original performance that included a story told three times, each time using a different method of communication: a primitive method, an evolved method, and a futuristic method created by the team. The team created signals that indicate a stage in the earth system, which they displayed for each communication method. The presentation also included a narrator or host and a stage set. Divisions I, II, III, and IV.

(4) *Crazy Columns.* Teams used only balsa wood and glue to create a structure that would be tested for its ability to balance and support as much weight as possible. But there were some twists: the parts of the structure did not have to be connected, although they could be if the team wished. In addition, the structure would rest on surfaces at three different heights, but the top of the structure had to be at least eight inches from the tester base. The two outer surfaces had to be 10½ inches apart. Placement of

the third surface was determined by the team, but within a specified area. Divisions I, II, III, and IV.

(5) *Laugh-a-Thon.* Teams created and presented a humorous performance that had team members portraying a puppet, a mime, and an image and its reflection. The performance also included a comedy routine or humorous sketch and the effect of something happening much faster than usual. Teams were to add two humorous features of their own that are meant to entertain. Divisions I, II, III, and IV.

In addition to the five long-term problems, student teams also solve *spontaneous* problems; these are not supplied in advance. Answers are judged on-the-spot as *common,* earning one point, or *creative,* earning five points. Two recent practice spontaneous problems were as follows.

(1) *Animal Rhymes.* Students had one minute to think and two minutes to respond. Questions counted against their time. They could not talk to each other. They received one point for each common response and five points for each creative or humorous response. They were to take turns responding. They could not skip a turn, repeat a response, or pass. If one member was stuck, the team was stuck. Once time began, it was not stopped. If a judge asked a student to repeat a response, clarify it, or give a more appropriate response, it counted against their time. They were to speak loudly and clearly.

The problem was to make a rhyme using a name or species of an animal. For example, you might say, "I think mice are nice" or "There's a cat in the hat."

(2) *Names and Occupations.* Preliminary instructions were the same as above.

The problem was to use a word or words to make a first and last name. The students had to relate this name to an occupation. For example, Budweiser could be split into "Bud" as a first name and "Weiser" as a last name. Bud Weiser could be a beer distributor. Or saliva could become "Sal" and "Iva." Sal Iva could be a dentist. The first word had to be a real name or nickname.

Junior Great Books

The popular (and non-competitive) Junior Great Books (JGB) program is used in gifted programs in all 50 states and many foreign countries. Teachers, in one- or two-day JGB workshops, learn to ask thought-provoking questions that require students to interpret literature. Modern and traditional literature is carefully selected for students in kindergarten through high school. The readings are understandable, rich in ideas, and enjoyable to read and discuss. For example, fairy tales and folk tales are used with children in kindergarten through fourth grade. Modern short stories and children's classics are for those students in grades four through nine. High school students read selections from fiction, philosophy, economics, or political science.

Typically, teachers and students discuss the readings in depth in three to five periods per week. Only high school students complete homework assignments.

The Junior Great Books program strengthens vocabulary and skills related to listening, interpretation, and inquiry—in addition to helping students obtain an expanded self-awareness and a greater understanding of psychological and social problems. For information, visit www.greatbooks.org/progs/junior.

United States Academic Decathlon

The United States Academic Decathlon (USAD) thoughtfully includes average high school students as well as outstanding ones. Each six-person high school team includes two "A," two "B," and two "C" students from grades 11 and 12. The USAD involves regional, state, and national competitions, with schools allocated to one of three categories depending on school size.

Students compete in conversation skills, formal speech, essay writing, language and literature, economics, fine arts, social studies, mathematics, physical science, and a Super Quiz, which has a topic that is supplied in advance—for example, "The History of Flight." For information, visit www.usad.org.

Competitions

The book *Competitions: Maximizing Your Potential*, by Frances Karnes and Tracy Riley, contains remarkably valuable descriptions of more than 275 competitions for students in grades 2 through 12.[33] The four categories of competitions are *Academic, Fine and Performing Arts, Leadership,* and *Service Learning* (i.e., community service). For each individual competition, the book supplies information such as the competition name, sponsor, purpose, description, eligibility requirements, dates for applications, how to enter, judging criteria, dates of awards, and the awards themselves—certificates, ribbons, medals, ambiguous "prizes," scholarships, and/or cash—sometimes lots of cash.

The large section of *Academic* competitions includes the categories of Business, Foreign Languages, General Academics (with three subcategories), Languages Arts (10 subcategories), Mathematics, Science (seven subcategories), Social Studies (six subcategories), and Technology.

As a Foreign Languages example, the National Greek Examination is sponsored by the American Classical League and Junior Classical League, Department of Classics, University of Massachusetts. Its purpose is to allow high school students studying classical and modern Greek to compare their achievement with that of students in other schools. Each of seven exams includes an original Greek passage with 40 multiple-choice questions that assess students' grasp of meaning, syntax, and vocabulary. The registration deadline is in early January, and students enter by contacting a school counselor, principal, or teacher. Exams are given in mid-March. Winners are contacted at the end of April and receive blue, red, or green ribbons and hand-lettered certificates.

As a *Leadership* example, the Discover® Card Tribute Award Scholarship is sponsored by the American Association of School Administrators and (who else?) Discover® Card to recognize high school students who exhibit excellence in areas of their lives other than academics. The applicant must demonstrate accomplishments in three areas: (1) Leadership, (2) Obstacles Overcome, and (3) Community Service. The competition is for high school juniors with at least a 2.75 high school grade-point average. The deadline to enter is mid-January, and students enter by submitting to the sponsor a two-page "criteria statement" discussing their accomplishments. Winners are notified in May. Nine students from each state, Washington D.C., and American schools abroad receive scholarships for any career path—college or trade schools: three scholarships for $1,000, three for $1,500, and three for $2,500. Nine national awards include three scholarships for $10,000, three for $15,000, and three for $20,000.

Most of the academic competitions reward academic excellence, usually—but not always—accompanied by evidence of leadership. As non-leadership examples, the Advanced Placement Scholar Awards, sponsored by the Educational Testing Service, bases awards strictly on AP exam scores. Also, the German, Latin, and Greek competitions are based strictly on acquired language proficiency.

Many competitions directly challenge students' creativity. Several examples follow.

(1) The Young Inventors and Creators Program asks for inventions or creations in the categories of health, business/office, household/ food, agriculture, technology, leisure time/entertainment, and environment, plus short stories, poems, music compositions (classical and popular), drama/video, and printing/graphics.

(2) The Business competition (under Academics) asks students to create a business plan in 10 pages or less.

(3) Mothers Against Drunk Driving (MADD) sponsors a competition that includes essay writing and poster design.

(4) The National Council of Teachers of English sponsors a creative writing (poems, short stories) competition.

(5) Duracell® asks students to design and build working devices powered by Duracell® batteries, then submit to them a description, a photograph, and a wiring diagram/schematic.

(6) In the Fire Fighting Home Robot Contest, students design and build a computer-controlled robot that can find and extinguish a fire in a house.

(7) The Young Game Inventors Contest asks for board game inventions.

(8) SuperScience Blue asks students to begin with a SuperScience Blue toy and improve its performance. Their motivation is clear.

(9) The U.S. Fish and Wildlife Service asks for paintings of North American ducks, swans, or geese to be used on Federal Duck Stamps.

(10) The American Automobile Association™ asks students to create a traffic safety slogan that is illustrated on a poster.

(11) The Reflections Cultural Arts Program simply asks students (preschool to grade 12) to submit their creations—related to a given theme—in the area of literature, music, photography, or visual arts.

Karnes and Riley's *Competitions: Maximizing Your Potential* is guaranteed to incite motivation and creativity.

Computers and the Internet

Computers and the Internet supply unlimited possibilities for valuable enrichment activities, from acquiring keyboarding and endless word processing skills to researching absolutely any topic, with worldwide resources. For example, information about *gifted and talented* is available at www.hoagiesgifted.com. *Creativity* is explained at http://members.ozemail.com.au/~caveman/Creative/index2.html.

The National Association for Gifted Children assembled a list of potentially helpful websites for students and teachers.[34] A sample of the topics and websites appears in Table 6.2.

Table 6.2. Websites for Teachers and Gifted Students[35]

Using the Internet for a variety of learning experiences	http://edweb.sdsu.edu/webquest/webquest.html
Locating and using Internet resources	http://execpc.com/~dboals/boals.html
Lesson plans for teachers	http://ericir.syr.edu (includes ERIC lesson plan collection) www.col-ed.org/cur
Research project assistance (e.g., locating experts)	www.tapr.org/emissry
Spanish resources, online scavenger hunts	www.4teachers.org
Library resources	www.awesomelibrary.org www.educationworld.com
Music education	www.childrensmusicworskhop.com
Art, art museums	www.artsednet.getty.edu
Mathematics	http://mathforum.org (with link to Ask Dr. Math) www.c3.lanl.gov/mega-math (math challenges) www.figurethis.org (math challenges) www.execpc.com/~helberg/statistics.html

Science	http://powayusd.sdcoe.k12.ca.us/dolly (cloning Dolly the sheep) http://hea-www.harvard.edu (astrophysics, astronomy) www.astro.washington.edu (astronomy) http://chem4kids.com (chemistry and biochemistry) http://space.rice.edu/hmns/dlt/video.html (Ask the Scientist, news)
Environmental education	http://envirolink.org/enviroed
Geography, weather	www.nationalgeographic.com/xpeditions http://quake.wr.usgs.gov
Social studies	www.thehistorynet.com (world history, daily quiz) http://socialstudies.com/online.html (projects) http://education.indiana.edu/~socialst (history, geography, cultural diversity, etc.)
World health and welfare projects	www.iearn.org
Cross-cultural e-mail, pen pals	www.iecc.org
UNICEF activities and quizzes	www.unicef.org/voy
90,000 kids in 103 countries	www.kidlink.org

Home Schooling: Acceleration and Enrichment

Based on her own experience with a gifted son, Lisa Rivero prepared a marvelous book that summarizes everything you ever wanted to know about home schooling gifted students.[36] Said Rivero, "Home schooling is an educational path that can provide the intellectual, social, and emotional support necessary for a fulfilling life,"[37] and, quoting Annemarie Roeper, "We home school to educate for life rather than simply to educate for success."[38]

Remarkably, a typical week for Rivero's son, at age eight, included exercise in a home gym, meeting with children of all ages, playing with friends ages five to 13, bowling with friends, participating in a book discussion group, participating in a Saturday College for Kids program, playing chess on Sunday with other children in a bookstore, and a weekly meeting with other home-schooled children who also were bright, intense, and sensitive.

Of course, parental instruction requires a significant amount of time and effort. Nonetheless, highly concerned and committed parents—most often moms, but sometimes dads—home school gifted students because home schooling allows flexibility in that the child's education:

- Is not focused on the child's age, school grade, and school history.

- Is custom-tailored to fit advanced curriculum to an advanced child.

- Avoids the massive time waste and busywork in regular classrooms.

- Is tailored to fit a child's unique learning styles, interests, and abilities to question and think abstractly.

- Provides an escape from being "out of sync" with classmates and feeling different from others.

- Allows a child to achieve for the sake of achieving, thus becoming more inner-directed.

- Allows a child to advance rapidly in areas of strength—the child can study and learn at several levels simultaneously.

- Can include watching history documentaries and conducting science experiments.

- Permits custom, self-chosen, and interest-based assignments, such as making a chronological list of Isaac Asimov's short stories.

- Provides a warm, nurturing, and accepting atmosphere in a self-paced education.

- Controls the values to which a child is exposed.

- Supports a child's self-confidence and self-directedness in learning.

- Provides an escape from bullying, if necessary.

- Accommodates a child's motivation and intensity.

- Can help a child understand that sensitivity, idealism, perfectionism, and extreme motivation are valuable strengths, not handicaps to be corrected.

- Reduces or eliminates a child's fear of making mistakes.

- Supports, rather than limits, divergent and creative thinking.

- Allows—and encourages—socializing with various groups and ages.

- Helps a child understand him- or herself and discover who he or she wants to be.

Rivero adds two reasons for home schooling based on personal preference and convenience: home schooling creates more family time, and it supplies freedom for family travel!

Summary

- Enrichment activities teach expanded academic content and strengthen thinking processes.

- Much enrichment is good for all students, not just the gifted.

- Enrichment goals (activities) for gifted students include, for example, content and activities consistent with students' abilities and needs; high content complexity; in-depth research; inspiring educational and career motivation; exposure to a variety of fields; stimulating interests; meeting social and psychological needs, including good self-concepts; and developing thinking skills.

- Kaplan's instructional goals included teaching accountability, curiosity, perseverance, a risk-taking attitude, a thirst for knowledge, active participation, and inner reflectiveness.

- School projects and activities include library and Internet research projects; creative writing, art, and drama; science projects; and independent projects.

- Learning centers allow individual work in, for example, reading, math, science, foreign languages, art, music, and creative writing.

- Educational field trips may be to such places as museums, planetariums, manufacturing plants, newspaper companies, research labs, or foreign restaurants.

- Service learning includes helping others and solving real community problems, which strengthens social responsibility, empathy, sense of justice, concern for the environment, self-actualization, leadership potential, and more.

- Global awareness—educating students regarding world cultures and problems—stimulates an international concern for others.

- Renzulli's social capital—mainly concern for others—is highly similar.

- Project REACH puts elementary students in contact with others around the world.

- Saturday programs typically are mini-courses taught by university faculty or students or by community experts, as in Purdue University's Super Saturday program.

- The NAGC lists summer programs on its website. Most cities offer summer programs open to all students.

- The Logan School for Creative Learning in Denver offers a Summer Musical Theater Workshop and a Creative Learning Camp for ages six through 12.

- Governor's School Programs are selective, state-supported summer residential schools mostly for high school students. They focus on math, science, arts, social sciences, and humanities.

- Many universities offer summer programs, such as Berkeley's Academic Talent Program, the University of Wisconsin's College for Kids, Purdue University's programs at four age levels, and the University of Iowa's three programs for elementary, junior high, and high school students.

- Camp Invention for middle school students promotes creative thinking and teamwork by inventing, for example, new devices that fly or make beds.

- Study-abroad summer programs include travel plus study of at least one country's language and culture.

- Many universities offer summer programs (clinics, institutes, retreats, camps) that focus on areas such as music, language, art, foreign languages, or computers.

- Benefits of Saturday and summer programs include: students are taught at a faster, more complex level; they cover non-traditional topics; independent research strengthens thinking skills; students interact with other gifted students; they come to better understand their abilities; they learn about college life; and instructors are good role models.

- With secondary school mentorships, students learn about the activities, problems, training, and the lifestyle of the role-model mentor. Mentors and mentees should be matched in gender, ethnicity, background, and values.

- College students have been mentors for high school students; they are matched in such traits as gender, economic status, or minority or underachieving status. They also may be matched in areas of interest (e.g., geology, drama).

- With elementary students, college-age mentors have taught, for example, study skills, library, and writing skills.

- Groups of elementary students can also visit mentors who are professionals.

- The Internet allows contact with mentors around the world, as at the Ursuline Academy.

- The Future Problem Solving program follows seven steps, from researching the problem and brainstorming solutions to selecting criteria, evaluating the 10 best solutions, and describing the final best solution in essay form. FPS holds state and international competitions.

- With Odyssey of the Mind, students work all year on long-term problems, such as building Stunt Mobiles, and are also given short-term spontaneous problems, such as making rhymes using animal names.

- Junior Great Books exposes students at three age levels to modern and traditional literature that is enjoyable and filled with ideas.

- Teams for the U.S. Academic Decathlon are composed of "A," "B," and "C" students, who compete in such areas as speech, essay writing, economics, fine arts, social studies, math, and a Super Quiz.

- The book *Competitions: Maximizing Your Potential* describes national competitions that reward high achievement, community service, or creative imagination.

- The Internet supplies endless possibilities for researching any topic, including *giftedness* itself.

• Rivero itemized dozens of benefits of home schooling gifted children. Chief advantages are: it is a self-paced education custom-fitted to the learning styles, interests, and abilities of an advanced child; it avoids the busywork and wasted time of regular classes; and it promotes self-confidence, self-directedness, and motivation.

7

Grouping Gifted Students

*Experts have concluded that untracking [not grouping
students by ability] brings no guarantee of high-quality
instruction for everyone, but may instead lead all to a
common level of educational mediocrity.*

~ James J. Kulik

[**Scene**: *Morning at the forest cottage of the Seven Dwarfs. Happy, Doc, Sneezy,
Dopey, Grumpy, Sleepy, and Bashful watch Snow White fix pancakes for breakfast.*]

Snow White (speaking softly with a happy smile): Well boys, breakfast
is almost ready.

Grumpy: It's about darn time!

Sleepy: Huh? What? Where's my hat?

Snow: Now let's seat you all at the table according to groups. Let me
see....

Dopey: How about short people on the left and tall people on the right.

Grumpy: That'd put everybody on the left, you nitwit! We'd be sitting
on top of each other, and Snow White would have a whole bench! She
could eat breakfast lying down!

Snow: Now let's be kind, Grumpy! Happy, what do you think?

Happy (smiling cheerily): I think it's a beautiful day!

Doc: What about beard length? We'll start at this corner and go around
the table. People with no beards are first—I think that'll be Snow White,
Sleepy, and Dopey. Then we'll have Bashful and...

Snow: I have an idea! What about sitting together in clusters? Based on what we're interested in! Then we could have marvelous chats about the nice things we like!

Happy: That would be so wonderful!

Grumpy: But these dodos don't have any interests!

Sneezy (loudly): Ah-choo!! It's the pancake dust! I don't suppose sneezers and non-sneezers would work. Then I'd have a whole bench!

Bashful (softly): Gosh, I like Snow White's idea. I'm interested in soft little bunny rabbits and rainbows. Grumpy, do you like little bunnies and rainbows?

Grumpy: Oh, shut up!

Snow (happily): I know! Let's have temporary grouping. Today we'll sit together based on our interests. Tomorrow we'll sit based on our beard length. And the next day we'll think of something else…maybe our favorite Disney™ movie! This will be so much fun!

Sleepy: Wha's happenin'?

Benefits and Problems of Grouping

We already noted the social benefits of grouping gifted students—for example, in Saturday and summer programs, where they meet equally talented age-mates for friendship and support. Bright and talented students must know that they are not alone.

Normal students stretch their normal minds by gabbing about rock and rap music, a teacher's neat BMW, who's going with whom, appropriate bagginess of faded jeans, $125 running shoes, and whatever else might be the latest fad or topic.

Now imagine an extremely bright student in middle or high school. He is not able to communicate with average age-mates. After all, how many other students are interested in advanced math, physics, Shakespeare, world languages and cultures, cosmology, or building computers? How many worry about the meaning of their lives, AIDS, world hunger, war, terrorism, or children or elderly persons who are beaten, neglected, or abused?

Social exclusion for the extremely bright child can include name-calling and teasing—"geek," "nerd," "dork," and "teacher's pet" are common, along with the half-insulting "brain." Or maybe the gifted kid is simply ignored and excluded. Either way, he or she can hardly avoid feeling and believing, "I'm different. I'm odd. I have no friends."

Some gifted students try to hide their talents by not talking about lofty issues and not carrying too many books. They dumb themselves down, using slang and acting "ordinary" to fit in with peers, sometimes purposely underachieving and scoring poor grades. Some even give up on life. A classic case is Dallas Egbert. His brilliance led to acceleration through elementary and secondary school and early college entrance. Even so, he felt weird and alone, though he wanted desperately to be normal. Had he found peers even close to his abilities and interests, he might not have killed himself at age 16. The unfortunate 1980 event led to the creation of SENG—Supporting Emotional Needs of Gifted— founded by James T. Webb at Wright State University in Ohio.[1]

In addition to the social benefits, there are clear academic advantages to grouping gifted students. The entire group can move rapidly through standard subject matter and into more advanced, complex, and diverse topics. The smaller group size permits teachers to assist with individual library or Internet research, scientific research, creative writing, various art projects, or countless other possibilities (Table 6.1 in Chapter 6). A teacher of the gifted also can supervise activities that are designed mostly for gifted students—Junior Great Books, Future Problem Solving, Odyssey of the Mind, mentorships with professionals, or the competitions described in Chapter 6 in Karnes and Riley's book *Competitions: Maximizing Your Potential*.[2]

Grouping can be part time or full time. The classic criticism of part-time grouping is this: *it's a part-time solution to a full-time problem.* But part-time grouping is better than no grouping at all. The obvious disadvantage is that the remainder of the day—or week—may be occupied with too-easy class work and slower-thinking peers.

Full-time grouping presents the obvious advantage of accommodating the educational *and* psycho-social needs of gifted children all day every day. Two so-so disadvantages are, first, that gifted students interact less with average students—who are the sort of people that they will deal with for the rest of their lives. Second, many teachers object to losing their brightest students, who serve as high-achieving, motivated role models for the rest of the class. On the bright side, when the academic stars are gone, other students have a chance to shine.

Pullout Plans

Pullout programs, sometimes called "part-time special classes," "resource room programs," or just "resource programs," are the single most common educational strategy for gifted students, according to gifted leaders June Cox, Neil Daniel, and Bruce Boston.[3] They are popular because they are visible groupings that administrators can point to, even though the students generally meet only for a brief time each week.

Typically, gifted and talented elementary students are "pulled out" of their regular class once or twice per week for two or three hours of enrichment in a "resource room." Usually, one G/T teacher-coordinator, normally with college training in gifted education, serves all or part of a school district, traveling from school to school to meet with groups of gifted children in the resource room. The resource room provides, for example, special reading materials, art supplies, science supplies, and computers. As in other special classes for gifted kids, pullout activities are intended to expose students to more complex material; enhance language and communication skills; improve library, Internet, scientific, art, etc., skills; and strengthen self-concepts—including raising academic and career motivation.

Pullout plans, including the similar district-wide resource programs (next section), *are the only plans that gifted experts Cox, Daniel, and Boston adamantly dislike.* Said Cox and colleagues, pullout programs are a "fragmented" and "patchwork" approach to teaching gifted students, and "able learners need a program that matches their abilities every hour of the school day, not just once or twice a week."[4]

Further, pullout programs provide a "false sense of accomplishment [to teachers, principals, and district superintendents]....it is easy to establish such a program and believe that the needs of able learners are being met."[5] But what takes place in a pullout program does not happen in a child's regular class, and thinking skills—a core component "need to be incorporated in all of the child's classes—math, science, social studies, and languages."[6] In addition, many teachers dislike pullout programs because they disrupt regular classroom activities.

Cox and colleagues also note that pullout programs are expensive, considering the district G/T teacher's salary. Two additional—and perhaps minor—problems are that, first, students may not be comfortable separated from others and labeled *gifted*, and second, pullout programs have been accused of too much "fun and games," with little relevance to what goes on in the classroom curriculum.[7]

District-Wide Resource Programs

Even though pullout programs are sometimes called resource programs, a more accurate meaning of *resource program* is a district-wide plan in which gifted students are transported once or twice per week to a district resource room.[8]

A resource room for junior high school students, for example, can include books, magazines, a science lab, AV equipment, language learning centers, a piano, plants, games, lots of computers, plus materials for other independent research and art projects. Enrichment activities have included astronomy and building telescopes, building and launching rockets, film animation, journalism and creating a newspaper, learning American Sign Language, art, literature, theater, photography, oceanography, and more.[9] To avoid repeatedly missing the same class at their home junior high schools, teachers and students often vary the mornings, afternoons, and days of the week they attend the resource room.

Part-Time Special Classes

Gifted and talented students may attend a part-time special class, usually for 50 to 70% of *every* school day.[10] With the regular curriculum covered in the home-room class, the part-time special class can focus on other educational experiences—which might include accelerated math, science, or languages, or research activities that promote creativity, problem solving, or other thinking skills.

Enrichment Clusters

An *enrichment cluster* is a group of students—who may or may not be identified as gifted—all of whom want to learn about a particular topic.[11] Within a given enrichment cluster, students may specialize in a particular interest area—a sort of division of labor. For example, in a theater cluster, different students might pursue acting, writing, stage production, costume design, Japanese theater, and so on. Whatever a student's topic, he or she should have a specific problem to solve.

The enrichment cluster meets with an adult expert—usually a teacher, parent, or community specialist—at designated times during the week for about 10 or 12 weeks, and student projects normally go into considerable depth. For example, students interested in pyramids learn about important archeologists, archeological research methods, lots of

Egyptian history, and how to use libraries and the Internet to research pyramids and other topics.

As with virtually all enrichment experiences, the goal is promoting advanced knowledge, creativity, other thinking skills, self-motivated learning, and high educational and career aspirations.

Temporary Grouping for Reading and Math

Bright students, almost by definition, typically surpass their classmates in reading, math, or both. For reading or math instruction, students can be grouped according to ability. They can either be grouped within their classroom and taught by their regular teacher (*within-class grouping*, a common procedure anyway), or they can be grouped with students at the next higher grade only for reading or math (*cross-grade grouping*). Students like both grouping plans, especially cross-grade grouping. Most teachers prefer cross-grade grouping, which frees them to teach students more equal in ability.[12] With either grouping plan, math and reading achievement run higher than without the grouping.

After-School High School Clubs

Most high schools have in-school (co-curricular) or after-school (extra-curricular) clubs for like-minded students interested in German, French, Spanish, drama, math, computers, bridge, chess, or whatever. Motivated teachers who are aware of gifted or highly interested students can create the clubs and organize the after-school gatherings, field trips, meetings with experts, and competitions (e.g., in chess, bridge, perhaps math), and they can supply plenty of educational and career information.

Special Public Elementary Schools for the Gifted

In medium to large cities, one or more entire elementary schools may be designated for gifted students. These are dubbed *magnet schools* because they attract high-ability students from across the city or area. The curriculum follows district guidelines, along with enriched and accelerated training in areas such as science, art, literature, and social sciences.

One outstanding public elementary school for the gifted is the Golda Meier School in Milwaukee, Wisconsin. Third- to fifth-grade students are selected from the Milwaukee school system based on the federal definition of giftedness—general ability, specific academic aptitude, creativity, leadership, or talent in the visual or performing arts. A quota system balances gender, race, and district representation.

The remarkable assortment of enrichment and advanced activities in the Golda Meier School includes drama lessons taught by members of the Milwaukee Repertory Company; a school newspaper guided by reporters from the *Milwaukee Journal*; piano, violin, viola, and general music lessons; several foreign languages; 12 to 30(!) field trips per year to Milwaukee's financial and cultural centers; "MACS Packs" (Math, Arts, Crafts, Science), which are daily student projects; and "Lunch Bunch"— games, films, reading, or just visiting. A Classics Club reads above-age-level books. The school includes a chorus, a student senate, an Advanced Science Club, and sporadic infant-care classes, featuring somebody's baby sister or brother.

Private Schools for the Gifted

It's no secret that achievement often runs higher in private schools than in regular public schools. Therefore, private schools can be a good alternative for parents who want a more challenging environment for their bright child. Compared with public schools, classes are smaller— which means greater personal attention—and private schools can cover more material in greater depth, in addition to a variety of special topics.

Some private schools—including the following four examples— serve only gifted students.[13] Their admission policies and procedures vary just slightly. They normally include respectable ability scores, high grades, an at-school visit with the student and parent(s), a vacancy at the school, and a willingness to spend big tuition bucks, although most schools have generous scholarships when needed.

For example, the EAGLE School in Madison, Wisconsin, serves gifted students from age 5 (kindergarten) through 13 (eighth grade). According to co-founders Elizabeth Connor and Mary Olskey, class size is small (about 14), which permits students to be scientists or mathematical puzzlers or to become involved with explorers and other people in history who have solved problems.[14] This small class size helps students move quickly through basic subjects without unnecessary drill or repetition, which allows time to explore content and issues in greater depth and pursue related new areas. The curriculum includes language arts, science, math, art, drama, music, French, Spanish, word processing, computers, and gym, plus electives such as fencing, chorus, and math games.

Academic rigor is balanced with creativity. Students participate in book discussions, compete on current events or math problem-solving teams, and have time to write, invent, create, or pretend. They even help plan and evaluate their own learning, which strengthens skills of independent learning. Teachers accept the high activity levels of many gifted students. Counseling helps students cope with their uniqueness. Admission is based on individually-administered IQ scores (i.e., Stanford-Binet or Wechsler)—with no firm cutoff IQ—a visit with child and parents, a review of school records or other relevant information, and a vacancy. Tuition for the 2005-2006 year was $8,550. Aided by scholarships, an EAGLE School goal is to admit every qualified child, despite financial difficulties. Also, parents may serve as teacher aides for financial credit. For information, visit www.eagleschool.org.

The Logan School for Creative Learning in Denver, Colorado, whose summer program we summarized in Chapter 6, is "dedicated to the development of the whole child...[and] addresses the intellectual, emotional, and social needs of bright and imaginative students" ages five to 15.[15] The curriculum is individualized "for each child's unique readiness level, learning style, and personal interests." Compared with the traditional grades K through 8 in public schools, Logan School classes use four broad age groups: Entry Primary, Upper Primary, Intermediate, and Advanced.

"Logan supports experiential learning through its Unit Field Trip and Environmental Education Programs." Field trips can be for individuals(!) or small groups. They go, for example, to libraries, museums, businesses, art galleries, laboratories, and nature centers. They interview and learn from experts in the field. There are no limits to students' potential math accomplishment—even calculus is available in pullout classes or individual study.

Admission is based on test scores, a student visit to the school, teacher recommendations, and a vacancy. For 2005-2006, this school's tuition was $11,760. For information, see www.theloganschool.org.

Sycamore School in Indianapolis is the only private school in Indiana devoted entirely to gifted students. It serves students from age 2½(!) through eighth grade. Enrollment in 2004-2005 was 425. Its website boasts (emphasize *boasts*) many awards, honors, achievements, and recognitions. As just three examples, the school's Symphonic Band performed in a National Band Festival at Carnegie Hall, one graduate of Sycamore placed first in the high school Westinghouse Science Talent Search, and one eighth grader went directly from Sycamore to Purdue University. Admission is based on a parent recommendation, teacher recommendation, a classroom visit, and an IQ score above 130. Tuition for Sycamore School for the 2005-2006 school year was $11,390. For information, see www.sycamoreschool.org.

Conserve School in northern Wisconsin is a new (in 2002) and truly remarkable residential high school for gifted students.[16] It covers freshman through senior grades, 15 students per class, with a total of 135 students. Because it is a residential school, it virtually never accepts students younger than age 14 or 15.[17] The 1,200-acre campus includes woodlands, seven lakes, and 22 miles of hiking and biking trails. Offerings include English, mathematics, history, languages, science (with well-equipped physics and chemistry labs, plus lakes and woods for biology studies), visual arts (including studio space, a pottery kiln, and a photo darkroom), performing arts (with a 500-seat theater, a large music room, private practice rooms, and optional private music and voice lessons), and technology at the school's cutting-edge Technology Complex.

Physical education/recreation activities include not only the usual basketball, baseball, softball, volleyball, soccer, track, and wrestling, but also golf, skiing, canoeing, kayaking, sailing, fishing, ice skating, and rock wall climbing on the school's own indoor climbing wall. In addition to the above curriculum, the school stresses environmental conservation, ethics, leadership, creativity, and personal growth. Tuition at Conserve School for the 2005-2006 school year was approximately $27,000, which includes room and board. For information, see www.conserveschool.org.

Overlapping characteristics of good schools for gifted students appear in Inset. 7.1. Table 7.1 presents an (incomplete) list of public and private schools for the gifted.

Desirable Features of Schools for Gifted Students

In their excellent book *Genius Denied*, Jan and Bob Davidson and Laura Vanderkam itemized characteristics of desirable schools for gifted learners, such as Charter School of Wilmington, Delaware, whose simple philosophy is: *The curriculum will challenge all students.* All suggestions aim at meeting children's needs, not conveniencing teachers, schools, and districts. Said the authors, "These strategies aren't rocket science, yet few schools [e.g., for the gifted] have them in place."[18]

In desirable schools for gifted students:

1. Parents, teachers, and school administrators work together for the common goal of maximally challenging children's abilities.

2. Teachers group students by subject matter competence, not by age.

3. Schools do not require students to study what they already know, and thus avoid boredom and wasting of valuable time.

4. They use acceleration, allowing students to skip entire grades or, if more suitable, to go to higher grades for individual subjects (most often math).

5. They modify the curriculum in other ways to avoid wasting gifted children's time and talents. They may use independent study, mentoring (e.g., by a local professional), distance learning (correspondence courses), or dual enrollment (some classes in elementary and some in middle school).

6. They host competitions and encourage participation in Talent Search (Chapter 5).

7. They recognize special needs and problems of gifted students, particularly exploring favorite subjects in great depth, career planning, and counseling.

8. Learning is associated with excitement and joy.

9. The school culture values intellectual exploration, discovery, and rigor.

10. It is acceptable for students to discuss ideas and projects at lunch time.

11. The school recognizes and celebrates the accomplishments of high achievers.

12. Teachers nurture their own talent; they take college courses to learn strategies for meeting the needs of special learners.

Noted the authors, the *ideal* primary school would include "coordinating teachers," who permit students to move freely among different grades for different subjects, depending on students' particular abilities. Classes would thus contain students of various ages.

Table 7.1. Public and Private Schools for the Gifted[19]

Canada
Calgary, Alberta
Hillhurst Community Elementary School, grades 4 to 6
Prince of Wales Elementary School, grades 4 to 6
Queen Elizabeth Junior & Senior High School, grades 7 to 9
Westmount Charter School (formerly ABC Charter School), grades K to 12
Vancouver, British Columbia
University Hill Secondary, grades 7 to 12

United States	
Arizona	
Tucson	Gateways School (exceptionally gifted)
	Kino School, grades K to 12
	Satori School, age 2.5 to grade 5
California	
Encintas	Rhoades School, grades K to 8
Huntington Beach	Pegasus School, grades K to 8
Los Angeles	El Sereno Gifted/High Ability Magnet School, grades 6 to 8
	The Mirman School, to grade 8, (highly gifted; IQ 145+)
	Multinomah Highly Gifted Magnet
	Westside Charter School for the Highly Gifted, grades 1 to 8
North Hollywood	North Hollywood High School, public (with gifted magnet; IQ 145+)
	Reed Middle School, public (with Honors Program; IQ 145+)
Oakland	Baywood Learning Center, elementary and middle schools
	School of Choice, middle and high schools, grades 6 to 12
Orange	El Dorado School for the Gifted Child
	Emerson Honors High School, private, preschool to high school

San Diego	San Diego City Schools Cluster GATE (highly gifted)
	San Diego City Schools' "Seminar" program (highly gifted)
San Francisco	Nueva School, pre-K to grade 8
San Jose	School of Choice, middle and high schools, grades 6 to 12
San Mateo	The Odyssey School, middle school
San Rafael	Dunham Academy, grades K to 8
Santa Cruz	Spring Hill – The Advanced Elementary School of Santa Cruz, grades K to 6
Colorado	
Boulder	Rocky Mountain School for the Gifted and Creative
Colorado Springs	Renaissance Academy, preschool and elementary
Denver	The Discovery Program, grades 2 to 8
	The Logan School, grades K to 8
	Polaris Program at Crofton, grades 1 to 5 (highly gifted)
	Ricks Center for Gifted Children (at U. of Denver)
	Stargate Charter School, grades 1 to 8
Lafayette	Brideun School for Exceptional Children, grades 1 to 8 (specializes in gifted children with disabilities)
Littleton	Community School for the Gifted, preschool (age 2 ½) through middle school
	Macintosh Academy, preschool to grade 8 (accepts gifted students with disabilities)
Connecticut	
Avon	Talcott Mountain Academy, grades K to 8
Wallingford	Choate Rosemary Hall, grades 9 to 12
Westport	Pierrepont School, grades K to 8
Florida	
Osprey	Pine View School, grades 2 to 12
Georgia	
Atlanta	Pace Academy, pre-first grade to grade 12
	Paidaia, age 3 to grade 12
Gainesville	Brenau Academy (art school), grades 9 to 12 (females only
Roswell	High Meadows School, age 3 to grade 8
Hawaii	
Honolulu	Assetts, ages 5 to 18 (gifted, dyslexic, gifted-dyslexic)
Idaho	
Boise	Arrowrock Classical School, elementary
Illinois	
Aurora	Illinois Math & Science Academy, public residential high school
Chicago	Whitney M. Young Magnet High School, grades 7 and 8 and high school
Des Plaines	Science and Arts Academy, preschool to grade 8 (IQ 120+)
Downers Grove	Avery Coonley, grades K to 8
Elgin	DaVinci Academy, pre-K (ages 3 to 4) to grade 8
	Summit Academy, preschool to grade 8

Franklin Park	Renaissance Preparatory School, grades K to 12 (academic or artistic talent)
Palatine	Quest Academy (formerly Creative Children's Academy), grades K to 8
Springfield	Iles School, public, grades 1 to 5

Indiana

Indianapolis	Sycamore School, pre-K to grade 8
Muncie	Indiana Academy for Science, Mathematics, and Humanities, grades 11 to 12

Iowa

Des Moines	Central Academy, grades 8 to 12

Louisiana

Natchitoches	The Louisiana School for Math, Science, and the Arts, grades 11 to 12

Maryland

Annapolis	The Key School, pre-K to grade 12

Massachusetts

Danvers	Clark School, grades K to 8
Devens	Francis W. Parker Charter Essential School, grades 6 to 12
Foxboro	The Sage School, preschool to grade 8
Framingham	Wayland Academy, pre-K to grade 6
Salem	Phoenix School, grades K to 8
Springfield	Academy Hill School, grades K to 8
Worcester	Massachusetts Academy for Math and Science, grades 11 to 12 and college freshmen

Michigan

Detroit (Bloomfield Hills)	Roeper School, preschool to grade 12
Farmington Hills	Steppingstone School, grades K to 8
Interlochen	Interlochen Arts Academy, grades 9 to post-graduate (includes college preparatory academics)
Redford (non-graded)	Gibson School for Gifted Children, ages 5 to 13

Minnesota

Bloomington	Dimensions Academy, grades 4 to 7
Inver Grove	Atheneum Gifted Magnet School, grades 3 to 6 (highly gifted)
St. Paul	Capitol Hill Gifted and Talented Magnet School, grades K to 8

Missouri

Kansas City	Kansas City Regional Program for Exceptionally Gifted Students
St. Louis	St. Louis Regional Program for Exceptionally Gifted Students (PEGS), grades K to 12
	Thomas Jefferson School, grades 7 to 12 (boarding and day school)

New Hampshire

Concord	St. Paul's School, grades 9 to 12

Exeter	Phillips Exeter Academy, grades 9 to 12 and post-graduate
New Jersey	
Princeton	Princeton Friends, pre-K to grade 8
New York	
Huntington	The Long Island School for the Gifted, grades K to 9
New York City	The Anderson Program, grades K to 5, expanding to middle school (Manhattan)
	Bronx Science, high school
	Hunter College Elementary School (IQ 132+; must begin in nursery school and kindergarten only;
Manhattan)	
	Hunter College High School, grades 7 to 12
	Saint Ann's, preschool to grade 12 (Brooklyn)
	St. Thomas Choir School, grades 4 to 8 (academically and vocally gifted)
	Styvesant, high school
North Carolina	
Asheville	The Asheville School, grades 9 to 12 (boarding), grades 7 to 10 (summer)
Charlotte	Metrolina Regional Scholars' Academy, grades K to 8 (IQ 145+)
Durham	Camelot Academy, grades K to 12
Raleigh	Fuller Gifted and Talented Magnet, elementary school
	North Carolina School of the Arts, grade 7 through
college	
	North Carolina School of Science and Mathematics, grades 11 to 12
Ohio	
Cincinnati	The Academy of Greater Cincinnati, grades K to 11
	Schilling School for Gifted Children, grades K to 12
	School for the Creative and Performing Arts, grades 4 to 12
Oklahoma	
Tulsa	The University School, grades K to 8
Pennsylvania	
Devon	Devon Prep, grades 6 to 12 (males only)
Garnet Valley	Voyager Charter School, public, elementary
Lower Paxton	Infinity Charter School, public, elementary
Malvern	Malvern Prep, grades 6 to 12 (males only)
Texas	
Dallas	The Winston School (gifted, students with disabilities)
El Paso	El Paso Country Day School, grades K to 12
Fort Worth	The Anderson School for the Gifted and Talented
Houston	The Rainard School, ages 4 to 13 (non-graded)
Vermont	
Putney	Putney School, grades 9 to 12 (gifted, gifted students with disabilities; boarding and day school)

Virginia	
Alexandria	Episcopal High School, grades 9 to 12
Arlington	Randolph Elementary School, grades K to 6
Charlottesville	Peabody School, grades K to 8
Herndon	Nysmith School for the Gifted, pre-K to grade 8 (IQ 130+)
Richmond	The Governor's School, grades 9 to 12
Washington (state)	
Bellevue	Open Window, pre-K to grade 5
Kirkland	Springhurst, preschool to grade 6
Lacy	NOVA, grades 6 to 8
Lynnwood	Soundview, preschool to grade 8
Seattle	The Evergreen School, preschool to grade 8
	Seattle Country Day School, grades K to 8 (IQ 127+)
	University Child Development School, pre-K to grade 5
Tacoma	The Seabury School, pre-K to grade 8
Veradale	Prism, pre-K to grade 3
Wisconsin	
Land O' Lakes	Conserve School, grades 9 to 12 (residential)
Madison	EAGLE School, grades K to 8
Milwaukee	Golda Meier School, grades 3 to 5
	Samuel Morse Middle School, grades 6 to 8
	Wisconsin Center for Gifted Learners, preschool through elementary grades

Magnet High Schools

Public magnet high schools are mainly a big-city option. Magnet high schools are known to reduce dropping out by both low-ability students and disgruntled gifted ones. Individual magnet high schools focus on, for example, superior abilities, math and science, engineering, business, law, music, theater and drama, art, trade skills, or several of these areas. Students from around the city are bused to the high school that matches their abilities, talents, or aspirations. They often are placed in career-related part-time jobs for valuable experience (and a salary).

As one example, the Northeast Magnet High School in the Wichita Public Schools is a four-year program for students who wish to focus their education on science, visual arts, or law. Naturally, the school also provides basic high school courses in English, social studies, science, and mathematics. Admission? All prospective students complete an application. If they are freshmen, they participate in a district-wide lottery for admission. Upper-classmen are admitted based on available space.

Northeast's Science program prepares students to pursue college work in medical and engineering fields. The school's Science Department also helps students connect with mentors—physicians, engineers, lab technicians, and others. "Partners," who support and participate in the Science program, include the University of Kansas Medical School, Great Plains Nature Center, Lake Afton Observatory, Raytheon, the City of Wichita Water and Sewer Department, and others.[20]

The Visual Arts program focuses on sculpture and pottery, drawing and painting, fibers and weaving, glass blowing, silversmithing, photography, computer art, and video education. Students learn from and display their work in the Wichita Art Museum, CityArts (yes, one word), Wichita Center for the Arts, Wichita State University, and other organizations.

The law program prepares students interested in such fields as criminal law, civil law, law enforcement, and public or social service. Northeast Magnet High School prepared its curriculum in partnership with the Wichita Bar Association, the City of Wichita, United Way, and "many generous individual mentors."

Eighty-five to 90% of the graduates of Northeast Magnet High School go on to college. For information, visit www.usd259.com/high/ northeast.html.

School-Within-a-School

In the school-within-a-school plan, all students in a district identified as gifted and talented attend one particular school, along with regular students. Gifted students work in advanced and enriched classes for part of the day. For the rest of the day, they mix with other students—for example, in physical education, manual arts, home economics classes, and sports and social events.

As an example, in northern Minnesota, all gifted children in one medium-sized rural public school district are transported to a central magnet elementary school.[21] Gifted children are placed in one classroom per grade level and are taught by teachers trained in gifted education. The gifted specialists trade teaching responsibilities with specialists in other areas. For example, a teacher strong in science will teach science to all gifted students in all grades. Another teacher strong in social studies will teach social students to all gifted students. Gifted students mix with others for art, music, physical education, recess, and lunch.

Special Classes

At a regular elementary school, a special class may accommodate all gifted students at a particular grade level or, more likely, in a particular age range. As with temporary grouping for reading and math, teaching is easier when students are more uniform in ability.

One survey showed that almost 100% of teachers, G/T teacher-coordinators, and school administrators agreed that special classes are academically beneficial to gifted students.[22]

On the downside, as mentioned earlier, some gifted students do not want to be separated from other students. Also, other students may resent the special treatment, perhaps with quiet ostracism or not-so-quiet name-calling.

A recent study confirmed both positive and negative features of being grouped with other gifted students.[23] The subjects were 44 students, grades 5 to 11, in a summer residential program for gifted students. Students were asked, "What are the advantages [and disadvantages] of being in classes with other high-ability [or mixed-ability] students?" The following eight categories summarize academic advantages and disadvantages, then social-emotional advantages and disadvantages of both homogeneous grouping and mixed-ability grouping.

Academic advantages of homogeneous grouping—such as special classes—outweighed disadvantages about 3 to 1. The advantages included greater challenge, faster pace, more discussion, higher teacher competence, higher motivation, no repetition, positive competition, fun, covering more material, getting more help, and "you don't have to help the other kids."

Academic disadvantages listed were peers are too intelligent, pace is too fast, expectations are high, and the workload is heavier. All of the 44 students believed that there were at least some disadvantages.

Social-emotional advantages of homogeneous grouping included that peers think alike, there is no teasing or abuse, and teacher attitudes and attention are good.

Social-emotional disadvantages were lower self-esteem, negative peer attitudes, and peer intimidation. Of the 44 students, 10 felt that there were no disadvantages.

Turning to *academic advantages of mixed-ability grouping*, students felt that mixed-ability classes were easier and more relaxed, and there was more review and more free time. Six of the 44 gifted students listed no advantages.

Academic disadvantages included a too-slow pace, less challenge, boredom, repetition, having to tutor, learning less, and lowered motivation.

Social-emotional advantages of mixed-ability classes were an opportunity to help others, more friends, greater diversity, opportunity to adjust to others, high self-esteem (from their own top ranking), and fun/enter-taining. Six gifted students reported that there were no advantages.

Social-emotional disadvantages included bad teacher attitudes (intoler-ant, unappreciative), teasing and abuse, impatience, frustration, and disruptive peers.

This research by Adams-Byers, Whitsell, and Moon mostly—not entirely—confirms our observations about the positive effects of group-ing gifted students together.

In high school, of course, advanced and challenging classes (e.g., phys-ics, calculus, art, journalism, drama, languages) are a normal part of the program, and gifted and talented students self-select suitable programs.

Cluster Groups

Unfortunately, we have to distinguish between full-time *cluster groups*, discussed here, and part-time *enrichment clusters*, described earlier. *Enrichment clusters*, you may recall, refers to groups of students—gifted or not—who are keenly interested in a topic and who meet with an expert to learn more about a subject—for example, pyramids.

In confusing contrast, the proper meaning of *cluster groups* is placing five to 10 high-ability students in one regular elementary classroom at each grade level, along with 15 or 20 regular students. The teacher—hopefully trained in gifted education—supplies a differentiated, enriched curriculum to students in the gifted group.

The teacher can "buy time" by allowing the gifted students to test out of material they already know—a popular procedure known as *curriculum compacting*.[24] As usual, the enrichment activities include advanced, in-depth content plus creativity, research skills, and other thinking skills. For example, a teacher and student might prepare a learning contract that outlines a library/Internet research project, a science project, or an advanced math, computer, theater, or foreign language project.

Sandra Kaplan suggested these checkpoints for creating cluster groups:[25]

- Develop criteria for selecting the students.
- Define the qualifications and procedures for selecting teachers.
- Outline the teachers' responsibilities.
- Plan the differentiated experiences for the gifted students.
- Plan the support services (e.g., counselors) and resources (e.g., computers).

Grouping at the Roeper City and Country School

Annemarie Roeper's school includes preschool to age 12 gifted students. Since Roeper owned the school, she could group students as she wished. Her flexibility and sensibility in developing the school were astonishing.

Let's first consider Roeper's philosophy. Instead of "education for success"—as in public schools—Roeper embraces a humanistic "education for life." With a goal of self-actualization, her philosophy emphasizes "learning by experience, discovery, exploration, active involvement, and creative expression."[26]

Roeper assumed that individual children learn at their own pace, learn in different ways, hold different interests, and have other unique characteristics and needs. Her simple conclusion is that teaching and learning goals cannot be the same for all children, as they are in public schools. At the Roeper City and Country School, students learn in a global, experiential way instead of a linear, sequential way.

The school uses cross-age grouping, with remarkable flexibility within the groupings. The lower school is divided into three "stages," or age groups. The first stage consists of approximately three- to seven-year-olds, the second stage includes approximately seven- to eight-year-olds, and the third stage includes nine- to 12-year-olds. Each group thus includes students of several ages and (public school) grade levels.

As much as possible, students' needs are matched with specific strengths of individual homeroom teachers. However, if a child's placement at the beginning of the year seems unsatisfactory, he or she is moved to another group, after consultation with parents, teachers, and even the child.

The homeroom teachers teach language, social studies, math, and the arts. Consistent with Roeper's philosophy, learning is individualized—with plenty of flexibility. Learning goals are set for each child based on needs, interests, and characteristics. Therefore, homeroom teachers work with students in large groups, small groups, and even individually. They also serve as counselors. The learning environment thus involves students academically, physically, and emotionally.

In addition to homerooms, Roeper's lower school includes many special classes, which each draw children from different age groups. The children select their special classes and work with children from other age groups.

It is startling to compare Roeper's flexible grouping strategy—which considers needs and interests of both students and homeroom teachers, along with special classes open to students of various ages—with the mostly lockstep, age-determined philosophy of public schools.

Recommendations for Teaching Gifted Students in Part-Time and Full-Time Grouping

Consider these principles, or recommendations, for providing suitable enrichment experiences for grouped gifted students.[27]

- Accelerate the pace of instruction.

- Use independent, self-directed learning.

- Group students according to skill level or interest area.

- Use projects and assignments that strengthen thinking skills, such as creativity, problem solving, analysis, planning, evaluation, and others (see Chapters 11 and 12).

- Be sure that the learning assignments and projects require advanced-level thinking at greater depth—for example, emphasize interrelationships among knowledge areas.

- Use outside mentors for both elementary and secondary gifted students.

- Use curriculum compacting—letting students test out of already mastered material—to supply time for independent projects and learning.

Summary

- Grouping gifted students leads to friendships and social support. Such support may be needed to offset exclusion and sometimes insults from other peers.

- Grouping allows gifted students to learn rapidly and move into more complex topics.

- In pullout plans, gifted students benefit from enriched or advanced G/T experiences once or twice per week, normally in a separate resource room, and usually taught by a teacher trained in gifted education.

- Criticisms of temporary grouping include: such plans are "a part-time solution to a full-time problem"; they are a "fragmented" and "patchwork" approach; they give educators a "false sense of accomplishment"; they disrupt regular classroom activities; they are expensive; they may include excessive "fun and games"; thinking skills should be incorporated in all classes; and students may not like being separated from others nor labeled as *gifted*.

- In district-wide resource programs, students travel to another school for the part-time enrichment.

- Part-time special classes for gifted students allow them to receive advanced work for 50 to 70% of every day.

- In an enrichment cluster, a group of motivated students (gifted or not) pursue a topic of common interest—for example, various aspects of theater—guided by an adult expert.

- With temporary grouping, gifted students may meet together for reading and math within their regular classroom (within-class grouping), or they may move to the next higher grade for reading and math (cross-grade grouping).

- After-school high school clubs accommodate gifted students with strong interests in special areas, such as languages, chess, or computers.

- Full-time grouping plans include special public schools for the gifted at elementary and secondary levels—for example, Milwaukee's Golda Meier School.

- Achievement generally runs higher at private schools than regular public schools. Some private schools, such as EAGLE School, serve only gifted students, promoting high academic achievement and creativity.

- Magnet high schools draw students with common interests—for example, in math, art, theater, creative writing, business, law, or trade skills. The Northeast Magnet High School in Wichita offers college preparatory programs in science, medicine, engineering, the visual arts, criminal and civil law, and law enforcement.

- With the school-within-a-school plan, all gifted students in a dis trict attend one school. They do advanced and enriched work part of the day, then mix with regular students for activities such as physical education, manual arts, and sports.

- An elementary school may have a special class for gifted students at each grade level or covering an age range.

- In one study, academic advantages of homogeneous grouping included, for example, greater challenge, higher teacher competence, fun, and covering more material. But some students felt that the pace was too fast and the workload too heavy. Social-emotional advantages included less teasing and good teacher attitudes. A few social-emotional disadvantages included lower self-esteem and negative peer attitudes.

- With mixed-ability grouping, most gifted students felt that the classes were easier, more relaxed, and supplied more review and free time. Disadvantages included a slow pace, boredom, repetition, and lowered motivation. Social-emotional advantages included helping others, more friends, and high self-esteem. Disadvantages included bad teacher attitudes, teasing, and frustration.

- With cluster groups, five to 10 gifted students at each grade level are placed in one class and taught by a teacher (hopefully) trained in gifted education. Curriculum compacting—testing out of a topic—may "buy time" for enrichment projects.

- Kaplan listed guides for creating cluster groups that included, for example, developing criteria for selecting students and teachers, and planning the differentiated experiences.

- Roeper's lower school divides students, ages three to 12, into three stages. The goal is education for life (self-actualization) instead of education for success. Learning is individualized, based on needs, interests, and characteristics. Students are matched with homeroom teachers. Students from all groups (stages) take special classes.

- Recommended educational experiences for part-time and full-time grouped G/T students include, for example, accelerating instruction, permitting independent learning, grouping students according to interests or skill levels, using assignments and projects that strengthen thinking skills, using mentors, and using curriculum compacting and testing out of mastered material.

8
Planning a Gifted Program

An organized curriculum is a key ingredient in the
complex blending of circumstances so central to the
transformation of a gifted learner's initial capacity for
intellectual activity into a mature competence for academic
and professional accomplishment.

~ Joyce VanTassel-Baska

[**Scene**: *The first after-school meeting of the six-person gifted and talented com-*
mittee at the Hope and Crosby Elementary School. Committee members include
school principal Donald McRonald; school counselor Pansy Attention-Deficit;
two excited teachers, Thelma Belma and Roger Lodger; Ms. Shalena Lincoln, the
mother of a gifted fourth-grade girl; and committee leader Ms. Sonja Thorley. Ms.
Thorley opens the meeting.]

Ms. Sonja Thorley (with enthusiasm): Good morning everyone! I'm
so glad you're here! We have such an important task ahead of us—planning special opportunities for our bright and talented children!

Teacher Thelma Belma: That's a great idea! I'm sick of these suppos-
edly smart kids readin' novels and sleepin' through my class!

Ms. Thorley (smiling): And you know why, don't you? They already
know what you're teaching to everybody else!

Ms. Belma: But how could they? I ain't even taught it yet!

Ms. Thorley: Trust me! They're like that!

Counselor Pansy Attention-Deficit: Hey, I talk to these smart kids
all the time! They're bored out of their bleedin' skulls! They oughta' be
kicked up a grade or two—let 'em learn somethin' new for a change.
What kinda' plans you got in mind?

Ms. Thorley: Well, I think we should start with cluster groups. We'll put all of our bright third graders in one classroom—with an enthusiastic teacher who wants to give them advanced work and independent projects.

Ms. Belma: Count me out! And good riddance to the little...!

Ms. Thorley: And we'll do the same for fourth and fifth graders. And Pansy is right—we should grade-skip some of our children. They already think and learn like older children!

Teacher Roger Lodger: But with cluster groups, we'll lose our best students, our best role models! Besides, the smart kids help me teach the other kids! I've heard of pullout plans. For two hours a week they can research the sex life of jellyfish! That'll keep 'em interested (snicker, snort)!

Ms. Shalena Lincoln (calmly): My daughter Nateesha has a marvelous mathematical mind! But she's just average at everything else. Will there be something for her?

Ms. Thorley: Good point! She's in fourth grade? We'll let her study math with the fifth graders! It's called "single-subject acceleration" or "partial acceleration."

Principal Donald McRonald: So, how do we proceed? What's next? I mean, what's first?

Ms. Thorley: We'll have enrichment projects for students who finish their work early, subject acceleration for speedy math kids, and full-grade acceleration for our brightest. Next week we'll discuss our identification procedures. (She passes out copies of a five-page document.) This is a program plan that I based on the district office G/T plan.

Other committee members (in loud and disgruntled unison): Do we gotta' read this?

As mentioned on page 16, in 1998, the National Association for Gifted Children (NAGC) prepared a brief—and therefore delightfully usable—eight-page document entitled *Pre-K–Grade 12 Gifted Program Standards*.[1] The title itself presents a primary principle: programs for gifted students should extend across the entire pre-college years. This to-the-point document is the product of lots of thinking and discussion by lots of G/T experts.

The document consists of seven tables, one for each of seven *standards*. Each table includes a description of one critical program component, along with four to six *guiding principles*. With refreshing realism, each guiding principle includes a description of both *minimum standards*— rock-bottom "requisite conditions for acceptable gifted education programming practice"—and *exemplary standards*—"desirable and visionary conditions for excellence in gifted education programming practice."

Most current programs likely sit somewhere between NAGC's minimum and exemplary standards. Let's look at these landmark NAGC standards, then review some supplementary planning considerations.[2]

National Association for Gifted Children Pre-K–Grade 12 Gifted Program Standards

Curriculum and Instruction

"Gifted education services must include curricular and instructional opportunities directed to the unique needs of the gifted child."[3]

Guiding Principles

(1) *Differentiated gifted curriculum must cover grades pre-K to 12.* Curriculum and instructional modifications for gifted learners must be explained and integrated throughout the district. Ideally, "a well-defined and implemented curriculum scope and sequence should be articulated for all grade levels and all subject areas."

(2) *Regular curriculum and instruction must be modified or adapted—or replaced—to fit high-level learning goals for gifted students.* Objectives and instructional strategies must be different than for regular students. Ideally, district curriculum plans will specify content, objectives, and resources for gifted students in regular classrooms.

To aid acceleration, gifted students must have ways to demonstrate proficiency in regular classroom concepts and processes. Ideally, such information will suggest plans for more challenging educational opportunities that fit specific needs of individual gifted students.

(3) *A flexible pace of instruction must permit accelerated learning.* Advanced content and differentiated teaching strategies must fit the accelerated learning pace and advanced intellectual capabilities of gifted students. Ideally, continual opportunities for acceleration in gifted students' areas of strength should be available— with high ceilings that do not limit students' opportunities.

(4) *A program must provide opportunities for subject skipping and grade skipping.* Decisions about subject or grade skipping require a thorough assessment of each prospective student. Ideally, subject or grade skipping should be available to any gifted student showing relevant needs.

(5) *Learning opportunities for gifted students must include a variety of curriculum options, instructional strategies, and resource materials.* Ideally, each gifted student should be able to work at advanced levels and rates as determined by pre-tests and other assessment.

Flexible arrangements—special classes, resource rooms, mentorships, independent study, research projects, and seminars— must be available. Ideally, for pre-K through grade 12, the differentiated program curricula should be modified to match "students' interests, readiness, and learning style."

Program Administration and Management

"Appropriate gifted education programming must include the establishment of a systematic means of developing, implementing, and managing services."[4]

Guiding Principles

(1) *Qualified personnel must direct the services for gifted students.* The coordinator should minimally have completed coursework or staff development in gifted education and show leadership ability. Ideally, the coordinator should have an advanced degree in gifted education or have completed a certification program.

(2) *The gifted program must be integrated with the larger educational program.* Linkages between gifted and general education must be created at all school levels. Ideally, the linkages will be strong.

(3) *The gifted program must include positive, working relationships with constituency, advocacy, and compliance groups.* The school programming staff must maintain good communication with parents and other involved community members. Ideally, the program will distribute information regarding, for example, program policies and practices, identification procedures, and student progress to parents and other involved persons.

The programming staff will create an advisory committee that reflects the cultural differences and socio-economic levels of the community, and that includes parents, community members, school staff, and students. Ideally, parents can share ideas and make recommendations about program operations.

Program staff must communicate with other departments within the school. Program staff also must communicate with outside agencies involved in gifted education—other districts, school board members, the local board of education, and the state department of education. Ideally, the local G/T staff will regularly consider issues and concerns of the outside agencies.

(4) *Resources and materials must be available for the gifted education program.* These include technological support and library materials that reflect the needs of gifted students. Ideally, other resources— parent, community, vocational, etc.—will support the program. Technology should be state-of-the-art.

Program Design

"The development of appropriate gifted education programming requires comprehensive services based on sound philosophical, theoretical, and empirical support."[5]

Guiding Principles

(1) *A continuum of programming services must exist.* The services must be available to all gifted students. Ideally, a full continuum of educational options will permit matching services to the needs of individual gifted learners.

(2) *A program must be adequately funded.* The funding should be fair in comparison with other local education programs. Ideally, the funding will be consistent with program goals and sufficient to meet them.

(3) *Gifted programming must develop from a sound and comprehensive base.* A program must be regularly reviewed by an outside source. Ideally, input from informed experts should influence original program planning.

Programming must be guided by a stated philosophy, which includes goals and objectives.[6] Ideally, the school, district, or board of education will have a mission statement or philosophy statement that explains the need for gifted programs.

Gifted services must be provided across grades pre-K through 12. Ideally, the plan will include policies and procedures related to identification, curriculum, instruction, teacher preparation, formative (on-going, middle-of-year) and summative (end of year) evaluation, support services (e.g., counseling, consultants, speakers, mentors), and parent involvement.

(4) *Gifted programs must be a regular and essential part of the general education school day.* Ideally, gifted services will supplement and build on the regular skills and knowledge learned in regular classrooms at all grade levels to ensure continuity through the grades.

Appropriate opportunities must be provided in the regular classroom, resource classroom, or other optional environments. Ideally, school districts will offer a variety of service delivery options (and locations); no single service should stand alone.

(5) *Flexible grouping must be an integral part of gifted education in order to provide the differentiated instruction and curriculum.* Ideally, flexible grouping should be used in all content areas at all grade levels so that students can learn with and from other gifted students.

(6) *Policies for modifying or adding to the nature and operations of existing and future school programs are essential for gifted programs.* Ideally, policies should exist at least for early entrance, grade skipping, ability grouping, and dual enrollment.

Student Identification

"Gifted learners must be assessed to determine appropriate educational services."[7]

Guiding Principles

(1) *A fair and comprehensive process will be used to determine eligibility for gifted education services.* Information about characteristics of gifted

students in areas served by a district must be disseminated annually to all appropriate staff members. Ideally, the district will supply information in a variety of relevant languages for parents and committee members about the process for nominating students.

All students must comprise the initial screening pool. Ideally, the nomination process should be ongoing; student screening should occur at any time.

Nominations may be made by any source—for example, teachers, parents, peers, community members, or students themselves. Ideally, nomination forms and procedures should be available in a variety of languages as well.

Parents must be given information regarding characteristics of student giftedness. Ideally, parents should attend workshops or seminars to acquire a full understanding of giftedness.

(2) *Instruments used for assessing students must measure diverse abilities, talents, strengths, and needs in order to allow students to demonstrate any strengths.* Assessment instruments must measure student capabilities with provisions for the language in which the student is most fluent (when possible). Ideally, assessment should be in a student's most fluent language. The purposes of assessment must be clear and consistent across all grade levels.

Assessments must be culturally fair. Ideally, the assessment should consider students' economic conditions, gender, handicapping conditions, or other factors that might interfere with a fair assessment.

Assessment must be sensitive to students' current stage of talent development. Ideally, assessment should be sensitive to all stages of student talent development.

(3) *An assessment profile of each student's strengths and needs must be developed in order to: (a) evaluate eligibility for a gifted education program, and (b) plan appropriate intervention services.* Ideally, individual assessment profiles and plans should be developed for all identified gifted learners.

Assessment profiles must include a student's unique learning characteristics, performance levels, and potential. Ideally, the assessment profile also will include the gifted student's interests, learning style, and education needs.

(4) *All identification procedures and instruments must be based on current theory and research.* No single assessment instrument should deny eligibility for gifted programming services. Ideally, assessment data will come from multiple sources and multiple assessment methods.

All assessment instruments must show reliability and validity for the intended purposes and students. Ideally, assessment data should include a balance of reliable and valid quantitative (e.g., grades, test scores) as well as qualitative (e.g., verbal, written) evaluations.

(5) *Written program identification procedures must include (at the very least) provisions for informed (parental, guardian) consent, student retention, student reassessment, student exiting, and appeals.* District programming guides must specify procedures for assessing gifted students at least once during the elementary, middle, and secondary levels. Ideally, student placement information should include a balance of reliable and valid quantitative and qualitative measures.

District guidelines also must include specific procedures for student retention, student exiting, and parent appeals. Ideally, such guides and procedures will be reviewed and revised as necessary.

Guidance and Counseling

"Gifted education programming must establish a plan to recognize and nurture the unique socio-emotional development of gifted learners."[8]

Guiding Principles

(1) *Gifted students must have guidance to help them accommodate their unique socio-emotional development.* Counselors must be familiar with characteristics and social-emotional needs and problems of gifted students. Ideally, counselors will have training related to gifted students' characteristics and social-emotional needs—for example, related to perfectionism, underachievement, and multipotentiality.

(2) *Gifted students must receive career guidance related to their unique strengths and needs.* Ideally, gifted students will receive college and career counseling and guidance that is both different and delivered earlier, compared with that for regular students.

(3) *At-risk gifted students especially need attention, counseling, guidance, and support to help them realize their potential.* Ideally—or especially—at-risk gifted students who do not perform satisfactorily in regular and/or gifted classes should receive intervention services.

(4) *In addition to guidance and counseling services, gifted students must be exposed to affective curriculum as part of their differentiated curriculum and instructional services.* Ideally, such "affective curriculum" includes personal/social awareness and adjustment, academic planning, and vocational and career awareness.

(5) *Underachieving gifted students must be included in—not excluded from—gifted programs.* Underachievers must not be exited from a gifted program because of problems related to their underachievement. Ideally, underachievers should receive specific counseling that addresses issues and problems related to their underachievement.

Professional Development

"Gifted learners are entitled to be served by professionals who have specialized preparation in gifted education, expertise in appropriate differentiated content and instructional methods, involvement in ongoing professional development, and who possess exemplary personal and professional traits."[9]

Guiding Principles

(1) A *comprehensive staff development program must be provided for all school staff involved in the education of gifted students.* All staff must be aware of the nature and needs of gifted students. Ideally, ongoing staff development for all school staff will include the nature and needs of gifted students and appropriate instructional strategies.

Teachers of the gifted must attend at least one professional development activity per year related to teaching gifted students. Ideally, teachers of the gifted should continuously be engaged in the study of gifted education through staff development activities, college courses, or degree programs.

(2) *Only qualified staff should be involved in the education of gifted students.* Teachers of gifted students must be certified to teach in the area to which they are assigned. They also must be aware of unique learning differences and needs of gifted students at their particular grade level.

All specialist teachers (e.g., district G/T coordinators) must hold or be actively working toward certification (or the equivalent) in gifted education in the state in which they teach. Ideally, all specialist G/T teachers should possess certification or a degree in gifted education.

Any teacher whose primary responsibility includes teaching gifted students must have extensive expertise in gifted education. Ideally, only teachers with advanced expertise in gifted education will have primary responsibility for teaching gifted students.

(3) *School personnel should be supported in their efforts on behalf of gifted students.* Such personnel must be released from regular duties to participate in G/T staff development activities. Ideally, such staff development should be funded, at least partly, by districts or other agencies.

(4) *School staff must have planning time and other support for the preparation and development of G/T program plans, curricula, and materials.* Ideally, teachers of the gifted should receive regularly scheduled time, including release time and pay for summer work, for developing programs and organizing related resources (e.g., field trips, mentorships).

Program Evaluation

"Program evaluation is the systematic study of the value and impact of services provided."[10]

Guiding Principles

(1) *Program evaluation must be purposeful.* Collected information must relate to the needs and interests of most constituency groups. Ideally, the information will address questions and needs of all constituency groups and stakeholders.

(2) *A program evaluation must be efficient and not excessively expensive.* School districts must supply funds and other resources for program evaluation. Ideally, districts should allocate funds, adequate time, and personnel for evaluating gifted programs.

(3) *Evaluations must be conducted competently and ethically.* Persons conducting the evaluation should be competent and trustworthy. Ideally, the evaluators will be experts in evaluating gifted programs.

The goal of the evaluation is to determine if the program reaches its intended goals. Ideally, the evaluation will report both strengths and weaknesses of the program, along with critical issues and factors that affect program services.

Instruments and procedures for collecting data must be reliable and valid. Ideally, they should be suited to student age, developmental level, gender, and ethnic/economic diversity of the students.

Both ongoing formative evaluations and end-of-year summative evaluations will guide program development and improvement. (District or state policies may require summative evaluations only every five years, sometimes more often.)

Individual information must be confidential. Ideally, all persons involved in the evaluation should be permitted to verify information and its interpretations.

(4) *Evaluation results must be available in a written report.* The report must be clear and cohesive. Ideally, the results will provide clear and relevant information that encourages stakeholders (all teachers, school board members, school and district administrators, the city board of education, and perhaps persons in the state G/T office or department) to improve the program.

Again, the 1998 NAGC *Pre-K–Grade 12 Gifted Program Standards* are a thoughtful, carefully compiled, and authoritative guide for planning and conducting gifted programs. The remaining sections of this chapter will review, elaborate, and supplement the NAGC standards.

Acceleration, Enrichment, and Grouping Options

As we saw in Chapters 5, 6, and 7, there are many acceleration, enrichment, and grouping options for gifted and talented students. An abbreviated review list follows.

(1) In the regular classroom, teachers can supply enrichment activities for bright kids who finish class work early or already know the material. For example, gifted students can study at learning centers or work on independent projects, perhaps with learning contracts.

(2) Within-class groups are arranged for different levels of reading and math ability.

(3) Part-time acceleration to a higher grade supplies advanced math or reading without using the regular teacher's time.

(4) Pullout programs foster advanced learning plus library, Internet, and research skills. But they are only a part-time solution, and gifted children are gifted full time.

(5) District-wide resource programs have essentially the same activities and goals (and problems) as within-school pullout plans. However, materials and equipment normally are more sophisticated.

(6) Grade skipping places gifted students with intellectual peers—and replaces repetition and boredom with motivation and challenge.

(7) Cluster grouping is placing five to 10 gifted students in a classroom with 15 to 20 regular students. The teacher, trained or experienced in gifted education, supplies a differentiated and enriched curriculum to the gifted students.

(8) Part-time special classes—perhaps four hours every day—permit advanced work and individual projects.

(9) Full-time special classes also allow individual projects, along with grade-level and advanced academic work.

(10) Special schools for the gifted are just that.

In this chapter's opening dialogue, teacher Sonja Thorley noted that planning a gifted program for an individual school can include several options simultaneously; it can include both enrichment and acceleration.

Actually, in the 1980s, a small debate roared over the virtues of acceleration versus enrichment. Acceleration proponents Julian Stanley and Camilla Benbow consider most kinds o educational enrichment to be busywork and irrelevant.[11] Enrichment folks pointed out that enrichment supplies "the depth, breadth, or intensity of content and process as appropriate to the students' abilities and needs."[12] In addition, they happily reminded everyone that enrichment is by far the most common educational practice for gifted and talented students.

The truth, of course, is that *both* are needed. Both should be included in programs for gifted students.

Another program planning consideration is selecting enrichment that allows students *choices* of activities—which leads to higher interest and motivation, enjoyment, and feelings of achievement. Enrichment also should be *challenging*—with high-level content and requiring high-level thinking skills.[13]

Content, Process, and Product

Three words guide much program planning for gifted students: *content*, *process*, and *product*. The words are almost self-defining.

Content means information, knowledge. A key question is: What knowledge or academic skills should a gifted student possess after studying a subject area? Imagine of a pyramid with lots of facts and ideas at the base, more general concepts and principles in the middle, and a few broad theories and systems at the peak. All should be included.

Process virtually always refers to creativity and other thinking skills. Chapter 10 will look at dozens of important thinking skills. As we will see, all complex thinking skills (e.g., planning) are built of simpler thinking skills (e.g., analyzing, sequencing, predicting consequences). The premier thinking skill is *creative thinking* (see Chapter 11).[14]

The *product*, of course, is the visible result of the library, research, art, or other project. The product may be, for example, a paper summarizing a student's Internet research on Bonny Prince Charlie, posters on clean air for a shopping mall exhibit, a narrated slide show for the class, or an enthusiastic, costumed poetry reading.

Preparing a Written Program Plan

As suggested in our opening dialogue, a first step toward preparing a written program plan is forming a school gifted committee. Such a committee normally includes the school principal, a counselor (one acquainted with common issues and concerns of the gifted), a district gifted and talented coordinator, several interested and enthusiastic teachers, and one or more parents of gifted children. In secondary schools, a gifted student or two should be included.

The committee's job, of course, is to plan a sensible program for gifted students. The first task is to assemble a written *program plan*. An experienced G/T coordinator almost certainly will have a preliminary draft of a G/T plan filed in a folder somewhere. That program plan likely is a synthesis of program plans from other schools, district guidelines, and state policies or regulations. Written program plans typically define *gifted and talented* in accord with the federal definition presented in Chapter 3.

The plan normally addresses *who, what, where, when, why,* and *how* questions, all tucked neatly into (usually) four sections of the written program plan.[15] In one way or another, the plan will address most of the central NAGC program standards. The four parts—program philosophy and goals, definition and identification, instruction, and program evaluation—typically appear in the following order.

(1) *Program philosophy and goals.* The committee considers these types of questions:

- What is our attitude toward gifted children?

- Why are we doing this? Why do we need a G/T program?

- What are our goals? What are our objectives?

- What do we wish to accomplish?

(2) *Definition and identification.* These two terms are closely related, as we noted in Chapter 3. The committee considers:

- Who is the program for? Which grades?

- What exactly do we mean by "gifted and talented"?

- How many students will we include? One percent? Five percent (the most common proportion)? Renzulli's 15 to 20%?

- Exactly how will we identify gifted students? IQ scores? Achievement scores? Creativity test scores? Teacher nominations? Parent nominations? Peer nominations? Self nominations? Some combination of these?

- What will we do to ensure inclusion of minority students and students with disabilities?

(3) *Instruction*. The topic of instruction includes several interrelated problems and subtopics.

- *Students*:
  - What are gifted students' needs?
  - How can we best meet these needs?

- *Program format and location*:
  - What forms of acceleration, enrichment, and grouping should we use?
  - Which will produce the best results?
  - Which are cost effective?
  - Will students be in their regular (heterogeneous) classroom, with independent projects and learning centers?
  - Will they be cluster grouped in one classroom per grade?
  - Will we use a pullout plan?
  - A district resource center?
  - Will they be in a special G/T class?
  - Does our city have special schools for the gifted?
  - How will we use community and city resources?

- *Personnel*:
  - Who will oversee and coordinate the final design of the program?
  - Who will teach the gifted students?
  - Who will be on the permanent school G/T committee?
  - What inservice training/presentations do we need? Should they be for all teachers?
  - What visits to successful programs should we arrange?
  - How will counselors be used? For personal and social problems? Educational guidance? Career information?
  - Will we use mentors? Local professionals? College students?

- *Time considerations*:
  - When will gifted students receive the special services?
  - When they finish regular assignments?
  - When regular assignments are "compacted" (e.g., by students testing out of regular class work)?
  - Every Tuesday afternoon? All day every day? Saturdays? Summers?
  - Can we create timelines? For identification? For beginning the G/T program?

(4) *Program evaluation.* Regrettably, many gifted programs skip this critical step. They assume that good intentions plus enthusiastic teacher and student participation are adequate indicators of success. Actually, every program component can and should be evaluated and improved.

- How can we evaluate improvements in student knowledge and thinking skills?

- How can we evaluate student and parent satisfaction?

- How can we evaluate program progress during the year? How can we make adjustment and improvements?

- How can we evaluate the effectiveness of every single G/T program activity and component? Identification procedures? Teaching strategies? Student learning activities? Books, supplies, and equipment? Program organization? Others?

The written program plan does spell out *who* is gifted, *how* they are selected, *what* program activities are needed, *why, what*, and *how* they are taught, *when* they will receive these special services, and *how well* the plan works.

Eleven Areas of Program Planning

Most of the following more specific considerations for program planning relate to and partially duplicate the NAGC *Pre-K–Grade 12 Gifted Program Standards* and the main components of a written program plan (*philosophy and goals, definition and identification, instruction*, and *program evaluation*). Most problem areas are major considerations.

(1) *Preliminary staff education.* To avoid uninformed assumptions and innocent mistakes, program planners should be acquainted with the current status of gifted education in the local district, city, and state. Visits to schools with successful programs are especially enlightening. One learns how to implement various plans, how to handle common problems, and especially which arrangements and activities have worked well—and which have flopped.

Program planners certainly need a copy of the NAGC Program Standards. Also, your state probably has a state G/T director and a formal written statement (position, guideline) on gifted education—which probably does *not* promise financial help. What exactly does your State Department of Education's policy say? How does it define *gifted and talented*? Does it recommend particular identification and programming practices? Does it offer training services? Other resources?

Your school district also may have a written policy, along with one or more district G/T coordinators.[16] Learn about these also.

Other preliminary educational points a program planner should investigate are:

- Do other area schools have programs? What are they doing?

- What is the position of the district superintendent and school board members (mostly parents) regarding gifted education? The anti-gifted attitudes of "They'll make it anyway!" and "Give the help to kids who need it!" are not unusual among parents of average children—and also among some teachers and administrators.

- Do district policies allow early admission to kindergarten? First grade? Grade skipping? What are the criteria? For unknown reasons, some districts strictly forbid early admission and/or grade skipping.

- Can high school students take college courses in person or by correspondence? Are Advanced Placement courses available in high school? (The answer to both questions usually is "yes.")

- In your school, are *all* other teachers supportive? Is the principal enthusiastic? Is the district superintendent pro-gifted?

Do some teachers object to: (a) losing their best students, and/or (b) getting stuck with problem learners while the gifted teacher happily sails along with bright students and few problems?

● Are parents or parent groups agitating for services for their ignored gifted children?

State and national gifted conferences are extremely informative and guaranteed to confirm your pro-gifted attitude. Especially valuable are the national conferences sponsored by the National Association for Gifted Children (NAGC) and the Council for Exceptional Children—Talented and Gifted (CEC-TAG).

(2) *Identification: Which types of gifts and talents will be accommodated? How many students will be served?* Because the identification procedure will define the types of gifts and talents selected for a program, it also will influence the types of needed programs and services. Will the program accommodate only bright, intellectually gifted students? Or will it also serve students with academic talents in specific areas? Creative talents? Scientific talents? Communication (speaking, writing) talents? Artistic and musical talents? Other gifts and talents?

As we noted in Chapter 3, it is not unusual for a formal, written G/T plan to endorse the federal multiple-talent definition of giftedness, but then use only IQ scores, achievement scores, and/or grades for actual selection.

Regarding program size, we also mentioned earlier that programs have included as few as 1% of students to as many as 15 or 20%, with 5% a usual number. With some acceleration plans, setting a fixed percentage of participants is not as sensible as establishing criteria that will qualify *any number* of suitable students for the acceleration.

IQ or achievement test scores must not be used rigidly. Test scores always show random variability, and it is unfair and unreasonable to exclude a capable student who misses the G/T program's cutoff score by one or two points. Selection must include subjective judgments along with criteria scores. Experienced intuition is fine.

Of course, selection of students gifted in art, music, creative writing, drama, or other talent areas necessarily will be based heavily on subjective judgments, perhaps accompanied by self, peer, or parent nominations.

At the 2004 National Association for Gifted Children conference, a "Great Debate" was titled *Should the Field of Gifted Education Use Traditional* (e.g., ability tests, achievement tests, grades) *or Nontraditional Tools* (e.g., self-recommendations or recommendations by teachers or parents) *for Identifying Students for Program Services?* On the side of traditional measures, Nancy Robinson argued that such measures actually define giftedness—as advanced mental age—and the tests accurately predict further rapid mental growth.[17] The tests work, she emphasized. They predict real-life advanced behavior, for example, that parents report. She conceded that the measures are not perfect. They do not predict the effects of opportunity or motivation; they do not predict adult success; kids are not always in their best test-taking form, leading to possible score inaccuracy; and some student groups are discriminated against.

Donna Ford, an African-American, strongly pointed out that tests keep Black students out of gifted programs—which, she said, is inexcusable and unacceptable.[18] Selection must be flexible. We need not use the same criteria for all gifted students. Interestingly, she noted that a single IQ score will brand a student *gifted* for the rest of his or her life. Ford listed about the same imperfections in testing as did Robinson, ending with a strong emphasis on blatant racial unfairness.

Sylvia Rimm agreed that using test scores alone is unfair and that schools can use other methods—but they must be reliable and valid.[19] Parents, she noted, usually can identify giftedness in their children—even though sometimes they are wrong. Generally, traditional testing is crucial to identifying and helping gifted children.

Jack Naglieri noted that for 100 years intelligence has been defined by IQ tests.[20] He mainly emphasized that scores on intelligence and achievement test are too-strongly influenced by a person's vocabulary—that is, verbal achievement. He showed examples of vocabulary items on IQ tests and achievement tests that were virtually identical.

Discussant Joseph Renzulli noted the obvious: the speakers agreed that ability and achievement testing are important but not infallible, particularly in regard to unfair discrimination.[21] Said Renzulli, "Tests do not tell us all there is about talent." He also noted a "multiple-criteria smokescreen," in which the use of numerous formal test scores for identification creates the illusion of validity—and serves as a gatekeeper to dismiss some student groups.

(3) *How will underachieving students, culturally different students, poor students, and students with disabilities be identified?* Students in these groups must be fairly represented. The problem is not the absence of gifts and talents. The problem is that educators too often do not search for giftedness in these populations.

Susanne Richert accurately observed that "the more measures that are used and combined inappropriately, the more likely it becomes that disadvantaged students (poor, minority, creative, and others)…will be excluded."[22] Her strategy and philosophy? "Data from different sources should be used independently, and any *one* source should be sufficient to include a student in a program…. Students should qualify for a program by scoring high on any of several measures."[23]

Of critical importance: *Minority and underachieving students and students with disabilities will raise their educational and career aspirations as a result of participating in gifted programs.* Selection criteria must be broad and flexible—and never used to prove that the students are "not gifted." Because a low score on any one test (or other criterion) can be misleading, most states recommend using multiple criteria: a combination of IQ scores, achievement test scores, teacher nominations (by caring, informed teachers), parent nominations, peer nominations, and self nominations. Mary Frasier and Alexinia Baldwin each have created matrices that assemble lots of information designed to help select minority students for gifted programs.[24]

(4) *Staff responsibilities: How will the plan actually be carried out?* There is a difference between endorsing a gifted program and rolling up one's sleeves to do the work. An early issue is deciding who will be responsible for what and when. Accountability checks can include setting timelines and deadlines, for example, for obtaining information, preparing reports, purchasing tests and materials, conferring with district administrators, and so on. Weekly meetings help ensure that responsibilities are met on time.

(5) *How will the program use school psychologists? School counselors? Consultants?* School psychologists are trained to administer individual intelligence tests — the Stanford-Binet and the Wechsler tests—whether or not they are well-versed in gifted education. The psychologist also can administer and interpret individual achievement tests, personality inventories, and (career) interest inventories, such as the *Kuder Preference Record.*

Counselors help students cope with academic and personal problems. They also help educate parents about the child's academic strengths, weaknesses, and personal difficulties. If parents are reluctant to allow their child to participate in a gifted program ("My kid ain't no egg-head!" "My kid's gotta' be with normal kids!"), counselors can explain the program and urge participation. They can also recommend summer programs in, for example, art, music, language, or science, or computer camps or workshops, or "college for kids" programs.

A counselor versed in gifted education can help G/T students know and understand their abilities, develop good self-concepts, understand similarities and differences between themselves and others, improve social skills, become more self-directed, and set realistic goals.[25]

Outside consultants—for example, experienced G/T teachers, state or district G/T coordinators, or professional G/T consultants or workshop leaders—can help:

- Prepare written program plans and other statements.

- Obtain funds.

- Design suitable acceleration and enrichment activities.

- Install a particular G/T program (e.g., Schoolwide Enrichment Model).

- Select or create rating scales, nomination forms, or questionnaires for identification.

- Ensure representation of various (e.g., minority) student groups.

- Design program evaluation procedures.

- Promote public relations.

(6) *What are the goals?* Chapters 5, 6, and 7 described specific acceleration, enrichment, and grouping methods for gifted students. Some high-level goals that should guide the selection of acceleration and enrichment plans include:

- High achievement.

- Advanced academic content and skills.

- Creative, critical, and evaluative thinking and other thinking skills (Chapters 10 and 11).

- Complex, abstract, and theoretical thinking.

- Library and computer research skills.

- Scientific thinking and research skills.

- Communication (speaking, writing) skills, including creative writing and report writing.

- Education and career information.

- Self-awareness and ethical and humanistic principles.

Interestingly, one panel at the 2004 NAGC conference debated the value of *cognitive* (intellectual/achievement) versus *affective* (emotional/social) education for gifted students. Feelings were strong. Jonathan Plucker, for example, argued that policy makers (e.g., district superintendents) are not interested in affective outcomes—they want to see cognitive gain, such as high achievement test scores.[26] Besides, said Plucker, affective gains are difficult to measure, and training effects do not last.

In contrast, Karen Rogers argued that gifted students must live in an affective environment.[27] She reminded us that Abraham Maslow's affective needs—love and belonging—must be met *before* cognitive needs can be met. Further, the common overexcitability syndrome experienced by some highly gifted students certainly is affective. Gifted students need such (affective) components of self-actualization as good interpersonal relations, self-acceptance, and high moral/ethical attitudes—plus passions and motivations.

Sandra Kaplan supported the cognitive, curricula position.[28] Sort of. Similar to Plucker's main point, she noted that students are recognized for their gains in knowledge and skills—for example, in Advanced Placement classes. But she also conceded that values—affect—are learned within academic content. For example, teaching thinking and problem solving includes teaching responsibility. Concluded Kaplan, "You cannot separate cognitive and affective."

James Gallagher, the final pro-affective speaker, simply insisted that we must teach affect (e.g., values, attitudes, motivations, other affective components), even if we can't measure it.[29] Can we imagine a world without affect? It would be colorless! Affect—high motivation—is the fuel that drives accomplishment. Said Gallagher, "Schools should emphasize affect, with cognitive dragged along behind!" He quoted one student: "Studying is great [cognitive], but there is more to life [affective]!"

(7) *Organizational and administrative problems.* Even simple elementary and secondary programs will require administrative reshuffling to provide, for example, the necessary funds, supplies, time, space, facilities, inservice training, record-keeping, and coordination with the rest of the school. A district- or city-wide program will require even broader planning and coordination.

It is common for larger cities to have one or more full-time G/T personnel in the central office to help plan and manage programs. At each local school, of course, one or more staff members must assume administrative responsibility for overseeing the program in that school.

(8) *Money.* While some programs are relatively cheap, especially early admission and other acceleration plans, the following are more-or-less predictable expenses:

- A district teacher-coordinator

- Texts and workbooks

- Equipment and supplies (e.g., computers, digital cameras, video cameras, art supplies, laboratory equipment)

- Transportation

- Consultants and inservice trainers

- Secretarial services, office supplies, duplicating expenses

- Travel to other programs

- Travel to state and national conventions

On one hand, program planners should consider cost-benefit matters from the beginning. On the other hand, and regrettably, little or no research compares the effectiveness of various program types with actual program cost. As mentioned above and several times in this book, early admission to kindergarten and later grade skipping almost guarantee a suitable educational challenge and the end of lazy study habits—at virtually no dollar cost.[30]

Note that while general funding for G/T programs may be scarce, a specific request for funds for minority or disabled gifted students; improving math, science, and computer skills; or fostering arts and the humanities can improve chances for financial support.

(9) *Accommodating the anti-grouping, detracking movement?* Rena Subotnik discovered that several anti-grouping leaders actually *favored* a suitable education for gifted students.[31] They just didn't like visible groupings—such as pullout programs and special classes—that announce "I'm gifted, but you're not!" Perhaps program planners should consider: Will the program include highly visible grouping? Highly visible enrichment and acceleration activities in mixed-ability classrooms? Should we worry about the matter?

If gifted students are to be taught in the regular classroom, teachers will need updating in such topics as identifying student differences, differentiating the curriculum, G/T learning strategies (e.g., self-paced instruction, solving problems, computer learning), suitable teaching strategies, acceleration, mentoring, and assessment.[32] Ideally, regular teachers will be enthusiastic supporters of the G/T effort and want to accommodate student differences.

(10) *Transportation needs.* Transportation arrangements and costs are part of many gifted programs—for example, for elementary students who participate in district-wide resource programs, elementary students who take middle school math classes, high school students who take college courses, or for any students who must travel to other schools that have special resources. Transportation also must be considered for field trips, mentoring programs, after-school projects and clubs, and Saturday and summer programs.

(11) *Program evaluation.* Program evaluation directly affects the survival of the program, the continuation or improvement of funding, and program improvement. Evaluation should be part of every program plan—right from the beginning. As noted earlier, the effectiveness of each and every program component can—and should—be examined, evaluated, and improved: identification methods, program type, enrichment and acceleration activities, changes in student knowledge and skills, teacher training, teaching strategies and activities, materials and equipment, student satisfaction, parent satisfaction, and so on.

Even the evaluation procedures can be evaluated and improved. For selected insightful comments and recommendations by Cox, Daniel, and Boston regarding many aspects of program planning, see Table 8.1.[33]

Table 8.1 Observations and Recommendations from the Richardson Study

(Cox, Daniel, & Boston, 1985)

Philosophic Considerations	~ Our school systems, public and private, most often reward patterns of behavior inappropriate for independent thinking, researchers, or artists.
	~ Some educators embrace a counterfeit notion of democracy in which everyone is not only equal in opportunity but in achievement.
	~ Abilities of able learners often are not challenged, leading to boredom and dropping out.
Program Planning and Administration	~ Develop a written philosophy for educating able learners that is compatible with the values of the school district.
	~ Select one or more G/T coordinators early in the program planning stages. The coordinator(s) will participate in the planning.
	~ Assess current G/T programs. Successful programs and components can be retained and expanded. Other options can be added.
	~ Allow for flexible pacing. Individual students should advance at a natural, challenging pace as they master skills and content.
Identification	~ "Cast a wide net." Select a larger population of able learners than is usually identified as gifted. [Cox, Daniel, and Boston recommend 25%.] Keep requirements modest. Avoid arbitrary cutoffs.
	~ Use a wide range of testing strategies, including out-of-level testing.
	~ Recognize creativity and problem solving as indicators of interest and ability.
	~ Recognize multiple measures of multiple types of intelligence.
	~ For minority groups, avoid tests that depend on standard English.
	~ Supplement testing with evaluations of characteristics of giftedness.
	~ We often overlook disadvantaged students and students with disabilities.
	~ With young children, use puzzles and games to discover talents.

Identification (cont.)	~ Use the results of identification to guide programming decisions.
	~ Avoid labeling children as "gifted," which implies that others are "not gifted." [Cox, Daniel, and Boston prefer "able learners."]
	~ Create a psychologically safe environment so that students will value, not hide, their abilities.
Program	~ A comprehensive program will include a collection of options for students of high ability, including enrichment and acceleration programs, and programs that permit continuous progress, especially in reading and math.
	~ Do not try to assemble all program elements at once. Create a mosaic, piece by piece.
	~ Programs must be sequential, carefully integrated, and communicated throughout the school system.
	~ Offer programs that reach beyond the normal boundaries—across disciplines, grade levels, and higher intelligence levels.
	~ Balance acceleration with enrichment for students with different types and degrees of ability.
	~ Use counselors for assessment, caring for students' affective needs, program selection, and career and college counseling.
	~ Encourage projects that involve real methods of inquiry and produce real products.
	~ Encourage thinking and questioning.
	~ Use concurrent/dual enrollment: elementary/middle, middle/high school, and high school/college.
	~ Allow capable students to enter college early.
	~ Use community resources, including mentorships and (in high school) internships, which aid educational and career decision making.
	~ Use educational options outside of the school, such as museums and art galleries.
	~ Encourage participation in Saturday, summer, and after-school programs.
	~ Consider residential and specialized schools.
Staff Development	~ Assume staff development to be continuous for all teachers and administrators.

Teacher Support	~ Coordinate teaching with students' learning styles.
	~ Help teachers develop an efficient record-keeping system for monitoring student progress.
	~ Use nearby colleges as a resource for staff development.
Evaluation	~ Plan program evaluation early in the program development stages.
	~ Establish baseline data for later comparisons.
	~ Regularly evaluate the success of every program element and its impact on student achievement and growth.
	~ Use internal and external program evaluators to ensure objectivity and credibility.

Why Gifted Programs Survive and Thrive

J. H. Purcell described three disarmingly simple yet pivotal factors in the survival and growth of gifted programs: (1) good state economic health—so that gifted programs are not eliminated by budget cuts, (2) state mandates for gifted education, and (3) enthusiastic support for gifted education by teachers, principals, and district superintendents.[34]

Supporters of gifted education agree that gifted programs normally provide marvelous academic stimulation. The programs not only relieve boredom, but they also improve social and emotional maturity. Bright students are able to explore their own interests. There is a feeling of community among participants in a G/T program. There are greater educational opportunities, for example, for creativity, independent research, or exploring other cultures and languages.

Why Gifted Programs Die

Despite good intentions, gifted programs disappear. The following problems and concerns have alienated some teachers, administrators, and parents of non-gifted students, leading to the termination of G/T programs.[35]

- The program appears to be a fun-and-games waste of time.

- Other teachers believe that gifted students are easy to teach, while they are stuck with problem students.

- Other teachers and parents complain that the gifted activities "would be good for all students."

- Teachers who are not trained in gifted education may be unaware of the educational needs of gifted students and appropriate curriculum for them.

- Parents believe that rich kids receive opportunities not available to their children—the programs seem "welfare for the rich."

- All parents want the best teachers for their children.

- Aggressive parents tend to get their children into G/T programs.

- G/T students are put under too much pressure.

- G/T students become arrogant and snobbish.

- G/T students develop neurotic, perfectionistic habits (elaborated in Chapter 12).

- Students not selected are resentful and have poor academic self-concepts.

- Classes are disrupted by pulling out the G/T kids.

- Gifted students' contributions to class (e.g., as role models) are lost.

- Identification may be too restrictive (e.g., based only on IQ scores).

- Gifted students are supplied with expensive equipment, field trips, and other opportunities denied to regular students.

- Gifted programs have been charged with racism and elitism.

- Some teachers believe that the focus should be on less capable students—the clear majority.

- The program seems to be a reward for high cooperation and high-achievement—a status symbol.

- High school students seem successful without having participated in an elementary school G/T program.

Summary

- In 1998, the NAGC prepared its *Pre-K–Grade 12 Gifted Program Standards.* Seven summary tables outline program planning guides in the areas of:

    1. Curriculum and instruction, which must be differentiated for gifted students and include accelerated learning.

195

2. Program administration and management, including such matters as qualified personnel, integration with the larger program, and working relationships with various groups.

3. Program design, with attention to a continuum of services, funding, stated goals and objectives, and flexible grouping.

4. Student identification, focusing on a fair and comprehensive process that measures diverse abilities and talents, culturally fair assessment instruments, an assessment profile for each student, and guides for student exiting.

5. Guidance and counseling that accommodates students' unique socio-emotional development and career guidance, and that considers at-risk and underachieving gifted students.

6. Professional development of qualified staff, with time provisions for program planning and curriculum development.

7. Program evaluation, which must be purposeful, efficient, ethical, related to interests of constituency groups, and available in a written report. Instruments must be reliable and valid.

- Planning a gifted program will involve acceleration (Chapter 5), enrichment (Chapter 6), and grouping gifted students together (Chapter 7).

- A 1980s debate argued the virtues of acceleration versus enrichment. Both are needed.

- Content (knowledge, skills), process (creativity, other thinking skills), and product (the results of student projects) guide much of program planning.

- A school gifted committee usually includes the principal, a counselor, a district G/T coordinator, several enthusiastic teachers, one or more parents of gifted children and, in secondary school, one or two gifted students. They plan a gifted program.

- Four parts of a written program plan include: (1) program philosophy and goals, including goals and attitudes toward gifted children; (2) definition and identification of students to be in the program; (3) instructional considerations, such as student needs, program format, personnel involved, and time considerations; and (4) program evaluation, an often-skipped step that examines, for example, student gains in knowledge and thinking skills, and student and parent satisfaction.

- Eleven additional areas of program planning to consider include:

    1. Preliminary staff education: What are other schools doing? What is the position of the school superintendent?

    2. Identification: What types of gifts and talents are to be accommodated? How many students? What selection criteria?

    3. How will we identify underachieving, disabled, culturally different, and poor students, as well as students with disabilities?

    4. Staff responsibilities: How will the plan be carried out? What are timelines and deadlines?

    5. What are the roles of school psychologists, school counselors, and outside consultants?

    6. What are the goals? Achievement? Creative and critical thinking? Library and computer skills? Career information? Ethical and humanistic principles? A 2004 NAGC panel debated the virtues of cognitive versus affective goals.

    7. Organization and administration—for example, time, space, funds, records, coordination with the rest of the school, and G/T personnel.

    8. Program expenses, such as a teacher-coordinator's salary, texts and workbooks, computers, art supplies, transportation, secretarial services, and travel to other programs and conventions. Little research exists comparing costs with benefits.

    9. Accommodating anti-grouping pressures (maybe). Visible groupings (e.g., pullout plans) may be problematic.

    10. Transportation needs—for example, to district resource programs, middle-school math classes, or college.

    11. Program evaluation—evaluating the success of every program component.

- Cox, Daniel, and Boston listed many Richardson Study observations and recommendations in the areas of: philosophic considerations (e.g., school systems often reward behavior inappropriate for independent thinking), program planning and administrations, identification (e.g., "cast a wide net," use out-of-level testing), program (e.g., include enrichment and acceleration options, carefully integrated), staff development and teacher support, and evaluation (e.g., using internal and external evaluators).

- Programs thrive due to good state economic health, state mandates for gifted education, and enthusiastic teachers and administrators.

- G/T programs provide academic stimulation and promote maturity.

- Many problems lead to the demise of gifted programs. For example, a program may appear to be "fun and games," teachers and parents complain that the gifted activities "would be good for all students," untrained teachers are unaware of gifted students' needs, the programs may be seen as "welfare for the rich," gifted students are put under excessive pressure, they may become arrogant, non-selected students are resentful, gifted students' contributions to regular classes are lost, there are charges of racism and elitism, and some teachers believe that the focus should be on less capable students—the larger majority.

9
Models that Guide Teaching the Gifted

*We have become accustomed to using a variety of
paradigms or models as a way of organizing this complex
field. We have had one paradigm for intelligence, another
for our public education system, and still another for how
we should educate students high in intelligence.*

~ James J. Gallagher

[*Scene: Living room of eccentric inventor Alexander Graham Schnell, creator of
the automatic talking chicken. TV cameramen have set up microphones, cameras,
and floodlights. GBC News correspondent Barbara Waters enters and sits down
facing Mr. Schnell. The floodlights are turned on, and the director counts "3, 2,
1!" and points to Ms. Waters.*]

Barbara Waters (smiling): Mr. Schnell, is it true that you are stark
raving mad? A brilliant lunatic in the true classic sense?

Alexander Graham Schnell: Mad? Well, sometimes I think funny!
Right now I'm working on invisible tennis balls for players who keep
saying, "I sure didn't see that one!"

Waters: When you were in school, Mr. Schnell, did any of your school
experiences help you become what you are today—a truly innovative,
independent and, some would say, crazy inventor?

Schnell: Now that you mention it, I was in a special program for gifted
kids. We did stuff based on the enrichment triad model, invented by
some clown named Joseph Ben Zuly-Zuly–or something like that. The
activities helped me think funny.

Waters: How exactly did Ben Zuly-Zuly's program help you think
funny, Dr. Schnell?

Schnell: Easy! I learned lots of stuff. Most important to me, they taught us to think—you know, different than everybody else. They called it *thinking creatively*. I call it *thinking funny*. Maybe even *thinking crazy*.

Waters: What did they ask you to do? What led you to think funny?

Schnell: Easy! We practiced thinking funny. Every day. We looked for new ideas, new ways to solve problems. I usually got carried away!

Waters: I think I understand, Mr. Schnell. They helped you learn to be an independent innovator. A person who contributes truly creative ideas to society. Is this correct?

Schnell: Absolutely!

Waters: Now about those chickens. Do they really talk? Or are you just a ventriloquist?

Schnell: They talk. Absolutely! No hanky-panky here. I start them off as chicks with vowels—long "e," short "a," that sort of thing. Then we get to consonants and whole words. For most, their first sentence is "Wake up, you handsome devil you!" This is for people who can't stand all that cock-a-doodle-do stuff at five o'clock in the morning!

Waters: I see. Now, Mr. Schnell, just one more item. Would you tell our viewers at home how you would like to be remembered?

Schnell: As somebody with a little humor, a little independence, a little imagination, and who isn't afraid to talk to a chicken.

Planning activities for gifted students requires thoughtful ideas about *what* one will teach, *why* it is worthwhile, and *how* to teach it. This chapter describes seven models that help guide the selection of valuable learning activities for students in gifted programs.

Enrichment Triad Model

In 1977, Joseph Renzulli published the book *Enrichment Triad Model: A Guide for Developing Defensible Programs for the Gifted and Talented*.[1] The Triad Model currently is the best known and most widely adopted curriculum model. Why? Because it's simple to understand, not difficult to implement, and makes extremely good sense.

The Triad Model is used almost exclusively at the elementary level. Students initially are exposed to Types I, II, and III enrichment, mostly in that order. But flipping around and back and forth is necessary and useful. Also, it's common to explain to students the differences between, and rationale for, enrichment Types I, II, and III.

Type I Enrichment

Type I enrichment, General Exploratory Activities, exposes students to topics, disciplines, persons, places, events, interest areas, occupations, and more that are not part of the regular curriculum. Type I enrichment experiences can include independent reading, chats with experts, videotapes/DVDs, field trips and visits, or any other valuable source of information—such as the G/T teacher.

A long but incomplete list of possible Type I enrichment topics and activities appeared in Table 6.1, Chapter 6. Peek again. Gifted students also might find an idea in Table 6.1, if they do not already have one, for a later Type III independent project.

Type II Enrichment

Type II enrichment is called Group Training Activities. It mainly includes: (1) school learning skills—for example, listening, note taking, outlining, and organizing information; (2) thinking skills, such as analyzing, classifying, planning, evaluating, thinking creatively, and thinking critically;[2] (3) communication skills in the areas of writing, speaking, and visual communication;[3] (4) interpersonal skills, which includes dealing with important life incidents; (5) general skills related to Type III independent projects—especially how to research a topic using the library or the Internet, and how to locate community resources; and (6) specific skills related to a student's particular Type III project—for example, in photography (camera operation, composing a picture); writing a short story, play, or movie script (format, creating suspense, conflict, hope, surprise ending); or using a microscope or other scientific equipment.

Type III Enrichment

Type III enrichment is Individual and Small Group Investigations of Real Problems. A student, or sometimes two or three students, pursues an original research project. The topic (see Table 6.1) might be in art, theater, science, repairing or building computers, culture and social sciences, business, world pollution, or any other of endless possibilities.

The problem begins with a question to be answered, and it should end with a product. The final product might be a report—perhaps a written report, a newspaper-like article, a radio broadcast, a demonstration of candle-making for the class, a manual entitled "Computer Troubleshooting for Dummies," or any type of art project. As Renzulli emphasized, students should be producers, not just consumers, of knowledge. The teacher serves as "guide on the side," helping clarify the problem, design the project, and locate information sources and equipment.

Type III projects should help students: (1) learn about the content and methodology of a particular area, (2) develop self-directed learning skills (e.g., planning, using resources, managing time, evaluating progress, and evaluating the final outcome) and, importantly, (3) develop self-confidence and feelings of accomplishment.[4]

Beyond a gifted student's own class, a wider audience is desirable for the Type III projects. For example, displays of student projects might be set up in shopping malls, hospital foyers, children's museums, the district school office building, the state capitol, or at the very least, the halls of the students' own school. Children's magazines and local newspapers publish children's writing and articles about research or other interesting Type III projects. Newspaper publicity is great support for the gifted program. Also, an enthusiastic G/T teacher can create local art shows and science fairs, if they are not already part of the school agenda.

Secondary Triad Model

It's more complicated to install the Enrichment Triad Model in middle and high schools, but it can be done. School administrators and interested teachers in disciplines such as math, physics, biology, English literature, French, or art can create a *talent pool class*, composed of students in the top 15 or 20% in general ability or ability specific to the particular discipline. Of course, students must have strong interest in conducting a Type III project. The class would speedily cover the regular curriculum, leaving time for Types I, II, and III enrichment.

In secondary schools, Type I enrichment is greater breadth and depth in the particular discipline. Type II again focuses on learning, thinking, and communicating skills, plus specific skills related to Type III projects. Secondary school Type III projects may require help from outside professionals. Audiences again are essential—perhaps publication in professional journals or presentations to suitable local groups.

Schoolwide Enrichment Model

As we noted, the high-impact Enrichment Triad Model first appeared in 1977—before Jeannie Oakes and others raised alarms about unfairness to excluded students. A key question then and now is: *Wouldn't that be good for all students?* Wouldn't *all* students benefit, for example, from training in creativity and thinking skills or visits to museums, industries, and art galleries? Or personal coaching in art or creative writing? Too often, the answer is an embarrassing *yes*.

Enter the Schoolwide Enrichment Model, which brings much of the Enrichment Triad Model to all students.[5] The following is an effort to compress two fat books into a few paragraphs.[6]

To begin, enrichment Types I and II are considered good for all students. Therefore, a school district or individual school or teacher who wishes to bring gifted education content into the regular classroom will find Types I and II activities, as described above, a good source of ideas.

Type III enrichment—independent projects—is considered suitable for students identified as gifted. In accord with Renzulli's Talent Pool Identification Plan described in Chapter 4, a generous 15 to 20% of the school would be selected for the talent pool. They would meet once or twice per week (remember the pullout strategy?) in a resource room to work on their Type III projects.

Back in the regular classroom, all students receive an explanation of Types I and II enrichment. All students also learn about the talent pool and Type III independent projects. It is very important that all students are advised that if they get excited about conducting an independent project, they should tell their teacher. Then they prepare and submit their ideas. If approved, the students become part of the talent pool.

A brief form, called an Action Information Message (or "Light Bulb"), simply asks for: (1) the student's name and teacher's name, (2) the general curriculum area of the proposed project, and (3) a three-line description of the independent investigation/study. At the bottom of the Light Bulb page, the teacher will comment on the student's "high levels of interest, task commitment or creativity…[and] suggested resources or ways to focus the interest into a first-hand investigative experience."[7]

As a final note on the high-impact ideas of Joseph Renzulli and Sally Reis, they distinguish between *schoolhouse giftedness* (lesson learning and test-taking giftedness, accompanied by a high IQ) and *creative-productive giftedness* (developing original ideas and products that have an impact on people). History forgets persons with schoolhouse giftedness, but it remembers "the creative and productive people of the world."[8]

Parallel Curriculum Model

The National Association for Gifted Children sponsored the development of the Parallel Curriculum Model (PCM).[9] "The purpose of this exciting new model is to challenge high-ability learners while upgrading the curriculum for all learners."[10]

Briefly, teachers follow four parallel principles that help gifted and regular students more profitably explore and understand a discipline. First, the *Core Curriculum* principle emphasizes teaching central (i.e., core) concepts and principles of a discipline. The *Curriculum of Connections* directs teachers to help students connect the core concepts within and across disciplines, times, places, and cultures. The *Curriculum of Practice* stresses helping students to understand and use key concepts and skills much as a practitioner in the discipline would understand and use them. Finally, the *Curriculum of Identity* invites students to use information about a discipline not only to understand the discipline itself, but to clarify their own ways of seeing, organizing, and relating to the world.

The four principles—*Core, Connections, Practice, Identity*—may be used singly or in combination to develop sound units or courses of study for individuals or groups. The "parallels" help ensure increasing intellectual demand upon advanced—and advancing—learners.

Autonomous Learner Model

George Betts' Autonomous Learner Model (ALM) resembles Renzulli's Enrichment Triad Model in that both are comprehensive programming guides.[11] Both spell out what to do, and in what order, to further the educational needs of bright kids.

In Betts' model, an underlying purpose is to help students become responsible, independent learners—that is, *autonomous* learners—by giving them progressively more responsibility for their own education. Other goals are to help students understand themselves and their giftedness (which leads to better self-concepts), improve their social skills, increase their knowledge in subject areas, and develop creativity and other thinking skills. Note that Betts' goals are shared by most programs for gifted and talented students.

The five-part ALM is summarized in Figure 9.1. Parts of the ALM may be used in the regular classroom with all students. At the same time, an advanced ALM may be used with gifted students in a resource room (pullout) program that meets for perhaps three hours twice per week. In secondary school, the ALM would be an elective course.

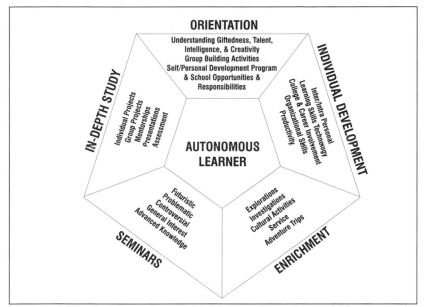

Figure 9.1. The Autonomous Learner Model. From George Betts and Jolene K. Kercher (1999). Reprinted with permission of ALPS Publishing.

Orientation. In the regular classroom, the Orientation dimension of the ALM emphasizes multiple intelligences, creativity, and talents of all children.[12] For gifted students, the Orientation dimension acquaints students (and parents) with the nature of giftedness, creativity, the goals and details of the ALM itself, and what the program can do for them.

In both the regular classroom and the resource room, self-understanding and group building exercises help students learn about themselves and each other. For example, one exercise is "Find Someone Who…." Each student has a 32-cell matrix with such entries as "has a job," "has been to another country," "writes poetry," "plays chess," and so forth. They walk about asking others to sign any square that fits them. Afterward, students discuss what they learned and how the activity benefited them.

Individual Development. The Individual Development dimension jumps right into strengthening skills, concepts, and attitudes that lead to independent, self-directed learning. This component also focuses on social skills, self-understanding, thinking skills, research skills, organizational skills, productivity (improved study habits, goal-setting), the use of technology, and information about college and careers. To aid cognitive and emotional needs, Betts recommended that gifted students talk about "what it's like being gifted."[13]

In the regular classroom, a teacher would focus on self-understanding, thinking and feeling, productivity, and exposure to careers. Most of the school year, in fact, would focus on the first two ALM dimensions of Orientation and Individual Development.

Enrichment. Enrichment, by definition, is content and activities beyond the regular curriculum. The G/T teacher thus presents enriched and differentiated curriculum. Also, each student explores a "passion area," researching the area and presenting findings to the group. Students also may see plays, visit art displays or museums, attend concerts, or hear speeches.

They also perform services, such as visiting the elderly or collecting food for the needy. Students might even study the geology of the Grand Canyon or the socio-cultural aspects of New York, San Francisco, or Washington, DC.

Seminars. In the Seminar component, each person in a small group of three to five students researches a topic and presents it to the rest of that group. Students learn the three steps of: (1) presenting information to promote understanding of a topic, (2) facilitating group discussion to promote involvement and thinking, and (3) bringing the activity to a close.

In-Depth Study. Betts' In-Depth Study component is about the same as Renzulli's Type III independent projects. Students become engaged in the highest level of independent, autonomous learning. They work on individual or small-group research studies. They decide what will be researched, what help will be needed, what the final product should be, how it will be presented, and how the entire episode will be evaluated.

The Betts and Kercher book, *Autonomous Learner Model: Optimizing Ability*, presents lots of classroom activities and helpful forms.[14] As brief examples, a self-understanding exercise elicits answers to "Today I am...," "Tomorrow I want to be...," "I am insecure when...," "My main strength is...," "When I am upset with others...," and more. Self- and teacher-rating forms evaluate social attitudes (e.g., "Needs to be more accepting of others"), abilities (e.g., "Solves problems effectively"), behavior (e.g., "Works independently"), and other areas.

Integrated Curriculum Model

Joyce VanTassel-Baska's Integrated Curriculum Model (ICM) underlies her curriculum programs for gifted learners in language arts, science, and social studies.[15] An assumption is that gifted students—and, in fact, all students—should receive a meaningful and organized sequence of educational experiences. Such an organized curriculum should transform a gifted learner's initial mental capacity into a mature competence for academic and later professional accomplishment.

VanTassel-Baska specifically criticized the models of Renzulli (Enrichment Triad), Betts (Autonomous Learner Model), Feldhusen and Kolloff (Purdue Three-Stage Enrichment Model), and Treffinger (Individualized Programming Planning Model).[16] Their common difficulty is that they are not derived from, nor directly applied to, such academic disciplines as science, social studies, or languages.

VanTassel-Baska's Integrated Curriculum Model assumes that:

- Gifted learners have different needs, and curriculum must be designed or modified to meet these needs.

- The needs of gifted learners require attention to cognitive, affective, social, and aesthetic areas of curriculum.

- Gifted learners require both accelerated and enriched learning experiences.

- Curriculum experiences for the gifted must be carefully planned, implemented, and evaluated.

Along with these four, the ICM includes other features of good teaching and learning. It emphasizes depth (not breadth) and concepts (not just facts). It is rooted in real-world issues and problems, which maintains interest. The ICM also promotes active learning and problem solving, stimulates higher-order thinking, helps students see interdisciplinary connections, promotes thinking about thinking (metacognition), and develops modes of thinking similar to those of professionals.

Further, the ICM is said to consider important characteristics of gifted students (precocity, intensity, and complexity); to work well in self-contained special classes for the gifted; and, by embedding higher-order thinking skills into the subject matter itself, to help students transfer these skills to new situations.

The main thrust of the ICM itself is its three dimensions of curriculum:

- The Advanced Content Dimension emphasizes (what else?) the advanced content of disciplines—for example, advanced literature.

- The Process-Product Dimension includes presenting problems that elicit higher-order thinking, reasoning, and learning.

- The Issues/Themes Dimension focuses learning experiences on important real-world themes, systems, issues, and cause-effect relations.[17]

All three dimensions are built in to VanTassel-Baska's National Language Arts Curriculum Project, her National Science Curriculum Project for High Ability Learners, and her untitled social studies project. According to VanTassel-Baska, her ICM meets criteria for exemplary curriculum design, exemplary content, and suitable differentiation for gifted learners.[18]

Pyramid Model

In Chapter 8, we looked at many insights and recommendations by June Cox, Neil Daniel, and Bruce Boston in regard to program planning, all based on findings from their elaborate Richardson Study.[19] This study included visits to gifted schools and, especially, a survey of various programs and their procedures for identifying and teaching gifted and talented students, whom Cox, Daniel, and Boston prefer to call *able learners*.

The Richardson Study itself reviewed and evaluated these kinds of gifted programs, most of which are described in this book: early entrance, moderate acceleration, radical acceleration, enrichment in the regular classroom, independent study, itinerant (traveling) teachers, resource rooms (e.g., libraries, computer rooms), full-time special classes, mentorships, Advanced Placement classes, International Baccalaureate programs, concurrent (dual) enrollment (elementary school/middle school, middle school/high school, high school/college), fast-paced courses, special schools for the gifted, pullout programs (weekly two- to three-hour classes), and district-wide resource (pullout) programs.

Cox and colleagues endorsed all of the plans, except (as noted in Chapter 7) pullout plans and the district-wide resource programs—which, you may recall, they described as "fragmented," "patchwork," and "part-time solutions to a full-time problem." They also recommended quality summer programs, such as Talent Search (Chapter 5) and Governor's School programs (Chapter 6).

Resembling Renzulli's generous talent pool approach to identification, Cox and colleagues concluded that about one-fourth of the students in the study (and presumably one-fourth of all students) are able learners and need special educational accommodations. As other noteworthy conclusions: existing programs ignore the needs of *extremely* bright and/or creative students, rigid cutoff scores (e.g., IQ numbers) exclude many creative and capable learners, and flexible pacing based on mastery is "the single most important concept for educators designing programs for able learners."[20]

Their three-section Pyramid Model appears in Figure 9.2. It accommodates students' educational needs at three levels of increasing giftedness. The bottom section, which they named *Enrichment in the Regular Classroom*, refers to the largest group of able learners, who are "above average" in ability. These students receive enrichment in their regular classroom—for example, via within-class and cross-grade grouping for math and reading, cluster grouping, individualized instructional methods (including learning centers), curriculum compacting (testing out of material they already know), and using resource centers such as libraries and computer rooms.

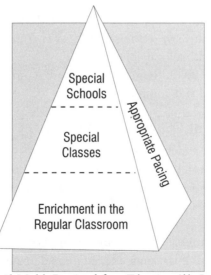

Figure 9.2. The Pyramid Model. Reprinted from Educating Able Learners: Programs and Promising Practices, by June Cox, Neil Daniel, and Bruce O. Boston. Copyright © 1985. Reprinted by permission of J. Cox, Gifted Students Institute, and the University of Texas Press.

The middle section of the pyramid, named *Special Classes,* refers to a smaller group of more able students who attend full-time special ("honors") classes. They also may participate in concurrent/dual enrollment plans.

The top section of the pyramid, *Special Schools,* refers to the smallest number, the most highly able—that is, the most gifted and creative—students. They attend special (magnet) schools for the gifted at both elementary and secondary levels. At the elementary level, Cox and colleagues named the Oaks Academy in Houston and Windsor Park Elementary School in Corpus Christi as good examples. Special high schools for the gifted emphasize science, math, languages, the arts, and an International Baccalaureate program. Cox, Daniel, and Boston listed the Walnut Hills High School in Cincinnati, the Houston High School for the Performing and Visual Arts, and the Bronx High School of Science as examples. They mentioned just one special school that serves gifted middle school students: Cincinnati's School for the Creative and Performing Arts, which includes grades 4 through 12.[21]

Cox, Daniel, and Boston conceded the obvious: one needs a very large city to justify special magnet schools for the top few percent of able learners. As a remedy for smaller cities, they suggested that elementary students in the top *two* levels of the pyramid could be placed in special classes and participate in dual enrollment. Secondary schools can create advanced classes, for example, in science, math, language arts, history, social studies, and fine arts—along with honors courses, AP courses, and dual enrollment with a local college.[22]

While likely difficult to implement, the Pyramid Model is extraordinarily thoughtful and comprehensive.

Programming at Four Ability Levels

The Pyramid Model recognized three levels of giftedness plus regular students, for a total of four categories. By coincidence—or from a similar penetrating analysis—Donald Treffinger and M. R. Sortore also itemized teaching suggestions for about the same four categories: regular students plus students at three increasing levels of giftedness.[23]

As in the Pyramid Model, Treffinger and Sortore acknowledge that different levels of ability, talents, and interests demand different instructional activities and challenges.

Level I, Services for All Students. At Level I—students in the regular classroom—the authors recommended:

- Creative and critical thinking.
- Thinking skills in the top levels of Bloom's Taxonomy (application, analysis, synthesis, and evaluation; see Chapter 10).
- Independent projects—individual and small group.
- General exploratory activities (as in Renzulli Type I enrichment).
- Individualized learning and progress in basic skills areas (particularly math and reading).
- Exposure to new topics and areas—for example, fine arts and foreign languages.
- Activities based on student interests.

Level II, Services for Many Students. Level II is the first level of giftedness, comparable to the bottom section in the Pyramid Model. Treffinger and Sortore suggested:

- Curriculum compacting.
- Junior Great Books.
- Odyssey of the Mind.
- Future Problem Solving.
- Solving real problems (problems students feel strongly about, not artificial workbook problems).
- Math competitions.
- Computer explorations.
- Science fairs.
- Young inventors' activities and competitions.
- Creative writing activities, conferences for young authors.
- Performing and visual arts, band, chorus, theater, debate
- Clubs and academic interest groups.
- After school, Saturday, and summer enrichment courses or programs.
- Personal, educational, and career counseling.

Level III, Services for Some Students. With an even smaller number of students—comparable to the middle of the Pyramid Model—Treffinger and Sortore proposed:

- Advanced classes in academic areas.
- Testing out of courses; credit by examination.
- Summer Talent Search programs and other special programs sponsored by universities.

- Individual drama, music, or art lessons.
- Complex or extended projects—individual or small group.
- Guest speakers and in-depth follow-up seminars.
- Solving community problems.
- Internships (or shadow-a-professional) experiences.
- Peer teaching.

Level IV, Services for a Few Students. Finally, with extremely capable students—comparable to the Pyramid peak—Treffinger and Sortore recommended:

- Grade acceleration, perhaps multiple grade acceleration.
- Enrollment in higher level courses within the high school or in college.
- Developing and conducting research or service projects.
- Presenting student work to outside groups (e.g., historical societies, government agencies).
- Publication of student work in outside sources.
- Mentors.

Taylor's Multiple-Talent Totem Poles

We introduced Calvin Taylor's multiple-talent totem poles in Chapter 3 in relation to definitions of giftedness. Taylor's main point was that if we examine a variety of abilities, different students will be at the top of different totem poles—which complicates deciding exactly who is "gifted." In Chapter 3, Figure 3.2, Taylor identified the nine abilities—totem poles—which he labeled *academic* (acquiring information and concepts), *productive thinking* (creativity), *communicating* (verbal and nonverbal), *forecasting* (predicting), *decision making* (weighing information, making judgments), *planning* (designing), *implementing* (putting a plan into action), *human relations* (social skills), and *discerning opportunities.*

Carol Schlichter's Talents Unlimited program aims at training teachers to recognize and strengthen student abilities in six of Taylor's talent areas.[24] Taylor had referred to these six talents as "one imitating, non-thinking, reproducing type of talent [*academic talent*] along with five thinking talents...ways of actively processing and working with knowledge in order to acquire it [*productive thinking, planning, communicating, forecasting,* and *decision making*]."[25]

In agreement with Taylor's distinction, Schlichter used a picture of a "McTalent Burger" to help convince students that the imitative, non-thinking academic talent (the plain bun) can be made a lot more interesting, valuable, and tastier when we add the other five creativity and thinking skill talents (extra ingredients): productive thinking (the juicy burger), planning (a slice of tomato), communicating (a lettuce leaf), forecasting (a tasty slice of onion), and decision making (melted cheese).

While not a major gifted program overhaul, Taylor's multiple-talent totem poles and Schlichter's cheeseburger clearly stress a thinking skills emphasis in programs for the gifted.

Comment

The models described in this chapter—Joseph Renzulli's Enrichment Triad Model, Secondary Triad Model, and his broader Schoolwide Enrichment Model; NAGC's Parallel Curriculum Model; George Betts' Autonomous Learner Model; Joyce VanTassel-Baska's Integrated Curriculum Model; June Cox, Neil Daniel, and Bruce Boston's Pyramid Model; Donald Treffinger and M. R. Sortore's classification of activities at four ability levels; and Calvin Taylor's multiple-talent totem pole model—all provide frameworks for planning worthwhile learning activities for gifted students. Some models specify the particular activities recommended, most obviously the Treffinger and Sortore four lists. Also, the valuable books by Renzulli and Reis, and Betts and Kercher include dozens of specific activities and exercises.[26]

This list of curriculum models is not exhaustive. For example, the text by Davis and Rimm summarizes 11 models; Renzulli's book of readings includes 15 models.[27] However, these seven seem the most informative and helpful for a brief guide for what can—or should—be done in programs for gifted and talented students.

Summary

- Renzulli's 1977 Enrichment Triad Model guides many gifted programs worldwide. With Type I enrichment (General Exploratory Activities), gifted students learn about topics, persons, events, and interest areas that are not part of the curriculum. Type II enrichment (Group Training Activities) includes school learning skills, thinking skills, communication skills, and interpersonal skills. Type III enrichment (Individual and Small Group Investigations of Real Problems) is the individual (or small group) study of real problems, which results in a final product that is presented to an audience. Table 6.1 in Chapter 6 listed suggestions for Type I enrichment and Type III projects.

- The Secondary Triad Model, for middle and high school, requires a talent pool class for each discipline.

- The Schoolwide Enrichment Model brings Type I and II enrichment into the regular classroom. Type III projects are considered suitable only for talent pool students (top 15 to 20%), but other enthusiastic students can submit Action Information Messages and join the talent pool.

- Students with *creative-productive giftedness* will make greater contributions to society than students with *schoolhouse giftedness*, noted Renzulli and Reis.

- The NAGC-sponsored Parallel Curriculum Model includes four principles that help students explore and understand a discipline. The *Core Curriculum* principle emphasizes teaching central concepts, the *Curriculum of Connections* helps students connect the important concepts, the *Curriculum of Practice* helps students understand concepts and skills as would a practitioner, and the *Curriculum of Identity* helps students clarify their own ways of relating to the world.

- Betts' Autonomous Learner Model helps students become independent learners. Five parts include Orientation (e.g., to the nature of creativity and giftedness), Individual Development (e.g., of skills and attitudes leading to self-directed learning), Enrichment (beyond the regular curriculum), Seminars (in which students research and present a topic), and In-Depth Study (independent, autonomous learning). The Betts and Kercher book includes lots of classroom activities and useful evaluation forms.

- VanTassel-Baska's Integrated Curriculum Model assumes that gifted students should receive meaningfully sequenced educational experiences, gifted students have different needs (e.g., in cognitive, affective, social, and aesthetic curriculum areas), gifted students' curriculum should be enriched and accelerated, and curriculum experiences should be carefully planned and evaluated. Gifted students' characteristics include precocity, intensity, and complexity. Three main points include presenting advanced content, eliciting higher-order thinking and processing skills, and focusing on important issues, themes, and ideas.

- Cox, Daniel, and Boston's Richardson Study evaluated many types of gifted programs. Their Pyramid Model divides "able students"—about one-fourth of all students—into three groups. The largest group of able learners (the pyramid base) are accommodated in the regular classroom. A smaller group of more able learners (middle of the pyramid) attend special classes. The smallest group of most highly able students (pyramid peak) attend special elementary and secondary schools when possible. Cox and colleagues suggested modifications for smaller cities.

- Treffinger and Sortore suggested classroom activities for all students and, like Cox, Daniel, and Boston, for students at three increasing levels of giftedness.

- Taylor's multiple-talent totem pole model emphasizes examining nine abilities, which will likely have different students at the top of each totem pole. Schlichter's Talents Unlimited program trains teachers to strengthen student abilities in six of Taylor's talent areas. Taylor referred to academic talent as an "imitating, non-thinking, reproducing type of talent." Others are "thinking talents."

- All seven models guide the selection of worthwhile activities for gifted students.

10
Thinking Skills

*Curriculum for gifted students should be modified in a
variety of ways, including an emphasis on higher levels of
thinking. Gifted students should spend the majority of
their time critically examining, synthesizing, and
evaluating ideas, rather than memorizing and applying
information and procedures.*

~ Shirley Schiever and C. June Maker

[**Scene**: *Gepetto's toy-making shop. He speaks with his son, Pinocchio, who earlier that day became a real boy.*]

Gepetto (thrilled and excited): Oh, Pinocchio! I can't believe it! You're a real boy, not the brainless, woodenhead puppet I whittled last week!

Pinocchio (happily): Yes, Father, I'm a real boy! Where's Cleo? I'd like to feed her to a fish!

Gepetto: Gosh, Pinocchio, do you mean feed a fish to Cleo? Maybe our thinking skills are still made of wood! We have to get our words in the right order. But Cleo will be so happy!

Pinocchio: And after we feed Cleo, can we go watch seagulls? Because I'd like to blow bubbles and learn to ride a bike!

Gepetto: Now Pinocchio, that's what I mean about thinking skills. We have to think about causes and effects. We have to be logical. Watching seagulls won't help you blow bubbles or learn to ride a bike.

Pinocchio: Okay, Pop. I get it. I think. Gosh, I'm hungry! Can we have dinner soon? I'd like a hot dog, a root beer, a broom, and a dustpan.

Gepetto (sadly): My darling little boy! Your thinking skills…well… they just aren't right! We have to classify things correctly! Hot dogs and soda are things to eat. A broom and dustpan…

Pinocchio (interrupting): I know! They're for cleaning up your sawdust!

Gepetto (happy and excited): Oh yes! Yes! Jiminy Cricket that's wonderful!

Pinocchio: And a broom and dustpan will get me to school on time! And I won't get chewed up by termites anymore!

Gepetto (again sadly): No, no, Pinocchio. Your logic is still...just a little strange. Your causes and effects...and detecting relevance and irrelevance.... We've just got to work on your thinking skills!

(Suddenly, a flash of light and puff of smoke. A lovely magical princess appears, smiling widely. She wears a flowing light blue dress, a glistening tiara, and waves a sparkly magic wand. Startled, Gepetto jumps back. Pinocchio shows a silly grin.)

Magical Princess (in high, laughing voice): Hello, I'm Pinocchio's Fairy Godmother. I made him a real boy! That was his reward for getting you both out of that awful whale Monstro! He's been such a pain lately! He might have digested you both! I do hope you're happy now!

Gepetto: It's wonderful to meet you, Fairy Godmother! We're both so excited that Pinocchio is a real boy! [In lowered voice.] But between you and me, I still wish he had a brain!

Thinking Skills and Intelligence

We have mentioned *thinking skills* many times. The topic is sufficiently important that expert Arthur Costa uses "thinking skills" interchangeably with "intelligent behavior" itself.[1] It follows that teaching thinking skills should help students to think more intelligently. It should not be surprising that thinking skills are included in every program for gifted students.

We can view thinking skills as intellectual abilities. And when we understand and practice thinking skills, they become stronger and more habitual, just like our math, piano playing, and tennis abilities.

In Chapter 3, we briefly reviewed Robert Sternberg's Triarchic Theory, or theory of successful intelligence.[2] It includes three important and broad types of thinking. His *analytic giftedness*—basic academic ability—is measured especially by tests of reading comprehension and analytical reasoning. *Synthetic giftedness* refers to creativity, with lots of intuition, insightfulness, and novel thinking. *Practical giftedness* is the ability to apply analytic and synthetic giftedness to everyday situations—to figure out what must be done for success in a venture.

This chapter will review several other interpretations of "thinking skills," all of which overlap with Sternberg's model.

Creativity

The most commonly noted thinking skill is *creativity*, sometimes called *creative ability*. This complex thinking skill—the sole topic of Chapter 11—includes lots of component thinking skills, which themselves are important. For example, teaching creativity (creative thinking, creative problem solving, creative ability) can include teaching students to analyze, compare, think flexibly, apply past knowledge, generalize, discriminate, hypothesize, synthesize, infer, plan, predict, see cause-effect relations, think logically, think critically, evaluate, communicate clearly, and probably more.

Joseph Renzulli often mentions that, compared with intelligent students who earn high grades, persons with *high creativity, high motivation*, and at least *above-average intelligence* will make the most significant contributions to society.[3]

Thinking Skills as Personality Traits

Some complex thinking skills resemble personality traits. For example, Arthur Costa named these as thinking skills: managing impulsivity, listening with understanding and empathy, taking responsible risks, thinking independently, persisting, striving for accuracy and precision, responding with wonder and awe, and remaining open to continuous learning.[4]

Are these thinking skills? Personality characteristics? Both?

Teaching Thinking Skills

There are three primary approaches to teaching thinking skills.

(1) *Metacognition.* This is *thinking about thinking.* In the classroom, metacognition means helping students understand their own and others' thinking.

(2) *Direct approach.* Students can learn conscious and deliberate strategies, for example, for solving problems, reasoning, or thinking

critically. Students can become quite aware of the thinking skills they are using.

(3) *Indirect approach.* Thinking skills also may be strengthened through practice and exercise. But the students may be unaware that they are learning thinking skills—for example, when they are asked to compare, evaluate, or classify.

Let's look more closely at each of these.

Metacognition

Metacognition—thinking about thinking—includes self-reflecting and self-monitoring. Some high-level thinking activities virtually require an awareness of one's thinking processes, such as when we plan, set goals, organize, sequence activities, select a strategy, evaluate, or combine ideas for a new creation.

Both learning and self-understanding may be promoted with metacognition. Leader, for example, asked her students to respond to such self-questions as: What did I learn? How did I learn it? What do I still need to find out? What ways of learning are easiest for me? Why? What are my strengths? What are my weaknesses?[5]

Metacognition also can help students better understand their own ideas, viewpoints, and values—and how and why they were learned. Why do I dislike rude people? Why do I plan to attend college?

An awareness of thinking—metacognition—also helps students understand where others' values, viewpoints, and ideas come from. For example, one can ask students to explain and defend the positions of others: The local high school students want a new swimming pool and a bigger student parking lot. Why are school district officials and local taxpayers opposed?[6]

As a final note, metacognitive operations control the selection and use of thinking skills: "I'm going to compare the quality of these shirts and their prices"; "I gotta figure out how to drive to California!"

Direct Approaches to Teaching Thinking Skills

As a teacher, using a thoughtfully constructed commercial program—which required many years to develop and evaluate—might be simpler and more sensible than trying to create one's own list of important thinking skills (there are hundreds) and then devise exercises and strategies to teach them. However, without actually buying the programs, the following descriptions of commercial materials and teaching strategies suggest many thinking skills that are worth teaching.

CoRT Thinking Program

Edward de Bono's CoRT (Cognitive Research Trust) Thinking Program is perhaps the best published material for teaching conscious, deliberate ways to solve problems.[7] The CoRT program takes a direct approach. Students understand each thinking skill and when and why it should be used. Sixty workbooks teach 50 important thinking skills. A sample of CoRT thinking skills appears in Table 10.1.

Table 10.1. Sample of CoRT Thinking Skills

O Considering all factors when making choices or decisions.
O Thinking of goals and objectives, including other people's goals.
O Planning, which includes considering all factors and itemizing goals and objectives.
O Thinking of consequences (short-term, medium-term, long-term) of actions.
O Identifying good points (pluses), bad points (minuses), and interesting points of ideas, suggestions, and proposals.
O Prioritizing—for example, relevant factors, objectives, and consequences.
O Thinking of many alternatives, possibilities, and choices.
O Making decisions, which requires considering the factors involved, objectives, priorities, consequences, and possible alternatives.
O Seeing other points of view, which exist because others may consider different factors, see different consequences, or have different objectives or priorities.
O Organizing by analyzing what needs to be done, what is being done, and what is to be done next; one may need to consider all factors and think of alternatives.
O Focusing on different aspects of a situation—that is, knowing when you are analyzing, considering factors, thinking of consequences, etc.
O Concluding a thinking project, perhaps with ideas, a problem solution, an answer to a question—or conceding an inability to solve the problem.
O Recognizing facts versus opinions as two types of evidence.
O Recognizing evidence that is weak, strong, or key.
O Recognizing points of agreement, disagreement, and irrelevance.
O Challenging existing ways of doing things as a means of stimulating new ideas.
O Improving things by identifying faults and thinking of ways to remove them.

○ Solving problems by thinking about problem requirements.
○ Recognizing information that is given versus information that has been omitted but is needed.
○ Recognizing guesses based on good information (e.g., the sun will rise tomorrow) versus guesses based on little information (e.g., the score of a future baseball game).
○ Recognizing contradictory information.
○ Distinguishing between ordinary emotions (e.g., love, fear, anger, sorrow) and emotions concerned with one's view of oneself (e.g., pride, insecurity).
○ Understanding that values determine thinking, judgments, choices, and actions.

Consider this magazine report:

The place is Maracaibo, Venezuela. There is a meeting of about 20 people (doctors, parents, government officials) to discuss the setting up of a new medical clinic. For three hours arguments flow back and forth.

Suddenly, a 10-year-old boy who has been sitting quietly at the back of the room, because his mother could not leave him at home alone, approaches the table. He suggests to the group that they "do an AGO (set the objectives), followed by an APC (outline alternatives), and then an FIP (set priorities) and, of course, and OPV (analyze other people's views)." In a short while there is a plan of action.

That 10-year-old had participated in the routine thinking skills program that is mandated by law in all Venezuelan schools.[8]

Most of the CoRT workbooks include five sections. First, an *Introduction* defines and explains each thinking skill. For example, with *Consider All Factors* (CAF), students learn that there are always many factors to consider before making a decision. Students also learn that omitted factors can lead to bad decisions. In addition, they learn to watch for factors that others have ignored.

Next is an *Example*, a sample problem. For instance, a new law in London, England, required all new buildings to provide parking space—which led to increased traffic congestion. What factors were ignored?

Practice includes four or five practice problems. For example, what factors should you consider when interviewing a potential school teacher?

Process refers to a class discussion that increases understanding of each thinking skill. For example, students might consider whether it is easy to leave out important factors. They also might discuss differences between CAF and other thinking skills.

Principles refers to usually five reasons for using a particular thinking skill. For example, the PMI (Pluses, Minuses, Interesting points) technique teaches evaluation. Students learn that ideas or activities may be evaluated by looking the good points or pluses (P), the bad points or minuses (M), and points that are neither good nor bad, just interesting (I). The five PMI principles are:

1. By using the PMI approach, one will not hastily reject an idea that initially looked bad.

2. One will not too quickly adopt an idea that has serious but overlooked disadvantages.

3. Some ideas are neither good nor bad, just interesting and relevant. Such ideas may lead to other ideas.

4. Without using a PMI, one's emotions may interfere with clear judgment.

5. With a PMI, one passes judgment on an idea after it is explored, not before.

With the CoRT program, thinking skills are taught as an independent subject—as a conscious and deliberate metacognitive skill. For information, see www.edwdebono.com.

Philosophy for Children

Mathew Lipman's *Philosophy for Children* takes the form of six storybooks for students age five to 17, each with a teacher's manual.[9] The books teach reasoning and critical thinking. They help children and teenagers understand ethical, moral, aesthetic, and philosophic matters. They also improve interpersonal relations. Follow-up discussions are a critical feature. Teachers help clarify the thinking skills and ethics that students have studied.

The six books are: *Lis,* for students ages five and six; *Rebecca,* for ages six to eight; *Thinking Stories,* for ages nine and 10; *Lisa,* for ages 11 and 12; *Suki,* for ages 13 and 14; and *Golden City,* for ages 15 to 17. The story characters spend a lot of time thinking about thinking, with lots of examples of good and bad thinking.

The following are examples of some of the thinking skills and ethical/moral concepts taught in Lipman's *Philosophy for Children* series:

- *Identifying underlying assumptions.* For example, what is the assumption underlying, "I love your hair. What beauty parlor did you go to?"

- *Cause-effect relationships.* Does this statement imply a cause-effect relationship: "He threw the stone and broke the window"?

- *Analogical thinking.* What is the correct answer? "Germ is to disease as candle is to: (a) wax, (b) wick, (c) white, (d) light."

- *Independent thinking.* Should we always follow the majority?

- *Taking other perspectives.* Can you see this issue from another point of view?

- *Caring.* Should we concern ourselves with the welfare of others?

- *Recognizing consistent and contradictory statements or ideas.* Can you be a true animal lover yet still eat meat?

- *Making generalizations.* What generalization can be drawn from these facts? "I get sick when I eat raspberries. I get sick when I eat blueberries. I get sick when I eat strawberries."

- *Learning part-whole and whole-part relationships.* Is this necessarily true? "If Mike's face has handsome features, Mike must have a handsome face."

- *Syllogistic reasoning.* What inference can we draw? "All dogs are animals; all Lhasa Apsos are dogs."

- *Reversibility and non-reversibility.* "No" statements are reversible: "No kangaroos are airplanes; therefore no airplanes are kangaroos." "All" statements are not reversible: "All housecats are felines, but not all felines are housecats."

- *Moral thinking.* Students consider, for example, "What is goodness?" and "What is fairness?"

- *Philosophic thinking.* Questions that stimulate philosophic thinking include, for example, "What is reality?" and "What is the mind?"

Other thinking skills exercises in Lipman's *Philosophy for Children* books promote creativity and help students understand descriptions versus explanations, universal versus particular statements (e.g., "All birds can fly" versus "This bird can fly"), hypotheses, impartiality, consistency, reasons for beliefs, and many other thinking skills.

For information, contact the Institute for the Advancement of Philosophy for Children, Montclair State College, Montclair, NJ 07043, or visit http://cehs.montclair.edu/academic/iapc/thinking.shtml.

Indirect Approaches to Teaching Thinking Skills

Project IMPACT and Feuerstein's *Instrumental Enrichment* program both take an indirect approach to teaching thinking skills. Learners almost certainly are unaware of the specific thinking skills being strengthened by practice and exercise.

Project IMPACT

Project IMPACT (Improve Minimal Proficiencies by Activating Critical Thinking) is another excellent published program for teaching thinking skills.[10] One teacher reported, "Students enjoy the lessons so much that they request them!"[11] Briefly, an entertaining series of puzzles teaches students to observe, compare, contrast, group, classify, order, sequence, prioritize, question, reason, and infer meaning. Students learn to recognize facts versus opinions, relevant and irrelevant information, reliable and unreliable sources of information, cause–effect relationships, generalizations, predictions, assumptions, and points of view, including prejudice.

As an example, the "Can You Zooley?" exercise in Figure 10.1 focuses on deductive reasoning. The subsequent series of questions require the learner to analyze the illustration and deduce information about the critters. Do not try this exercise. And if you get stumped, the answers are at the end of this chapter.

Figure 10.1. "Can You Zooley?" Lesson from Project IMPACT. Reprinted by permission of S. Lee Winocur, Ph.D., Center for the Teaching of Thinking, Project IMPACT.

1. Which family is visiting the polar bears?

2. Which is the family of spiders?

3. Whose son has Mr. Crocodile just swallowed?

4. Which swimming family has only three sons?

5. Which family has just three daughters?

6. Is the polar bear's cub male or female?

7. Which is a family of snakes?

8. Which is the family of kangaroos?

9. What will be the surname of the elephant's baby that is soon to be born?

10. What is the zookeeper's name?

For information, contact Project IMPACT, Orange County, CA, Department of Education.

Instrumental Enrichment

Reuven Feuerstein spent several teenage years in a Nazi concentration camp.[12] Later, in Israel, he examined the educational needs of immigrants, too many of whom would be classified as retarded by IQ tests. He constructed his *Instrumental Enrichment* program to help them become more independent, capable thinkers.

For example, his *Organization of Dots* exercise presents a page of dots. The task is to identify and outline specific geometric figures—diamonds, squares, stars, and others—by connecting the dots. Remarkably, this seemingly simple exercise: (1) reduces impulsivity, as well as strengthens (2) planning, (3) determining a starting point, (4) discovery strategies, (5) taking different perspectives, (6) discriminating form and size, (7) use of relevant information, (8) labeling, (9) accuracy and precision, and (10) motivation.

With Feuerstein's *Orientation in Space* exercise, imagine a simple three-dimensional line drawing of a front lawn. There is a house at the back, flowers at the front, a bench on the left, and a tree on the right. A separate drawing shows a boy, who we are to imagine is in the center of the lawn, facing the house (back), or the flowers (front), or the bench (left), or the tree (right). By filling information in on a table, a person describes the position of each object relative to each position of the boy (i.e., on his left or right, in front, or behind). Again, remarkably, this exercise teaches: (1) the ability to use stable systems of reference (which may be concrete, abstract, or personal) for orientation in space, (2) problem defining, (3) using several sources of information simultaneously, (4) working systematically, (5) using inferential thinking to reach logical conclusions, (6) communicating information precisely and accurately, (7) summarizing data using a table, and (8) reducing egocentric thinking.

These and other exercises also help learners to: recognize, define, and solve problems; analyze, make comparisons, and categorize; plan and test hypotheses; recognize the need for logical evidence; and use time and space dimensions. Said instrumental enrichment workshop leader Frances Link, "It's fantastic! It changes teachers!"[13]

Other Ways to Teach Thinking Skills

Apart from the above four programs, Joyce VanTassel-Baska et al. also described strategies for teaching thinking skills.[14] For example, to teach *critical thinking*, teachers can ask students to: (1) evaluate problems, issues, or situations; (2) compare ideas (e.g., that students themselves have suggested); (3) generalize from concrete information to more abstract meanings and conclusions; and (4) summarize information. Similarly, Sandra Kaplan found that we can strengthen critical thinking by teaching students to prove with evidence, make logical predictions, create classifications, and identify main ideas.[15]

To strengthen *research-related thinking* skills, noted Van Tassel-Baska, a teacher can: (1) require students to gather information from many sources (e.g., print, Internet, interviews, student surveys); (2) have students analyze data and represent the information in charts, graphs, or tables; (3) ask questions that assist students in drawing inferences and conclusions from data; (4) ask students about implications and consequences of research findings; and (5) have students communicate their procedures, findings, and conclusions in formal reports and/or presentations.

To reinforce *creative thinking*, a teacher can: (1) solicit many ideas and thoughts about a topic or issue; (2) engage students in exploring diverse points of view and then reframe or simplify the ideas; (3) promote open-mindedness and tolerance for imaginative, perhaps playful ideas; and (4) give students opportunities to develop and elaborate their ideas.

Creative problem solving may be strengthened by: (1) encouraging students to identify and define problems (which may be "fuzzy"), (2) having the class brainstorm solutions to problems, and (3) having students evaluate the problem solutions.

Bloom's Taxonomy

Any discussion—or list—of thinking skills must include Benjamin Bloom's taxonomy of six educational objectives, which extends from simpler "low-level" objectives to increasingly more complex "high-level" objectives.[16] The eye-opening observation—novel in 1956—was that the low-level objectives of *knowledge* and *comprehension* were routinely taught in schools, but the progressively higher-level objectives—thinking skills of *application, analysis, synthesis,* and *evaluation*—were not. One recommendation was that "regular" students might invest most of their effort mastering lower-level knowledge and comprehension objectives; faster-learning gifted students could spend more time exploring higher-level objectives—applying, analyzing, synthesizing, and evaluating.

Teachers can use questions to teach at each of Bloom's six levels. See the (abbreviated) list of "key words" for questioning in Table 10.2.

Table 10.2. Asking Questions at Each of Bloom's Six Levels[17]

Level	Key Words for Questioning			
Knowledge	What	When	Who	Which
	Identify	Name	Define	Tell how
Comprehension	Compare	Conclude	Contrast	Predict
	Explain	Rephrase	Illustrate	Give examples
Application	Plan	Tell us	Demonstrate	Develop
	Test	Apply	Build	Indicate
Analysis	Explain	Distinguish	Analyze	What
	Categorize	Compare	Support your reasoning	assumption? Relate
Synthesis	Create	Propose a plan	Think of a way	Put together
	Suggest	Develop	What conclusion?	Formulate a solution
Evaluation	Evaluate	Choose	Decide	Judge
	Select	Defend	What is most appropriate?	Which would youl choose?

Other Thinking Skills

There are many lists of thinking skills. Further, as noted in Chapter 1, complex thinking skills (e.g., creativity, problem solving, planning) always are built of simpler ones (e.g., analyzing, sequencing, questioning, drawing inferences, predicting consequences, evaluating). When you think about it, the simpler thinking skills are themselves composed of still simpler thinking skills. For example, evaluating includes analyzing, comparing, seeing cause-effect relations, and thinking logically. Most thinking skills require such subskills as, for example, recalling, discriminating, classifying, and comparing.

Table 10.3 shows an incomplete list of thinking skills, drawn from many sources. Note that the list includes ethical and moral thinking, which appear in both the de Bono and Lipman programs. Some sections of Table 10.3 overlap, perhaps duplicate each other in spots. For example, it should not be surprising that problem solving, reasoning, evaluating, and scientific thinking are similar and interrelated. Table 10.3 presents a fair picture of the types of thinking skills that we all use—and the types of thinking skills that many teachers try to strengthen.

Table 10.3. A Sample of Thinking Skills

Global Type of Thinking	Relevant Thinking Skills	
Creative Thinking	Fluency	Originality
	Flexibility	Visualizing
	Elaboration	Analyzing
	Synthesizing	Transforming
	Finding problems	Thinking intuitively
	Thinking logically	Thinking analogically
Critical Thinking	**Evaluating:** bias, credibility, consistency, qualifications, inferences, reasons for a claim, reliability of information, relevance of objections, appropriateness of conclusions	
	Identifying: assumptions, opinions, claims, missing parts of an argument, ambiguity, contradiction	
Problem Solving	Defining and clarifying the problem	
	Selecting relevant information	
	Setting goals	
	Recognizing assumptions	
	Making inferences	
	Evaluating alternatives	
	Detecting causes and effects	
	Drawing conclusions	
Ethics, Morality	Empathy, understanding others' problems	
	Honesty	
	Respecting others' rights	
	Responsibility	
	Accepting differences	
	Caring, compassion	
	Patience, pleasantness, courtesy	
	Accepting consequences	
	Valuing education and achievement	
Reading	Finding main ideas	
	Explaining authors' intentions	
	Detecting implications	
	Making inferences, predictions	
Writing	Stating and defending an idea	
	Sequencing information	
	Elaborating	
	Communicating clearly	
	Expressing feelings, values	
	Arguing logically and persuasively	
	Developing story plots	
	Summarizing	

Global Type of Thinking	Relevant Thinking Skills
Science and Research	Asking good questions, guessing Identifying needed information Formulating hypotheses Observing, measuring, estimating, extrapolating Applying principles Discovering trends and patterns Reading charts, graphs, tables Recognizing mathematical relationships (e.g., weight, time, distance) Detecting cause-effect relationships
Reasoning	Deductive, inductive thinking Logical thinking Verbal, spatial thinking Analyzing and justifying assumptions Identifying implications Synthesizing, combining, elaborating Identifying relationships and patterns Explaining
Classifying	Comparing, contrasting Sequencing Part-whole relationships Overlapping classes Explaining exceptions Diagramming classes
Planning	Following rules and directions Prioritizing, planning steps Setting goals and objectives Considering implications Predicting outcomes
Evaluating	Asking questions Identifying errors Making inferences Predicting consequences Recognizing assumptions, beliefs, opinions Making decisions Recognizing essentials, nonessentials Detecting relevance, irrelevance Setting criteria Verifying outcomes

Selecting Thinking Skills to Teach

Several experts have suggested guides to help teachers select worthwhile thinking skills and thinking skill programs.[18] Some main suggestions are:

- A thinking skills program, or specific thinking skills, should not require extended teacher training.

- The program should be usable by all teachers, not just the highly qualified.

- If some parts of a program are skipped, the remainder should be usable and valuable.

- The program, and specific thinking skills, should be enjoyable and suited to students' interests.

- The program and thinking skills should help students better understand their own thinking—that is, the materials should improve students' metacognitive "thinking about thinking."

- Important thinking skills should be taught.

- There should be practical examples of each thinking skill.

- The learning experience should be "active," with opportunities for practice and application of the thinking skills.

Summary

- Developing students' thinking skills is a goal of every program for gifted students.

- Sternberg's model includes analytic giftedness, synthetic giftedness, and practical giftedness.

- Creativity is a central thinking skill that includes many component thinking skills.

- Renzulli notes that persons high in creativity, motivation, and at least above-average intelligence make the most significant contributions to society

- Some thinking skills, such as independent thinking and persistence, resemble personality characteristics.

- Metacognition is thinking about thinking. Teaching metacognition includes helping students become aware of their own thinking and learning, as well as others' thinking. Metacognitive thinking also controls the selection of thinking skills.

- Edward de Bono's *CoRT Thinking Program* takes a direct approach; students are fully aware of the thinking skill(s) they are learning. *CoRT* teaches 50 thinking skills in 60 workbooks. Each lesson includes an explanatory introduction, a sample problem, practice problems, process (class discussion of the skill), and a list of usually five principles (reasons for using the skill).

- Mathew Lipman's *Philosophy for Children*, also a direct approach, uses six storybooks for students from age five to 17. The books teach concepts related to identifying underlying assumptions, cause-effect relationships, thinking independently, taking other perspectives, caring, moral and philosophic thinking, and more. Teacher follow-up discussions are important.

- *Project IMPACT* uses a series of entertaining puzzles to teach, for example, comparing, prioritizing, inferring meaning, and recognizing assumptions and unreliable sources of information. This program takes an indirect approach—that is, thinking skills are exercised and strengthened without directly telling students that they are learning, for example, to compare, prioritize, question, infer meaning, etc. The entertaining "Can You Zooley?" strengthens deductive reasoning.

- Reuven Feuerstein's *Instrumental Enrichment*, also an indirect approach, includes reasoning problems, such as *Organization of Dots* and *Orientation in Space*, to reduce impulsivity and egocentric thinking, as well as to strengthen problem solving, planning, working systematically, analyzing, defining problems, testing hypotheses, communicating information, and more.

- Van Tassel-Baska suggested teaching critical thinking by having students, for example, use evidence and logic. To promotes research skills, students gather information, analyze data, make inferences, think of implications, and communicate findings. For creative thinking, students think of many ideas, explore diverse points of view, become more open-minded and imaginative, and develop and elaborate on their ideas. Creative problem solving is strengthened when students identify problems, brainstorm solutions, and evaluate problem solutions.

- Bloom's taxonomy of six educational objectives includes low-level objectives of knowledge and comprehension and higher-level objectives (thinking skills) of application, analysis, synthesis, and evaluation. A recommendation is that gifted students focus more on Bloom's higher-level objectives.

- Complex thinking skills always are built of simpler subskills.

- Table 10.3 presents an incomplete list of sometimes overlapping thinking skills, including ethical and moral thinking.

- Guides for selecting thinking skills to teach include, for example: a program should not require extended teacher training, it should be easily usable, and it should be enjoyable and suited to students' interests. The skills should improve students' metacognitive understanding of thinking. Important thinking skills should be taught.

Solutions to "Can You Zooley?"

1. The **Zuff** family. It is the only family group outside of the cages. The polar bears must be **Tricks**.

2. **Lesger**. They have eight legs.

3. The **Beeze** son. And the crocodiles must be **Gobbies**. This is the only small animal inside a different type of large animal. We learn that males are rectangles.

4. The **Squeal** family. They have fins and three little sons (rectangles).

5. The **Lesger** family. They have three little circles (females) and no rectangles (males).

6. **Male**. It's a rectangle.

7. The **Slizz** family. They have no legs.

8. The **Swifts**. They seem to have two legs and a big tail, with a little one attached to the front of the mother.

9. **Ample**. This is the only family with a small animal inside of an adult female.

10. **Glup**. He is the only adult by himself outside of the cages.

11
Creativity and Teaching for Creative Growth

Almost from the beginning, modern research on creativity,
intelligence, and achievement showed that although,
as a group, students with high IQs obtained good grades
both at school and university, they were consistently
outstripped by those with not only a high IQ
but also high creativity.

~ Arthur J. Cropley and Klaus K. Urban

[*Scene*: *Cottage of Cinderella, her stepmother, and her two ugly stepsisters Drisella and Esmerelda. Stepmother and stepsisters will soon brainstorm ideas for making Cinderella's life as wretched as they can.*]

Stepmother: Come now girls! We've got to find new ways to make you-know-who as miserable as we possibly can!

Drisella: Yes, Mama. I'm so tired of her lovely hair, pretty face, and sweet personality. Why can't she be like the rest of us?

Esmerelda: OH PIPE DOWN, DRISELLA! WE'RE JUST AS DAMN CHARMING AS SHE IS! AT LEAST I AM!

Stepmother (hastily): Girls! Girls! Don't let the little twit upset you like that! Now, you both know the brainstorming rules!

Drisella: Of course, Mama. We don't criticize. We don't evaluate. And we toss out...

Esmerelda: Honestly! You airhead! Everybody knows that! Oh well, go on! Let's hear the rest!

Drisella: We toss out whatever ideas occur to us, and the wilder the better. We list lots of ideas. We modify and combine ideas so we'll have even more ideas. Let's hide her apron!

Esmerelda: That's the dumbest idea I ever heard of, you nincompoop! If we're going to hide something, let's be more creative. Let's hide her broom and mop—then tell her to clean up the floors, the front sidewalk, and the street!

Stepmother: Now really! That's the WORST idea I ever heard, you nitwit! She'd just find another broom and mop and have everything spiffy in a few minutes! Why don't we strangle her cat?

Drisella: That's really a dumb one, Mama! The cat would make a big fuss, and Cinderella would hear us. Let's put bread crumbs in her bed, syrup in her shoes, vinegar in her yogurt, break the teeth out of her comb, cut the strings on her vest, stomp on her sewing basket, send her to the next kingdom for some salt, and make her clean the chimney—from the inside.

Esmerelda: You ignorant, big-nosed toad, we did those last week! Look, let's have her take some soup and sandwiches over to Tom Tom, the piper's son. Tom Tom's got the plague!

Stepmother: She'd just bring the plague back home, you clumsy fool! I know! Let's stop her from going to the Prince's ball!

Drisella: Oh, Mother, you've got it! Isn't it wonderful how a warm, receptive, and encouraging atmosphere can stimulate creative thinking!

The topic of *creativity*—a core thinking skill—appears in 11 of the 12 chapters of this book.[1] Creative thinking is a central topic in giftedness and a fundamental goal of most gifted programs.

In Chapter 10, we noted also that creativity is a complex ability composed of lots of component thinking skills—for example, analyzing, comparing, recalling information, thinking flexibly, thinking critically, thinking logically, synthesizing, generalizing, discriminating, inferring, planning, predicting, detecting cause and effect, evaluating, and others.

We also mentioned Joseph Renzulli's sensible observation that, compared with intelligent grade-getters, highly motivated, highly creative students who are at least above average in intelligence eventually will make the most significant contributions to society.[2]

Characteristics

Chapter 4 described many abilities and characteristics of creative people in conjunction with creativity tests. For example, the original 1966 *Torrance Tests of Creative Thinking* measure *fluency, flexibility, originality,* and *elaboration* abilities, and the newer scoring system adds *humor, fantasy, expression of feelings or emotions, richness of imagery, colorfulness of imagery, movement or action, taking an unusual or internal perspective, extending or breaking boundaries,* and others.[3]

Of course, all creative people vary in their particular assortment of ability, personality, and motivational characteristics. However, many traits appear again and again in studies of creative persons. Note these desirable (positive) traits and their approximate synonyms:

- Flexibility (originality, unconventionality)
- Awareness of creativeness (creativity consciousness, values own creativity)
- Self-confidence (independence, non-conformity)
- Risk-taking (not afraid to be different, willing to fail)
- High motivation (energetic, adventurous)
- High curiosity (wide interests, questions norms and assumptions)
- Sense of humor (plays with ideas, childlike freshness in thinking)
- Attraction to complexity (attracted to novelty, tolerant of ambiguity and disorder)
- Artistic interests (aesthetic interests, attracted to beauty)
- Open-mindedness (receptive to new ideas, liberal)
- Sensitivity (reflectiveness, needs alone time)
- Good intuition (perceptive, finds order in chaos)
- Intelligence (articulate, logical)

Sometimes, we also find troublesome (negative) traits. Creative people may be:

- Egocentric (tactless, intolerant)
- Stubborn (resists domination)
- Rebellious (uncooperative)
- Capricious (careless, disorderly)
- Sloppy and disorganized with details and unimportant matters
- Arrogant (cynical, sarcastic)
- Impatient (demanding)
- Overactive physically and mentally
- Temperamental (emotional)

- Indifferent to conventions and courtesies
- Indifferent to rules, laws, and authority
- Absentminded (forgetful, mind wanders)
- Argumentative (argues that everyone else is wrong)

Our discussion in Chapter 2 of the overexcitability syndrome, shown by some highly gifted students, included high energy and high creativity (strong fantasy, visual imagery, metaphorical thinking). Perhaps it is not surprising that this combination of high energy and high creativity can lead to outstanding achievement and accomplishment. You also may recall that overexcitability includes high moral thinking—a concern for others' feelings and a keen awareness of social unfairness.

We also mentioned in Chapter 2 that the high energy of many gifted students has led to the often-incorrect diagnosis of Attention Deficit Hyperactivity Disorder (ADHD) and drugging energetic creative students into calmness.[4] An interesting consideration is that one-fourth to one-third of our historically eminent persons—particularly artists and writers—suffered bipolar disorders (formerly called manic-depressive illness).[5] Ruth Richards observed that if Vincent van Gogh had been given antidepressants, he might have exclaimed, "I feel like painting happy clowns on black velvet!"[6]

Creative Abilities

Distinctions between *creativity, creative abilities, creative thinking skills,* and sometimes *creative personality characteristics* can be anywhere from picky to invisible. For example, *originality* is our cornerstone creative ability (or creative thinking skill)—but the tendency for original thinking also is a personality trait. *Flexibility* is another creative ability—tightly related to originality—but also a personality trait.

Logically enough, creative abilities are partly genetic and partly learned. Consider Mozart versus most other piano players.

The following descriptions of creative abilities are from several sources, particularly the creativity man himself, E. Paul Torrance.[7]

Fluency is the ability to produce many verbal or non-verbal ideas in response to an open-ended problem.

Flexibility is the ability to take different approaches to a problem, think of ideas in different categories, or view a problem from different perspectives.

Originality is just that—uniqueness, nonconformity in thought and action, flexibility, or unconventionality in thinking. Dictionary synonyms include creativity, novelty, rarity, singularity, and innovativeness.

Elaboration is the ability to develop, embellish, improve, and even implement an idea.

Transformation virtually means *creativity*—changing one object or idea into another by modifying, combining, or substituting, or by seeing new meanings, implications, applications, or adaptations to a new use.

Sensitivity to problems is the ability to find problems, detect difficulties, detect missing information, and ask good questions. Albert Einstein emphasized that creative people are excellent "problem finders."[8]

Problem defining, related to problem sensitivity, includes at least the abilities to identify the "real" problem, isolate important and unimportant aspect of a problem, clarify and simplify a problem, identify sub-problems, think of alternative problem definitions, and define a problem more broadly.

Note that both *sensitivity to problems* and *problem defining* logically require *good intuition* and *perceptiveness,* listed earlier as personality characteristics.

Visualization is the ability to fantasize, to see things in the "mind's eye," to mentally manipulate images and ideas. The word *visualization* often is used interchangeably with *imagery* and even *imagination.* Visualization is an essential creative ability, and a complex one. Creative writing, for example, involves moving back and forth between mental images and the writing itself.[9] Also, imagery takes place in other senses, not just the visual one. Both Mozart and Beethoven first "imagined" their compositions.

Analogical (or *metaphorical*) thinking is the ability to borrow ideas from one context and use them in another. Or borrow a solution from a related problem. Or "see a similarity." Or "see a connection" between one situation and another. Deliberate metaphorical thinking—borrowing ideas—appears every day in the cartoon and political cartoon sections of your newspaper. See Figure 11.1.

Figure 11.1. Deliberate analogical thinking is a common way to find creative idea combinations for political cartoons and cartoon strips.

Analogical thinking is an extraordinarily common and effective technique for finding new ideas in science and invention, literature, movie making, architecture, clothes design, and other areas. A 2004 newspaper article reported that Hollywood finds movie plots in "books, plays, comic books, graphic novels, theme parks, video games, cartoons, radio, children's books, pulp novels, toys, TV, comic strips, folklore, and music."[10]

> *Predicting outcomes or consequences* is the ability to foresee the results of various solution alternatives and actions. It is related to *evaluation* (below).
>
> *Analysis* is the ability to separate details, or break down a whole into its parts.
>
> *Synthesis* is the ability to see relationships, to combine parts into a workable, perhaps creative whole.

Evaluation is the important ability to think critically, to separate the relevant from the irrelevant, to evaluate the "goodness" or appropriateness of an idea, product, or solution.

Logical thinking is the ability to make reasonable decisions and deduce reasonable conclusions. Logical thinking permeates all aspects of creative thinking and problem solving.

The ability to *regress* refers to "thinking like a child," whose mind is less cluttered by habits, rules, and conformity pressures.

Intuition is a little-understood capability to make "mental leaps" or "intuitive leaps"; to see relationships based upon little, perhaps insufficient information; or to "read between the lines." Intuition is related to *problem sensitivity* and *perceptiveness*.

Concentration is the ability to focus one's attention. Concentration . relates to one's "task orientation" or even Torrance's "blazing drive" of creatively productive people.[11]

Self-Actualized and Special-Talent Creativity

Abraham Maslow coined the phrases *self-actualized creativity* and *special-talent creativity*.[12] Self-actualized creativity refers to a general creativeness—a broad tendency to think creatively in a variety of life situations. Self-actualized creativity also implies good mental health.

In contrast, special-talent creativity refers to the sometimes immense creative talent in specific areas. As suggested earlier, many notable persons with marvelous special-talent creativity also are famous for their neuroses and psychoses. Plato called it "divine madness." In one study of "30 well-known creative writers…a remarkable 80% had a history of a major mood disorder."[13] Consider the names Vincent van Gogh, Howard Hughes, Edgar Allen Poe, Judy Garland, John Belushi, Janis Joplin, introvert Yves St. Laurent, and perhaps even Beethoven and Mozart. Can you think of others?

Some innovative individuals will be high in self-actualized creativity, some will be strong in special-talent creativity, and some will possess both. *An important point is that you do not need to have a marvelous and highly specialized creative talent to consider yourself a creative person.*

Two Models of Creative Thinking and Problem Solving: Wallas and CPS

One well-known model of creativity describes the creative process. The other equally well-known model outlines how to solve a problem creatively.

The Wallas Model

The time-tested, near-ancient model of Graham Wallas describes the four-step creative process of *preparation, incubation, illumination*, and *verification*.[14] The terms are almost self-defining.

Preparation is exploring and clarifying the situation, perhaps looking for the "real" problem, thinking about requirements for a good solution, reviewing relevant information, and acquainting oneself with innuendos, implications, and perhaps unsuccessful solutions. Wallas emphasized its conscious and deliberate nature.

Incubation is a little-understood process of fringe-conscious or maybe even unconscious activity that happens while the thinker is doing something else, like watching TV, jogging, or perhaps even sleeping.

Illumination is the abrupt "Eureka!" experience—a sudden change in perception, inspiration, idea combination, or idea transformation that seems to meet problem requirements. Excitement is common.

Verification is exploring the value or workability of the solution. The idea could be a dead end.

The four steps do not always follow a fixed, sequential order. For example, incubation may be absent or near-instantaneous. Or incubation might cycle the thinker back to further preparation. Or a failed verification usually leads to further preparation or incubation.

Creative Problem Solving Model

The Creative Problem Solving (CPS) model was created by Alex Osborn, inventor of brainstorming, co-founder of the Batten, Barton, Dursten and Osborn advertising agency in New York City, and founder of the Creative Education Foundation in Buffalo, New York.[15]

The CPS model is used in corporate problem-solving sessions and in school classrooms.[16] It also underlies the seven steps in the Future Problem Solving program (Chapter 6). Five steps guide the most popular CPS process.

(1) *Fact finding* is itemizing what you know about the problem or challenge. It includes visualizing and looking at the situation from many viewpoints. You might ask *who, what, when, where, why,* and *how* questions.[17]

(2) *Problem finding* involves thinking of alternative definitions of the problem. Note that the problem definition will determine the nature of the solutions. "In what ways might we...?" (IWWMW) statements can help. Also, ask, "What's the real problem?" "What do we really want to accomplish?"

(3) *Idea finding* is the divergent thinking, brainstorming stage. Ideas are freely proposed without evaluation.

(4) *Solution finding* (bad name; it should be called *idea evaluation*) includes listing criteria for evaluation, evaluating the ideas, and selecting one or more of the best ideas. Will it work? Is it legal? Are costs acceptable? Would grandmother approve?

For example, in evaluating different ways to teach creativity, some criteria might be: Will the strategy work? That is, will it strengthen important creative abilities? Will it raise creativity consciousness? Will it require too much class time? Will students enjoy the experience?

(5) *Acceptance finding* (another bad name; it should be *idea implementation*) is "thinking of ways to get the best ideas into action."[18] Acceptance finding may involve an action plan—a list of steps to be taken and a timetable for taking them.

Teaching Creative Thinking

As a first consideration, becoming more creative or helping others (e.g., students) become more creative means that *you must try to strengthen the (positive) creative personality traits and creative abilities mentioned earlier*—for example, originality, flexibility, open-mindedness, willingness to take a risk, and maybe curiosity.

Mainly, you and others absolutely must become more *creativity conscious.*

The rest of this chapter will evolve around five main personality and intellectual objectives related to becoming a more creative person—and helping others to become more creative thinkers and problem solvers.

1. Fostering creativity consciousness and creative attitudes
2. Improving our (and others') understanding of creativity
3. Exercising creative abilities
4. Learning creative thinking techniques
5. Becoming more involved in creative activities

Creativity Consciousness and Creative Attitudes

As noted above, the single most important component of creative growth is acquiring a *creativity consciousness* and related creative attitudes. Many creative people are aware of their own creativeness and the importance of deliberately seeking innovative ideas and problem solutions. In fact, the single best item on adult creativity inventories is the question, "Are you creative?"[19]

Ironically, creativity consciousness is not only the *most important* aspect of becoming more creatively productive, it also is the *easiest to teach*. Creativity conscious will be a natural outcome of virtually any type of creativity exercises or involvement—for example, reading this chapter.

Creativity consciousness and creative attitudes include:

- An awareness of the importance of creativity for personal self-actualization and for solving personal and professional problems more creatively.

- An appreciation of the importance of creative people and creative ideas in the history of civilization—which may be seen as a history of creative innovation in all areas.

- An awareness of blocks and barriers to creativity—our habits, traditions, rules, policies, and especially our social expectations and conformity pressures.

- A receptiveness to the novel, unconventional, tradition-breaking, and perhaps even wild, crazy, zany, and farfetched ideas of others.

- A predisposition to think creatively—to play with ideas, search for novelty, and get involved in creative activities.

- A willingness to take creative risks, make mistakes, and sometimes fail.

Every college course and professional workshop dealing with creativity
stresses creativity consciousness, creative attitudes, and removing barriers
to creative thinking.

If you believe that our innate creative abilities cannot be greatly improved, consider this: by changing our attitudes in a more creative direction, we at least can learn to use the abilities we already have.

Perhaps you have heard of a *creative atmosphere*—which contrasts, of course, with a repressive, fearful, and idea-stifling atmosphere. A creative atmosphere—in a company, a classroom, a home, or elsewhere—rewards creative thinking and helps it become habitual. Psychologist Carl Rogers called it *psychological safety*. If we feel safe exploring creative ideas and behaving creatively, we will. If not, we won't.[20]

Many professional creativity trainers use "warm-ups" as a quick way to change group attitudes in a more creative—and fun—direction. Wouldn't the following dopey five-minute creative thinking problems loosen up a group?[21]

- How can we get an elephant out of our bathroom? He likes it in there.

- What are some goofy names for a pet alligator?

- Why do you want to be a duck?

- How many ways could we quickly get a message to somebody a mile away?

- Make up breakfast and dinner menus for the six grizzly bears who are visiting you.

- Why would an elementary school principal announce that classes will begin at midnight?

- What would happen if elementary schools did begin at midnight?

- What are some crazy ways to remove a mayor from office? Use any meaning of "remove."

- Think of names for some delicious dishes that include raspberries and bear meat.

- It's Valentines Day in a fourth-grade class. What are some creative ways for students to deliver valentines to each other?

More exercises that can be used as warm-ups appear later in this chapter in the section titled "Exercising Creative Abilities."

Idea Squelchers

Over the years, several lists of anti-creative *idea squelchers* have appeared, including on the cover of one issue of the *Journal of Creative Behavior.* Do these sound familiar? Would you ever say any of these things?

It can't be done.	It won't work.
We've never done it before.	I'm telling you, it won't work!
We're not ready for it yet.	See? It didn't work.
Are you nuts?	It's a waste of time.
What will the parents think?	Won't we be held accountable?
Somebody would have suggested it before if it were any good.	It's been the same for 20 years, so it must be good.
Let's wait and see.	It'll mean more work.
Let's not bother.	Don't step on any toes.
You've got to be kidding!	That's not our job.
You don't understand the problem.	Be practical.
We have too many projects now.	We need more lead time.
Let's form a committee.	Let's use proven methods.
That's trouble.	Don't rock the boat.
It's not in the curriculum.	We did all right without it.
What bubble-head thought that up?	Don't forget the chain of command.

Improving Understanding of Creativity

An improved understanding of creativity will raise creativity consciousness, demystify creativity, and help convince children and adults that—given their present abilities—they are quite capable of hatching creative ideas and doing creative things.

Instruction on creativity can include such matters as:

- The importance of creative ideas to society and to ourselves. (Where would we be without creative thinking?)

- The nature of most creativity as modifications and combinations of existing ideas.

- The notion that creative people are not rigid. They look at things from different points of view and consider different possibilities.

- The presence of conformity pressures—which squelch creativity. (Remember idea squelchers?)

- The notion that creative people take risks, play with possibilities, and sometimes fail. (Want to avoid failure? Don't do anything— especially anything new!)

- The importance of analogical thinking. For example, the *Star Spangled Banner* was based on an English drinking song. Cockleburs inspired Velcro®. As we noted earlier, many (or most) ideas for inventions, music compositions, movies, cartoons, architecture, etc., stem from deliberate analogical thinking.[22]

- Biographies, personality characteristics, and thinking styles of creative people.

- How creative people use such techniques as brainstorming, analogical thinking, and the CPS model to extend their intuition and imagination, and to solve problems.

- What is measured by the *Torrance Tests of Creativity*—for example, fluency, flexibility, originality, elaboration, breaking boundaries, humor, fantasy, emotional expressiveness, synthesis of figures, internal visualization, and others.

- The nature of the creative process, as represented in the Wallas stages and the CPS model.[23] The creative process also can be described as a "change in perception" or "mental transformation." Visual puzzles, optical illusions, and political cartoons illustrate the sudden "seeing" of new ideas, relationships, and meanings. Shivvers sensibly described the creative process as beginning with an idea "seed" from which an idea grows and becomes more varied and complicated.[24] If it becomes too complex and confusing, recommended Shivvers, one should return to the seed and start over. Also, he warned that one should not get too inflexibly married to an idea.

- The notion that creative people use their talents, not waste them.

Exercising Creative Abilities

We itemized some creative abilities earlier in this chapter. We assume that these abilities—like virtually any other ability—can be strengthened through exercise.

Many creativity workbooks use open-ended "think-of-all-the-ideas-you-can" activities to exercise creative abilities—and at the same time strengthen creativity consciousness and creative attitudes. "What would happen if...?" (or just "What if...?") problems are a traditional divergent thinking exercise that strengthens at least fluency, flexibility, originality, elaboration, analysis, evaluation, predicting outcomes, visualization, imagination, and logical thinking. For example, what would happen if:

- We had no books?
- All of the pens and pencils in the world disappeared?
- The British had won the Revolutionary War?
- The only musical instruments were drums?
- Thomas Edison had become a swell plumber and never invented lightbulbs?
- The Wright brothers stuck to bicycles?
- Computer chips were never invented?
- There was no corn crop in the Midwest this year?
- Miami became the North Pole?
- Everyone looked exactly alike?
- You had an eye in the back of your head
- Everyone wasted school supplies?
- Everyone was dishonest? Rude? A litterbug?
- There were no fast-food restaurants? No cars? No electricity? No nuclear bombs? No peanut butter? No gravity?

As other traditional creativity exercises, students can think of *unusual uses* for any common object or characteristic (for example, old tires, a brick, clothes pins, ping pong balls, a walking cane, hair trimmings from a barber shop, a smile, etc.). Also, *product improvement* problems ask students to think of changes or improvements for a familiar object or characteristic (for example, a bathtub, a TV set, a bicycle, a pencil, popcorn, Jell-O®, helpfulness, promptness, school attitudes, etc.). *Design* problems ask students to design a dog-walking machine, a cat petter, a better trash collection procedure (for home or school), a burglary prevention system, etc.

Exercises aimed specifically at strengthening *flexibility* ask students to look at things from other perspectives. How does this elementary classroom look to a high school student? A hungry mouse? An alien from outer space? A visiting duck?

Many everyday problems need solutions. These kinds of problems also exercise creative abilities:

- How can the school lunch menu be improved?

- How can bicycle theft be eliminated?

- How can the school electric bill be reduced?

- How can traffic accidents be reduced?

- What can we do for a parent on his or her birthday for less than 10 dollars?

- How can we help the elderly in our neighborhoods?

- What would be an interesting independent project in the area of movie stars, automobile manufacturing, snakes, mountain climbing, opening a pet store, dairy farming, earthquakes, etc.?

Every teacher interested in stimulating creative attitudes and abilities will actively engage students in creative thinking and problem solving.

Teaching Creative Thinking Techniques

There are several creative thinking and problem-solving techniques that, in fact, originated with creative people.

(1) *Brainstorming.* Today, the term *brainstorming* is used loosely to describe any type of thinking ("Hey, let's brainstorm how to spend your 10 bucks!"). However, brainstorming is a classic creative problem-solving technique, usually involving only about six (e.g., management) people. Of course, we can brainstorm with more folks, but with larger groups (e.g., classrooms), not everyone will participate; some will be "free riders."[25] Alex Osborn's four brainstorming rules are:

- Criticism and evaluation are ruled out until later. This is the "deferred judgment" principle.

251

- "Freewheeling" is welcomed. It's best to be wild and creative first, then evaluate and "tame down" later.

- Quantity is wanted. A greater number of ideas improves the likelihood of finding useful ideas.

- Combining and improving others' ideas is encouraged and, of course, adds to the growing list of ideas.

Most or all problems and exercises mentioned earlier in this chapter (e.g., "What would happen if...?") could serve as classroom brainstorming exercises.

(2) *Reverse brainstorming.* Reverse brainstorming is effective and fun—and it *always* identifies what students and others currently are doing wrong:

- How can we be unpleasant to new students?

- How can we create more work for the school custodians?

- How can we waste lots and lots of electricity?

- How can we be rude to each other? Violate each others' rights?

- How can we avoid thinking creatively?

- How can we mess up the school grounds? Always be late? Never learn anything in school?

(3) *Attribute listing.* Attribute listing is built on this philosophy: "Each time we take a step we do it by changing an attribute or quality of something, or else by applying that same quality or attribute to something else."[26] We thus *modify* attributes, as in improving details for new refrigerators, trucking systems, or bag lunches; or we *transfer* attributes from one situation to a new situation. Attribute transferring is analogical thinking, as described earlier.

As an example of attribute modifying, students—or umbrella designers—could create ideas for new and better umbrellas by first identifying umbrella attributes (parts, qualities), then thinking of ways to change or improve each part. For example, consider attributes of size (e.g., small, large, purse-size?), shape (do they have to be round?), weight, fabric color, handle material

252

(design, color), opening mechanism (spring?), number of ribs, etc.

The attribute listing strategy also could be applied to most other problems—for example, local traffic safety, design of a zoo, or a school outing. What are the component parts? How could we improve each of them?

Most anything can be creatively improved. Attribute listing helps structure the improvement.

(4) *Idea checklists.* Osborn devised an idea checklist to help stimulate creative ideas. A shortened form of his "73 Idea-Spurring Questions" includes:[27]

- *Put to other uses?* (New ways to use? Other uses if modified?)
- *Adapt?* (What else is like this? What could I copy?)
- *Modify?* (Change meaning, color, motion, form?)
- *Magnify?* (Stronger, extra value, exaggerate?)
- *Minify?* (Miniature, lighter, streamline?)
- *Substitute?* (What else instead? Other ingredient?)
- *Rearrange?* (Other pattern? Other sequence?)
- *Reverse?* (Reverse roles? Turn it backward?)
- *Combine?* (A blend, an assortment, combine purposes?)

One creativity workbook for children called it the SCAMPER technique: Substitute, Combine, Adapt, Modify/Magnify/Minify, Put to other uses, Exaggerate, Reverse.[28]

Virtually every book on stimulating creativity will include techniques for creative thinking.[29] Bob Stanish's books are especially superb for teaching creative thinking to children.[30]

Involvement in Creative Thinking and Creative Activities

Finally, the most popular, natural, and probably most effective procedure for strengthening creativity in students (and ourselves) is involvement in creative activities—doing creative things.

Resource room activities often involve students in independent projects, with a major goal of promoting creative thinking and problem solving. The projects virtually always require defining the problem, exploring, discovering, considering possibilities, planning, solving small and large problems, and exercising plenty of other "outside the box" creative abilities.

Look again at the enrichment topics and suggestions in Chapter 6, Table 6.1. Project possibilities are almost unlimited, for example, in the categories of math; science; literature, writing, and communication; computers and the Internet; visual and performing arts; language, culture, and social sciences; business and economics; and interests, hobbies, and so on.

Note also that Renzulli's Type III enrichment described in Chapter 9 is titled "Individual and Small Group Investigations of Real Problems."

In Chapter 6 (Enrichment), we described the Future Problem Solving, Odyssey of the Mind, and Camp Invention programs, all of which were designed specifically to involve students in creative thinking and strengthen their creativity consciousness and creative abilities.

Creativity can be rewarded and exercised in gifted students—and all students—to the benefit of the students, their futures, and society.

Summary

- Creativity is a core goal of most programs for gifted students. Creativity is complex, comprised of simpler component thinking skills.

- Many traits of creative children are positive (e.g., originality, high motivation, curiosity, humor, artistic interests, open-mindedness), but some may be negative (e.g., stubbornness, rebelliousness, arrogance, being temperamental).

- The excitability syndrome includes high energy and creativity. Students with such traits may be incorrectly diagnosed with ADHD; some gifted students do have ADHD. Many historically eminent artists and writers suffered bipolar disorders.

- There are many creative abilities, including fluency, flexibility, originality, elaboration, transformation, sensitivity to problems, problem defining, visualization, analogical thinking, predicting outcomes, analysis, synthesis, evaluation, logical thinking, intuition, and others.

- Maslow's general, self-actualized creativity implies good mental health. His special-talent creativeness may include neuroses and psychoses. Some creative persons have both self-actualized and special-talent creativeness.

- The 1926 Wallas model of the creative process is summarized in four words: preparation, incubation, illumination, and verification. The order of the four steps is not rigid.

- Osborn's CPS model includes the five steps of fact finding, problem finding, idea finding, solution finding (idea evaluation), and acceptance finding (idea implementation).

- Teaching creativity includes strengthening creative personality traits and creative abilities. Five recommended steps are:

  1. Foster creativity consciousness and creative attitudes, which should happen with any creative involvement. Creative attitudes include an appreciation of creative people and ideas, an awareness of blocks to creativity, a predisposition to think creatively, and a willingness to take creative risks and sometimes fail. A creative atmosphere (Rogers' *psychological safety*) rewards creative thinking. Brief, far-fetched warm-up exercises aid creative attitudes and thinking. Idea squelchers include, for example, "It can't be done," "It won't work," "It's a waste of time," "That's not our job," "Don't rock the boat," and many others.

  2. Improve understanding of creativity to strengthen creativity consciousness and other creative attitudes. This includes instruction on, for example, the importance of creativity, the nature of creativity, flexible thinking of creative people, conformity pressures, taking risks and sometimes failing, analogical thinking, creativity techniques, the creative process, and more.

  3. Exercise such creative abilities as fluency, visualization, analysis, analogical thinking, and resisting premature closure. "What would happen if...?" problems, thinking of unusual uses for objects, and thinking of product improvements are common creativity exercises. Flexibility exercises include taking different perspectives on a problem. Finding solutions to practical problems (e.g., bicycle theft) is valuable.

4. Teach creativity techniques such as brainstorming, reverse brainstorming, attribute listing, and using idea checklists; they can benefit creative growth. Such techniques appear in many books on fostering creativity in adults and children.

5. Most important is involvement in creative thinking and creative activities. Projects and programs that involve students in creativity include Renzulli's Type III enrichment, Future Problem Solving, Odyssey of the Mind, and Camp Invention. Table 6.1 in Chapter 6 suggests creative projects in many areas.

12
Problems and Counseling Needs

Gifted students by their very advanced cognitive abilities
and intensity of feelings deal with issues about self and
others in ways that are different from those of the general
population and therefore require specialized understanding.

~ Nicholas Colangelo

[*Scene: Jockelyn College. The women's golf coach is trying to teach Kitty Woods to play golf. They're on the putting green. The coach places a ball three feet from the hole. Both are serious and concentrating.*]

Women's golf coach: Now putting is tricky, Kitty. Be sure to carefully line up the ball. Is it an uphill putt? A downhill putt? Will the ball roll left? Right? And don't hit it too hard; it'll roll too far past the hole. But don't leave your putt short either; "Never up, never in!"

Kitty Woods: But what if I make a mistake? I'll probably miss the hole. Or I might smack the ball too hard! I'll probably slug my foot! Maybe I'll drop the putter! I can't stand making mistakes. I know I'm stupid! I've never done this before. I really don't want to try! I just know I won't be perfect at it!

Coach (smiling calmly): Just line it up carefully and give it a try! Nobody's perfect.

(Kitty shrugs, then drops to all fours, tilts her head, squints, looks at the ball, looks at the hole, then nervously stands back up. She putts. The ball barely misses the left side of the cup.)

Kitty: See? I missed! I knew couldn't do it! It's not my fault! The hole's too small! And the grass leans the wrong way. And the ball hit a bump anyway. What about ring toss? I know I can do that! I'm really good if I stand close!

Coach: But that's just your first try! You'll get better, I promise! C'mon, Kitty, let's try again!

Kitty: But I tried and missed! I feel hopeless! I'm terrible! I'll never be any good! I'm getting queasy. I'm so upset! I need to lie down. I'll talk to my shrink about this tomorrow!

Coach (still smiling calmly): C'mon, let's just try a few more times.

Kitty: I'd only fail. But don't tell my parents! They think I'm perfect at everything!

Coach: Huh? Everything? But you've never putted before!

Kitty: I have an idea! I'll practice putting all night tonight, all day tomorrow, and all night tomorrow night! I'll work and work and work until I'm perfect! And then I'll be sinking these three footers every time! Maybe 20 footers. Can I see you day after tomorrow?

Coach (thoughtfully): Maybe you were right about ring toss.

Why Counseling?

Most gifted students tend to be better adjusted than average. After all, compared with their peers, school has never been a problem, and they usually—not always—have good social skills and adequate friends. In high school, they look forward to success in college, a pleasing future career, and a nice life. However, as mentioned in Chapter 1, Leta Hollingworth warned that *extremely* bright students can have serious school problems.[1] They are too different, too alone, too impatient with slow-thinking friends (and teachers), and often upset by the irrationality, unfairness, and hypocrisy in the world.

As we will see, there are other recurrent personal and social problems unique to giftedness. As Nicholas Colangelo noted, to help gifted students and their families deal with these problems, counseling is an essential part of every gifted program.[2] *And the greater the gift, the greater the need for counseling.*

Home and Peer Problems

With very bright students who score above IQ 150 or 160, one problem is a near certainty. They feel different because they *are* different. They may have problems with both family and peers. Home difficulties might include jealousy and resentment by siblings, due partly to the gifted child's special treatment. Or the gifted child might resist parental authority, which creates conflict and stress. Occasionally, the problems extend to drinking, drugs, and delinquency. Even suicide is possible.

As for peer problems, we noted at the outset of Chapter 7 that highly gifted students can be light-years ahead of age-mates in their educational, philosophic, idealistic, and humanistic concerns and worries. In contrast, other less-able students may be preoccupied with spending money, clothes, cars, and the opposite sex. A common outcome is some degree—perhaps a high degree—of social rejection. According to peers, the highly gifted child obviously is weird.

Boredom and Apathy

Without a challenging gifted program, very bright children often get bored in a school that ignores their academic, psychological, and social needs. The school environment can lead to apathy, feelings of isolation, depression, underachievement, rebelliousness, poor social skills, and poor learning and study skills. According to one estimate—and despite logic—up to one-fourth of all high school dropouts are gifted.[3]

Perfectionism

One recurrent problem of gifted children is *perfectionism*. To set the stage, *normal* perfectionism is a healthy characteristic that drives hard work and accomplishment. Healthy perfectionists find pleasure in their high effort and high achievement.

The problem is *neurotic* (dysfunctional) perfectionism. Such self-analytic, self-judging, and compulsive students cannot appreciate their own competency nor the adequacy of their work.[4] If they receive an "A-" (not an "A") on a test, they feel inadequate, self-critical, weak, ashamed, and they doubt their ability. They are overly precise. They become obsessive-compulsive workaholics—they study continuously and perhaps work all night on projects. They may turn in papers late because the reports must be perfect. They cannot tolerate mistakes or imperfect work. They stew about one slightly incorrect answer on a test, asking themselves, "Why didn't I...(write down this or that or study more)?" They may argue with teachers about test scores. Some of them make themselves sick (or even cheat) trying to do perfect work. They might have a fast heart rate and sweaty palms the morning of a test, or they might experience other physical or medical maladies. They always feel that more could be done.[5]

High achievement becomes identical to feelings of self-worth. Perfectionists feel excited and capable when they do well. They feel ashamed when they do not. They typically value high achievement more than fun, friends, sports, family activities, good health, and even sleep.

Even though they expect perfect success in everything they do, some failure is inevitable. Not surprisingly, these perfectionists avoid new experiences that could lead to failure. Some might ask, "What's wrong with me?" and look for themselves in descriptions of mental disorders.

For example, the perfectionism may occur with music lessons. The talented-but-compulsive violin or piano student practices every free minute, never satisfied even with a high level of performance. Many such students are impatient with other students' lack of perfectionism. They might not associate with non-straight-"A" students.

Recommendations for Teachers, Counselors, and Parents

Patricia Schuler recommended that teachers:[6]

- Learn to recognize perfectionism.

- Educate themselves regarding how (neurotic) perfectionism affects gifted students socially and emotionally.

- Discuss with students how high standards motivate excellent work, but neurotic, compulsive perfectionism is unhealthy.

- Encourage flexibility, creativity, and exploring *new* areas—where success and perfection are *not* assured.

- Use humor to lighten the classroom atmosphere and reduce any perceived threat to perfectionistic students.

Schuler suggested that teachers and counselors help perfectionistic students:

- Recognize their strengths and weaknesses—and understand that no one is superior in everything.

- Accept mistakes and reduce their feelings of failure.

- Develop a good attitude toward learning and school.

- Learn to help others and receive help from them.

- Develop a sense of humor in regard to accepting themselves and others.

Rosemary Callard-Szulgit, a former teacher of the gifted, recommended that parents of perfectionistic students can:[7]

- Plan regular times to sit and talk. Such lively children have plenty of thoughts and ideas rattling around in their heads. With bedtime talks, the chatty child sometimes must wake the sleepy parent in order to continue. The chats help restore a normal balance in the child's life.

- Take walks with their perfectionistic child. Walking is a wonderful stress reducer and supplies a great opportunity for talking.

- Make sure the child joins family outings and events—movies, pizza, a picnic, visiting a flea market, even watching a favorite TV show. The perfectionist can even select the event.

- Ensure that their child sees a school or private counselor. The child probably will be more inclined to discuss—and begin resolving—the problem with a trusted professional than with a parent or even a favorite teacher.

- Let their perfectionist child know that they care about him or her. Hugs, touches, and loving phrases supply important strength and balance.

Barbara Kerr suggested that a school counselor might use her (drastic?) *Perfectionism Behavior Change Contract* to break perfectionistic habits.[8] The contract includes these paraphrased instructions:

At bedtime, don't set your alarm. Get up late. If you wake up anyway, go back to sleep or read something until you truly are late. When getting ready for school, leave one item unfinished—for example, leave your hair unbrushed, shirt wrinkled, or wear unmatched clothes. Be late for a less-important class or meeting—and don't explain or apologize. At lunch, don't count calories—eat what you wish and take your time. In the afternoon, leave a task undone. Don't reply to an important message. In the evening, skip an expected duty, such as washing dishes or taking out the garbage. Don't finish your school work. Go to bed late—after reading something interesting, doing something fun, or talking to a friend.

Next morning, get up late and begin again!

Potential Diagnosis Errors

Attention Deficit Hyperactivity Disorder

We briefly described Attention Deficit Hyperactivity Disorder (ADHD) in Chapters 2 and 11. The central point was that highly active, excitable, and perhaps inattentive (due to class boredom) gifted children may be incorrectly diagnosed as having ADHD. According to James Webb et al., perhaps "half of gifted with the diagnosis of ADD/ADHD" do not truly have the mental disorder.[9]

A counselor's obligation is to help clarify whether the excitability and hyperactivity relate to a student's high giftedness—perhaps stemming from education misplacement—or whether it truly is an ongoing attentional, hyperactivity problem that might be helped with medication. Webb et al. listed these distinctions between children who truly have ADHD versus similar characteristics of many gifted children.

(1) *Not turning in work.* ADHD children may forget to do the work, not finish the work, or lose it. Gifted children *choose* to not complete the work or to not turn it in.

(2) *Not following rules.* Impulsive ADHD students may be unaware of rules and conventions, or else unable to follow them. Gifted students may question the rules, particularly if they seem unreasonable.

(3) *Difficulty with peers.* Hyperactive and impulsive ADHD children may be aggressive. Gifted children can be misperceived as aggressive because they try to correct others and/or blurt out answers.

(4) *Further characteristics.* The following are a few additional characteristics of intellectually gifted children that can be misdiagnosed as ADHD:[10]

- Gifted children might attend selectively to challenging and interesting tasks but avoid or "tune out" less interesting input and activities.

- They may not complete uninteresting tasks.

- When asked a question, they may wait to prepare a thoughtful response.

- They may blurt out answers, but they usually are correct.

- They may not quickly shift attention unless motivated to do so.

A complication is that gifted children *can* have ADHD, and the "twice-exceptional" diagnosis is difficult. Gifted children with ADHD can be extremely productive when motivation is high and the task is reasonably structured, but otherwise may be unable to complete even simple tasks. Such inconsistency is present in most ADHD children, including gifted ADHD children.

Asperger's Syndrome

Asperger's Syndrome includes high-functioning autism, defined in Webster's 2002 dictionary as "self-centered subjective mental activity (daydreams, fantasies, delusions, hallucinations), accompanied by withdrawal from reality." Typical behaviors in Asperger's Syndrome include linear and sequential thinking and a strong preference for order and predictability. Other symptoms are introversion, social awkwardness, and aloofness; attention problems; overexcitability; hypersensitivity (e.g., to bright lights and loud noises); repetitive patterns of interests, activities, and play; resistance to change; an inability to interpret interpersonal cues; talking at an early age; excessive talking and asking questions; concern with fairness; and a quirky sense of humor. Importantly, in Asperger's Syndrome, intellectual abilities are undamaged and typically fall in the normal to above-average range.[11]

Many of these descriptors, however, also fit a lot of gifted kids. Therefore, two related issues are: (1) misdiagnosing introverted gifted students as having Asperger's Syndrome, and (2) not identifying gifted children who *do* have Asperger's Syndrome.

James Webb et al. summarized cues for detecting non-Asperger's kids who simply are gifted:[12]

- Gifted children have normal friendships with those who share interests.
- They understand interpersonal situations and the emotions of others.
- Their own emotions are appropriate to the topic.
- They can show sympathy and empathy.
- They are aware of others' perceptions of them.
- They have little or no motor clumsiness.
- They tolerate abrupt routine changes.
- Speech and humor are more adult-like.
- They understand metaphors and idioms, such as "A stitch in time saves nine."

Schizotypal Personality Disorder

Schizotypal Personality Disorder is a precursor to full-blown schizo-phrenia and therefore has earned the nickname "Schizophrenia-lite."[13] Persons with Schizotypal Personality Disorder are eccentric, sensitive to criticism, and feel that they do not fit in. Not surprisingly, they keep to themselves. In school, they may underachieve.

Those with Schizotypal Personality Disorder have peculiar fantasies, superstitions, and magical beliefs. In Webb's example, such a person might explain that the strip on the newer 20-dollar bills is detected at supermarket scanners and ATMs so that the government can track their moves. They may also believe that they possess remarkable capabilities— for example, that they can read others' minds and predict forthcoming events.

Some similarities to giftedness leading to misdiagnosis are clear. The majority of gifted children are more sensitive than others. Many are intro-verted. Many have a lively fantasy life—for example, they may have imaginary playmates, which usually disappear when they enter kindergar-ten. In addition to reason and rationality, creatively gifted students will have "non-rational tendencies to be playful, fanciful, illogical, [and] far-fetched."[14] Thinking is unusual—even near psychopathological among adult artists, writers, and particularly poets. Gifted students may withdraw when reading or when engaged in creative thinking and activities.

Gifted students who may appear schizotypal will show these non-psychotic traits:[15]

- Emotional displays are appropriate to the situation.

- Gifted students may reduce visible emotions if they feel that those emotions are unacceptable.

- Paranoid thinking is absent.

- Gifted students are comfortable with peers who share interests.

- School achievement is high—if the gifted student likes the sub-ject and/or teacher.

- On many occasions, their creativity or curiosity has been unap-preciated.

- Unusual behavior/appearance reflects independence (or rebe-llion), not psychopathy.

Avoidant Personality Disorder

Persons with Avoidant Personality Disorder tend to stay away from situations that might lead to criticism or disapproval. The disorder includes being overly shy and inhibited. Such persons badly want close personal relationships, but—of course—they fear rejection. Avoidant Personality Disorder usually begins in infancy or childhood, caused by shyness plus a fear of new situations and strangers.

Gifted persons may be misdiagnosed as having Avoidant Personality Disorder since they tend to be sensitive and introverted. Because of previous easy success in school, they have not experienced failure and therefore may become afraid to fail. They easily become perfectionists and, in extreme cases, are paralyzed by their perfectionism. Gifted students also learn to avoid situations—such as high achievement or high creativity—that can lead to teasing or ridicule.

The following clues suggest that avoidance problems are due to giftedness, not a true Avoidant Personality Disorder:[16]

- With sensitive and shy gifted students, there will be no strong increase in, for example, shyness, isolation, and fear of strangers as the child grows older.

- With shy gifted students, there will be no "panic disorder" or "generalized social phobia."

- Shy gifted students are much less likely to show avoidance behavior with peers who share their interests.

Depression

Gifted students suffer depression with about the same intensity and just as often as the rest of us. High ability does not protect them. However, depression may become moderate to severe if a school system ignores a gifted child's capabilities and educational needs. One estimate is that gifted children enter each grade already knowing 60 to 75% of the material for that year.[17] Noted Webb and colleagues, the result is "boredom and impatience [which leads to a] low-grade depression."[18] Seligman named this depression *learned helplessness.*[19]

The reader with a college course in philosophy might remember existential depression. The term may be traced to Albert Camus and Jean Paul Sartre and appears in the writings of more recent philosophers and novelists. Gifted young adults—perhaps in middle or high school— may become "existentially depressed" because of their high-level intelligence, sensitivity, intensity, and idealism.[20] They realize that their own mentality is advanced and out-of-sync with that of others. They think about their futures. They think about their existence and its meaning, if any. They think about world problems that so strongly conflict with their idealism.

Existentially depressed students have a higher-than-average risk of suicide. Some situations further increase their depression and risk of suicide—especially rejection by both family and peers. Gifted children, for example, may be called "nerds," "geeks," or "dorks"—which hardly promotes marvelous self-perceptions and self-concepts.

Webb et al. proposed three recommendations for treating students with existential depression: (1) help the students realize that others understand their feelings, (2) emphasize that their ideals are shared by others and that they are not alone, and (3) encourage them to join social, political, or religious causes—which increases feelings of power and reduces feelings of aloneness.[21]

Gifted and Gay

Between one and three gifted students per 1,000 are both gifted and gay (lesbian, bisexual; GLB)—a double label.[22] Almost no GLB students admit to being gay until they are in college. Therefore, in elementary and secondary school they often have no peers, no role models, and no one to talk with about their sexual identity.[23]

Social exclusion and feelings of guilt, anxiety, rejection, and rock-bottom self-esteem lead easily to depression—perhaps revulsion and suicide. These negative feelings likely are amplified because of the gifted-and-gay students' overexcitability, sensitivity, and precocious awareness of social rejection. Even teachers and coaches may make homophobic comments, signaling their absence of support. The school climate is "uncomfortable at best, dangerous at worst."[24] Insults and violence may even come from the student's own family.

Some GLB students will direct their fears and poor self-identity into extreme academic, athletic, or extracurricular activities—a type of neurotic perfectionism. Others engage in self-destructive behaviors such as smoking, drug use, risky sex, running away from home, or other forms of delinquency.

One adult group of GLB persons, age 18 to 25, noted that GLB students: (1) badly need role models, and (2) have no support for coming out. They made these counseling recommendations:[25]

- Let GLB students know that they are all right—not bad, evil, or sick. Be compassionate.

- Let them know they are not alone.

- Never show disappointment in them nor dismiss their sexual feelings.

- Establish school, out-of-school, and distance (e-mail, Internet) support groups.

- Raise teachers' awareness that GLB students can be in every class-room—and they likely are confused, scared, and lonely.

- Raise staff awareness that drug abuse, dropping out, suicide attempts, or compulsive perfectionism may stem from homo-sexuality.

- Ensure that every classroom is respectful and safe—for example, from name calling.

- Try to eliminate staff homophobia.

- Train counselors to work with GLB students regarding such matters as sexual identity, daydreams and attractions, fears and emotional problems, and social problems.

- Create policies to combat discrimination and violence against homosexual students.

- Include gay historical and literary persons in the curricula.

Suicide

Remarkably, about 10% of all adolescents make at least "one suicide attempt or gesture."[26] Suicide rates for gifted students are not higher nor lower than for others, which is slightly surprising in view of gifted students' suicide risk factors—for example, social isolation, neurotic perfectionism, high sensitivity, and their keen awareness of world prob-lems, often accompanied by feelings of powerlessness and frustration because they cannot improve matters.[27]

Parents and teachers must watch for these warning signs:

- Suicide threats (e.g., "I wish I were dead")

- Changes in behavior (e.g., no longer caring how they look, weight changes, skipping school, losing interest in favorite things, withdrawing from friends, giving away possessions)
- Low self-esteem ("I'm dumb")
- Lack of energy and enthusiasm
- Greater irritability and rebelliousness
- Self-destructive behavior (heavy drinking, driving recklessly, carrying a gun)

Preventative measures must include family, school, and peers. For example, parents must:

- Learn more about adolescent suicide.
- Improve communication, approval, and trust.
- Respond to their children's needs and support their interests.
- Reconcile their own interests and demands with their children's interests.

The school can:

- Train personnel in suicide prevention (e.g., noting suicidal thoughts in essays).
- Teach suicide prevention to all adolescent students—who can identify suicidal classmates.
- Schedule individual and group counseling.
- Identify sources of student stress.
- Help gifted students accept themselves, understand their own strengths and weaknesses, and avoid over-commitment.
- Emphasize that suicide is an utterly horrible solution to one's problems; it's a foolish and permanent solution to a temporary problem.
- Create a (light, humorous) environment where students can talk about problems.

Multipotentiality

One often-cited reason that gifted students have difficulty selecting a career is called *multipotentiality.* Gifted students typically have both high ability and wide interests. They could succeed at a high level in any number of careers. They may agonize over narrowing their options to a single career goal. They may seem paralyzed in making a career—and therefore an educational—decision.

Some additional complications are these:[28]

- If the gifted student is a perfectionist, the agonizing is amplified by a search for the absolutely "perfect" or "ideal" career.

- Gifted students may feel strong pressure from parents and others to select only high-status, high-paying careers.

- They usually must make a long-term commitment to a graduate or professional school, which delays a good income and perhaps starting a family.

- After a few years of training, the long-term career goal may be difficult to alter if the student changes his or her mind.

Counselors can assist with multipotentiality problems by helping students:

- Explore the career as a lifestyle, not just a job or position.

- Understand that career changes are possible and common.

- Explore interests, abilities, and broad categories of life satisfactions.

- Discuss careers with other multipotential students so the student understands that others face the same difficulties.

Early Visibility of Intelligence and Talent

Many outstanding performers, athletes, scholars, artists, and other professionals displayed their strong interests and talents as children. They were *early emergers.*[29] As a child, Hollywood filmmaker/creator George Lucas watched old movies, built things (including a working roller coaster), and read lots of comic books. Pablo Picasso began painting as a very young child and could draw like Rembrandt at age 14.

The early emerging creative or academic genius (or athletic star) may show intense interest and capability in, for example, computer games, math, social studies, creative writing, or racing on bikes or skis.

269

Talent development is uneven; the young genius may show just average ability in other areas. Given a choice, the student prefers to write papers about or otherwise pursue the one captivating area. The early emerger will fantasize about success and fame in his or her interest area. In secondary school he or she will plan advanced training in the area, perhaps neglecting other academic obligations and social activities. The fascination continues into college and young adulthood, resulting in the quick choice of a college major, seeking out suitable mentors, and perhaps postponing marriage and avoiding community involvement.

Early emergence becomes a problem only when parents, teachers, or counselors ignore—or worse, criticize—an enthusiastic child's interest and talent in favor of that American goal of "well-roundedness." ("Now just knock if off, George Lucas! You're not going to be a great filmmaker! So just go outside and play soccer with the other kids!") Some parents and teachers even consider early emergence to be a sign of maladjustment and withhold suitable training. For example, they might prevent accelerating a child gifted in math, physics, social studies, music, art, or theater.

Early emergence is an opportunity. Parents and teachers must supply the necessary resources and training; they must think positively and flexibly about the future of the energetic and talented student.

Stereotyped Educational and Career Choices

Nicholas Colangelo and Barbara Kerr analyzed college majors and career choices of high school students scoring in the 95th to 99th percentiles on the ACT.[30] Of 196 possible college majors, half of the students selected just five stereotyped majors: pre-medicine, pre-law, engineering, business, and communications. However, their ACT scores did not correlate with their college majors. Less than 2% of students with *perfect* scores on the English subtest intended to major in English. Less than 3% of those with *perfect* scores on the math subtest intended to major in pure mathematics. Just 12% of students with *perfect* scores in the natural sciences planned to enter such pure science fields as physics, astronomy, or biology. Of 577 students with *perfect* scores in social studies, just two planned to major in history.

In response to this surprising data, Colangelo and Kerr decided that the problem centered on lack of career information—and therefore creates an obvious need for career counseling aimed at making informed choices.

Gifted Boys

Barbara Kerr and Sanford Cohn used the term "overwhelming" to describe the number of gifted boys who do not bother to complete homework, are bored in school, and ignore most school activities.[31] That is, they underachieve.[32] They also may worry about social rejection because of their superior mental ability—although if they happen to be athletic, they can hide their brains and be socially accepted.

Unfortunately, a caring teacher who creates special assignments to challenge gifted boys might raise the boys' visibility—and worsen the social problem.

Boy Code

W. Pollock described a four-part colorfully-named "Boy Code," which is simultaneously the code of boys' culture and a restrictive strait-jacket.[33] First, *The Sturdy Oak* advises that boys never show weakness, never have moods, and never depend on others for help. They should be stable, stoic, and independent. Second, *Give 'em Hell* requires that boys act macho and tough (at all times) and participate in daring, risky activities. Third, *The Big Wheel* demands that boys acquire dominance, status, and power; always be the leader; and freely mistreat others on their path to success. Fourth, the self-explanatory *No Sissy Stuff* requires absolutely that boys never show sympathy, empathy, warmth, dependence, or any similar emotional response to another person.

Gifted boys quickly learn the Boy Code and try to conform. If rejected anyway, however, they may become angry or even violent.

Young men normally accept society's prescription: go to college (and major in pre-med, pre-law, engineering, or business), stay current on and perhaps play sports, get a classy job, get a classy wife, and buy a big home with an elegant family room, a fireplace, a crazy-huge TV set, the most expensive two or three cars they can afford, and any other visible sign of financial success.[34]

A problematic irony is that gifted males are smart enough to understand that society's definition of masculinity may not be suitable for them personally. But they join the common pursuits anyway. Concluded Kerr and Cohn, "Men's emotionality, creativity, spirituality, and self-actualization have truly been limited by the traditions of masculinity."[35]

At her 30th high school reunion, Kerr discovered that boys she knew in high school who were highly intelligent "had somehow, against all odds, become—well—ordinary."[36] They were content, ethical, overly gentle, and usually overweight and balding, with little to say about their mid-level management or accountant jobs. As pre-college students, they seemed to feel that they had to lower or jettison their own dreams and aspirations to meet the expectations of their families, communities, and schools. The most creative ones had disappeared. Whispers suggested "got into drugs," "went to jail," "went crazy," or just "got lost."

Sissy, Fat Boy, Geek, Nerd, Dork, Brain

Thoughtless peers award these labels to gifted boys, perhaps accompanied by teasing and bullying. All of these slurs assume violation of the Boy Code. All are childhood insults suffered by a remarkable number of eminent men. Kerr and Cohn speculated that such rejection may have contributed to these individuals' later independent, creative accomplishment.[37]

Boys may become "sissies" by modeling females instead of males— their sisters, mothers, grandmothers, and others. Generally, gifted boys tend to be more androgynous than other boys. Some are gay, and the label *gay* is used as both an insult and a threat. Note that being both gifted and gay makes one a member of a minority-within-a-minority. The double label almost guarantees social and emotional problems.

Children's (and adults') weight problems are popular news items, often blamed on the low level of exercise required for watching cartoons and a strong appetite for McBurgers. Excessive weight also may stem from genetic predisposition, hormonal imbalance, excessive early nutrition, and over-eating junk food. Additionally, many gifted boys prefer to read—not exercise—particularly if rejected by peers.[38]

A classic perception of "nerds" ("geeks," "dorks," "brains") is that their intellect surpasses their social skills. They may show remarkable talent in, for example, chess or computers (games, programming, repair). But they are shy, awkward, and clumsy with words, especially around girls.

Minority Boys

The topic of gifted minority boys seems to include virtually all gifted boys who do not have white skin. The umbrella includes: (1) African Americans, (2) Asian Americans, (3) Hispanics, and (4) American Indians. Most are poor. Most are urban, except American Indians.

Each group presents problems and traditions common to most members.

Gifted—and virtually all other—African-American students experience peer pressure to underachieve. Do not be smart. Do not study. Drop out as soon as possible. If they do not do these things, they are accused of "acting White." High achievers may become "raceless;" other Blacks do not accept their achievement, while many Whites do not accept their blackness.[39] However, when formally identified as gifted, these minority students, their parents, and their extended families may become optimistic and supportive regarding school achievement and life success.

Asian boys learn strong family loyalty, respect for elders, and obedience to family traditions. They value honor and the notion that supporting family and community is more important than individual success. While many students are high achievers, visible pride in personal accomplishment may quietly be seen as inappropriate.

The families of gifted Hispanic boys encourage traditional roles for males and females. The "machismo" ideal requires that males be dominant and competitive. Terrific intellect does not prove manhood, and so a gifted boy must demonstrate his manliness in other ways. Family loyalty typically is extremely strong. Some young men even give up college scholarships because leaving home can be seen as abandoning their family. Discrimination against Spanish-speaking persons includes the belief that they can attain only low-level jobs.

The category *American Indians* includes hundreds of language and culture groups. Most live in poverty. For example, one gifted boy lived in a Hogan with no electricity, no running water, and no hospital within 100 miles.[40] American Indian communities stress harmony and cooperation. Individuals typically do not wish to stand out, including by showing their intellect. In or out of school, they tend not to be competitive or aggressive.

Gifted Girls

In recent decades, young high school men have drifted away from leadership roles—and more and more young women take over the school paper and the yearbook, often getting elected as school president and vice president. The parade of women college graduates accepting diplomas in law, medicine, business, and other fields happily confirms that, compared with 40 years ago, times have changed dramatically. Even so, young women generally avoid college courses in engineering and the hard sciences.[41] Interestingly, many also avoid teaching and nursing because these are stereotyped female areas—even if deep down inside they would just love to be a teacher or nurse. Parents and teachers also may push them away from these stereotyped occupations.

We mentioned at the outset of this chapter (and earlier) that young people with IQs above 150 or 160 often have adjustment problems. Girls at this level tend to suffer social isolation even more than gifted boys. To cope during adolescence, some hide their giftedness. A few lower their professional aspirations.

Many gifted girls resemble gifted boys in enjoying outdoor adventures, sports, and problem solving. Also like gifted boys, career aspirations tend to be adventurous—for example, they may wish to become astronauts, diplomats, Egyptologists, or great writers.

Most foresee a marriage-career lifestyle, which can cause problems with males who did not expect a mate whose life extends beyond wife, mother, and housekeeper. Sometimes, domestic burdens and responsibilities stretch the mental stability of the ambitious wife. It is not unusual for women—but it *is* rare for men—to reduce their career involvement to meet family obligations.

Kerr used the label "culture of romance" to describe strong pressures to value relationships with men at the expense of women's own career achievement.[42] One trend is that, as women's career identities become weaker, their romantic identities become more important.

A subtle and self-defeating aspect of many women is their superior ability to cope and adjust—for example, to a lower status career and a smaller salary. Said Kerr, "My own theory is that gifted women may be too 'well-adjusted' for their own good."[43]

At her 30th high school reunion mentioned earlier, Kerr discovered that many highly intelligent women, now age 50, had returned to their original interests and careers. Some—after discarding disagreeable husbands—also realized their dreams of travel to exotic spots.

See S. B. Rimm for good information how girls can flower into successful, professional women.[44]

Differences in Math and Science Ability?

In middle and high school, gifted females tend to avoid more challenging math and science courses.[45] Small wonder that, on average, more males than females score at the *very highest* levels on ACT math tests. Kerr emphasized that "Counselors should remember that the highest level of mathematical ability required by even the most rigorous math-related professions is well within the reach of gifted girls."[46] In fact, nearly two decades ago, Kerr and Colangelo studied high school students—males and females—who scored above the 95th percentile on the ACT.[47] Did they find gender differences in career aspirations? Not at all. As many females as males selected college majors in pre-medicine, pre-law, business, *and mathematics.*

Incidentally, females score higher than males on the English portions of the ACT.[48]

Counseling

School counselors can help close the male-female math gap by raising their own (yes, the counselors') expectations of females—for example, guiding talented females into harder math classes. Counselors also can help in the identification of very young gifted girls. Evidence of high intelligence, precocious math and reading, and high enthusiasm for school will support early admission to kindergarten or first grade, or later grade skipping.

Career counseling and career education should include biographies of highly successful women—including women with similar, perhaps troubled, backgrounds with whom the gifted girls can identify. The biographies should include the educational and other preparatory steps that led to success in the eminent women's professional areas.

Gifted females should personally meet with women role models—women who have succeeded in "math, politics, engineering, and other fields where women are rare."[49] Models should be selected who enjoy their lives and are passionate about their careers—not ones who complain about stress, being overworked, or having other career difficulties. Such inspirational women will illustrate how to successfully combine a career and a family. Many successful women have partners in the same career area who have the same values and goals.

Counselors also can help gifted girls identify barriers to their educational and career goals, as well as effective plans and steps (e.g., high school course-taking decisions) to overcome them.

Overall, noted Kerr, counselors can help gifted girls raise their aspirations, plan concrete future goals, analyze how relationships might affect their career development, understand how their interests and needs are unique, and realize the importance of selecting a career consistent with their values. Finally, Kerr also noted these two universal truths: "Choices made in late adolescence create clear limits on adult attainments,"[50] and "The rarer a woman's gift, the greater her responsibility to actualize that gift."[51]

Cultural Effects

Cultural circumstances are critical. Kerr studied "at risk" Arizona girls who had been earning "A's" in math, science, or both.[52] Problems of these gifted girls included being poor; victims of racism; involved in drugs, alcohol, or nicotine; or into early sex, sometimes with pregnancy. Some suffered from eating disorders or impulsiveness (e.g., openly calling the teacher a "slut"). Some took risks, such as having unprotected sex. Two-thirds were Hispanic or American Indian. They were smart, conceded Kerr, but made bad choices and were at risk for not achieving their goals. In her successful workshop, Kerr helped these girls believe in themselves and increased their ability to effectively control their lives. Kerr also explained to them that most eminent women had experienced problems and made some bad choices.

Recurring Problems

The following are some common psychological, social, educational, and career-planning problems of gifted students for which counseling is needed—sometimes desperately:

- Problems with social adjustment and social relationships
- Feelings of isolation, anxiety, depression
- In high school, worsening self-concepts of gifted girls
- Planning to drop out of high school
- Electing not to attend college
- Unrealistic expectations by parents
- Jealousy, resentment, and hostility by non-gifted parents and siblings
- Lack of challenge in school work
- Low achievement and poor study habits, due to rarely having to study
- Refusal to do routine, already-learned schoolwork.
- Nonconformity and resistance to authority
- Excessive competitiveness
- Difficulty accepting criticism
- Poor self-understanding
- Over-commitment with school and outside activities, resulting in excessive pressure
- Conformity pressures, including hiding talents in order to be accepted
- Name-calling by peers
- Believing that non-gifted peers—and sometimes teachers—dislike them

- Difficulty selecting a career
- Matching career interests with suitable universities
- Difficulty developing a satisfying philosophy of life
- Having a physical disability or a learning disability

Bibliotherapy: Aiding Emotional and Intellectual Development

Books can help gifted students at all grade levels to better understand their intellectual capabilities, emotions, and social circumstances. These are the goals of Judith Halsted's *Some of My Best Friends Are Books.*[53] Through reading, students discover others like themselves who have dealt with the same problems relating to feelings, emotions, social problems, and concerns for the future.[54] This is called bibliotherapy.

About one-fourth of gifted children—especially the highly gifted—have social and/or emotional problems. For example, they feel forced to fit in, but often do not. The result is reduced self-esteem. Reading aids understanding and coping with the problem. Partly for this reason, noted Halsted, *the first choice of enrichment for bright students should be reading books.*

Consider these age-related stages and challenges for high-ability children, all of which can be aided by suitable reading.

(1) Preschoolers must develop a positive self-concept. Books also aid intellectual growth.

(2) In the early grades, books can help children learn that they and others differ in ability. And while they need friends at their own high level, gifted children must value and enjoy all children.

(3) Upper elementary bright children sometimes choose between following their natural and easy enthusiasm for learning or concealing their ability to avoid alienating peers.[55] These children can read about topics that promote self-understanding, such as *giftedness, talent, motivations,* and *individual differences.*

(4) Middle school gifted students, if reasonably well-adjusted, cope nicely with common adolescent problems. They also should retain their good self-concept, which includes high intelligence and intellectual curiosity. Middle school students also learn more about their identities and social needs, perhaps in book discussions with other gifted students. By the end of middle school,

gifted students more clearly understand their capabilities, have a few close friends, and are quite comfortable with classmates of lesser ability.

(5) Bright high school students even better understand their high capabilities—and their weaknesses. They have the self-assurance to take risks, accept occasional failures, and continue working to better themselves. At this level, they must develop and use their capabilities without concern for what others think. Of course, they are keenly concerned with decisions that will shape their futures, particularly about college and career choices.

Important topics emphasized in Halsted's book recommendations are *achievement, aloneness, arrogance, creativity, developing imagination, differentness, drive to understand, identity, intensity, introversion, moral concerns, multipotentiality, perfectionism, relationships with others, self-image, sensitivity, using ability,* and *working alone. Some of My Best Friends Are Books* elaborates on these and other problems and then lists about 300 books in its extensive bibliography that deal with them, usually with a one-half to one-page description of each book.

Goals of Counseling

Counseling aims at self-discovery—helping gifted students understand their abilities, interests, values, and themselves generally. Counselors should become aware of gifted students' mental and emotional characteristics and their recurring problems. Counselors can help students deal with their personal and social difficulties, in addition to helping them make realistic educational and career plans.

The "counselor," incidentally, can be the teacher/coordinator for the gifted program or another teacher, mentor, or gifted peer, as well as the school counselor or school psychologist. All can help gifted students work through problems and understand that they are not abnormal, weird, nor alone.

Mary Landrum assembled counseling recommendations specific to elementary, middle, and secondary students in personal-social, academic, and career-vocational areas.[56] For example, counseling gifted elementary students involves helping them: (1) recognize their abilities, (2) understand similarities and differences between themselves and other children, (3) realize they cannot be superior in everything, (4) develop good attitudes toward school, (5) get along with others, (6) clarify their values, (7) find a good balance between educational and other activities, (8) experience a stimulating academic program, (9) strengthen problem-solving skills, and (10) resolve problems that interfere with learning.

A counselor can help middle school students: (1) understand and deal with the mental, social, emotional, and physical changes that happen in adolescence; (2) explore interests; and (3) select realistic educational and eventual career goals.

In high school, counselors can help gifted students: (1) clarify personal problems, (2) become more responsible for their futures, (3) analyze academic problems and needs, (4) develop study and test-taking skills, (5) select classes consistent with their interests, (6) explore possible career areas based on interests and strengths, and (7) consider universities consistent with their academic and career goals.

Counselors also can help gifted students resolve problems related to, for example, underachievement, social adjustment, or personal crises.[57] Counselors can help minority and low-income students deal with family or cultural value conflicts—for example, studying hard in school and being career-minded (e.g., "acting White") or aspiring to higher achievement than one's family. In addition, counselors can make arrangements for students to meet with mentors and other professional role models, which is doubly important for gifted minority students, who may rarely meet the highly successful members of their race. Again, bright females may need steering into math and science courses.

Counselors certainly should communicate with teachers and perhaps other school staff regarding the needs and problems of individual gifted students.

Group Counseling

With a trained counselor who understands both gifted youngsters and group dynamics, Colangelo concluded that "counselors can offer no more powerful tool for the social and emotional growth of gifted students than group counseling."[58] Such counseling provides gifted students the rare, safe, and open opportunities to share their struggles, insights, and questions about giftedness with other gifted students. How does it feel to be gifted? How does it feel to understand things (hypocrisy, human suffering, silly fads) that fellow students cannot? Gifted students can hardly discuss such matters with average peers.

Colangelo recommended the following types of questions to help students discover themselves and better understand their relationships with others: [59]

- What does it mean to be gifted?
- What do your parents think it means?
- What do your teachers think it means?
- What do other kids think being gifted means?
- How do you feel about being labeled "gifted"?
- How is being gifted an advantage? Today? In the future?
- How is being gifted a disadvantage? Today? In the future?
- If you were not gifted, what would be better for you? Worse?
- Have you ever deliberately hidden your giftedness? How?
- Have you ever deliberately underachieved?
- How is meeting with this group different from your regular school day?
- What does it mean to be gifted and Hispanic? Black? Asian? (Other race or nationality?)
- Would you rather be a gifted boy? A gifted girl?
- Is there a period of time in school—elementary, middle, or high school—when it is easiest to be gifted? More difficult to be gifted? Why?

Three final notes on counseling gifted students: first, some counselors may claim that "I'm too busy helping those who are almost certain to fail to be able to help those who are almost certain to succeed."[60] Second, in the counseling sessions many gifted students demonstrate a complex and articulate understanding of themselves—their abilities, personality, and likely educational and career goals. Third, some gifted students show a surprising interest in the counseling process itself. For example, they might analyze the counseling process and give the counselor constructive—and sometimes disconcerting—feedback on the counselor's effectiveness. The gifted students also may wish to know what the counselor believes and values.

Summary

- While most gifted students are better adjusted than average, the problems of extremely bright students include being too different from peers and uncomfortably aware of unfairness in the world.

- Counseling is an essential part of gifted programs, especially for the highly gifted.

- Very bright children may have problems with family, school, and peers. Home problems may include rejection by siblings or resisting parental authority.

- School problems can include social rejection due to their higher-level thinking, as well as boredom and apathy, depression, underachievement, and poor social and study skills

- Normal perfectionism drives high accomplishment. Neurotic perfectionism leads students to expect absolute perfection in everything. They become workaholics. Feelings of self-worth depend on high achievement.

- Teachers must recognize and understand perfectionism, encourage flexibility, lighten the class atmosphere, and help students accept mistakes. Parents can talk with their child and arrange counseling.

- Kerr's *Perfectionism Behavior Change Contract* includes, for example, deliberately being late for meetings and not completing tasks.

- Recurrent characteristics of gifted students include high activity, excitability, and sometimes inattentiveness. They may be incorrectly diagnosed as having ADHD. Webb et al. listed distinctions between ADHD children and gifted children.

- Some ("twice-exceptional") gifted children do have ADHD.

- Some characteristics of Asperger's Syndrome fit some gifted children: autism (fantasies), introversion, overexcitability, repetitive interests, talking early, excessive talking, and above-average mental abilities.

- Schizotypal personality disorder—and sometimes giftedness—includes, for example, eccentricity, sensitivity to criticism, underachievement, and having peculiar fantasies.

- Avoidant personality disorder includes, for example, shyness and fear of rejection. Gifted students also may be sensitive and introverted and may avoid high achievement that leads to teasing. But gifted students will not show a "panic disorder" nor avoid peers who share interests.

- Depression—from boredom and impatience—may be moderate or severe if a school ignores a gifted child's abilities and needs. Seligman called it *learned helplessness*. Existential depression stems from a gifted child's intelligence, sensitivity, and idealism. Webb et al. suggested helping such students realize that their feelings and ideals are shared by others.

- Gifted students who also are gay almost always have no peers, no role models, and no one with whom to discuss their sexual identity. Self-esteem usually is low, and the social climate may be dangerous. Recommendations include, for example, training counselors and staff to provide compassion, establish support groups, and reduce staff homophobia.

- Suicide rates for gifted students are no higher than for others, despite social isolation, high sensitivity, and awareness of world problems. Warning signs include, for example, suicide threats, low self-esteem, and self-destructive behaviors. Parents must learn about suicide, improve communication and trust, and support their children's needs and interests. The school can train staff and students in suicide prevention, schedule counseling, identify stress sources, and more.

- Multipotentiality refers to difficulty selecting a career due to gifted students' high ability and wide interests.

- *Early emergers* show strong talent and a focused interest at an early age. The focus continues into college and a professional career. Parents and teachers may worry about "well-roundedness."

- Kerr and Colangelo found that of 196 college majors, half of their high-ability high school students selected just five stereotyped majors. They concluded that there is a strong need for career counseling.

- Many gifted boys underachieve. They worry about social rejection due to their high mental ability. The "Boy Code" involves never showing weakness, acting macho, acquiring power and status, and not showing sympathy or other emotional responses. Meeting expectations of family and community may lead to forfeiting personal aspirations.

- The labels "sissy," "fat boy," "geek," "nerd," and "dork"—labels sometimes applied to students with high intellect—were suffered by many creative, eminent men.

- The category *minority* includes African Americans, Asians, Hispanics, and American Indians. Students within each group share cultural traditions and problems that often work against high achievement. American Indians typically are poor and isolated.

- Despite dramatic increases in women graduating in law, medicine, business, etc., women continue to avoid engineering and the hard sciences. They also may avoid (the stereotyped) teaching and nursing. A marriage-career lifestyle may be problematic. The "culture of romance" refers to valuing relationships with men over career achievement.

- Any math-related profession is "well within the reach" of gifted girls.

- Counselors can help identify gifted girls for early admission and acceleration. They also can help with career education and raising girls' aspirations.

- Problems of Kerr's Arizona gifted girls included being poor, drugs, pregnancy, eating disorders, and other risks.

- Other recurring counseling problems of gifted students include, for example, difficulties with social relationships, feelings of isolation and anxiety, planning to drop out of high school, planning not to attend college, problems with non-gifted parents and siblings, too-easy school work, poor study habits, resistance to authority, poor self-understanding, over-commitment and excessive pressure, conformity pressures, career selection, university selection, and having a physical or learning disability.

- Bibliotherapy helps gifted students, beginning at preschool age, to understand their capabilities, emotions, and social circumstances. Judith Halsted, author of *Some of My Best Friends Are Books*, feels that reading is the best type of enrichment.

- Counseling helps gifted students understand themselves and their abilities, deal with personal/social problems, and clarify educational and career plans.

- Landrum categorized counseling issues and recommendations at elementary, middle school, and high school levels.

- Counselors can help with values conflicts (e.g., "acting White"), arranging mentors/role models, and raising staff awareness of the needs of gifted students. Females may need steering into math and science courses.

- In group counseling, students share common problems and insights about giftedness.

References

Adams-Byers, J., Whitsell, S. S., & Moon, S. M. (2004). Gifted students' perceptions of the academic and social/emotional effects of homogeneous and heterogeneous grouping. *Gifted Child Quarterly, 48,* 7-20.

Adderholdt-Elliot, M. R. (1987). *Perfectionism: What's bad about being too good?* Minneapolis, MN: Free Spirit.

Adderholdt, M. R., & Goldberg, J. (1999). *What's bad about being too good?* Minneapolis, MN: Free Spirit.

Assouline, S. G., Colangelo, N., Lupkowski-Shoplik, A., Lipscomb, J., & Forstadt, L. (2003). *Iowa acceleration scale* (2nd ed.). Scottsdale, AZ: Great Potential Press, Inc.

Atkinson, J. W. (1978). Motivational determinants of intellective performance and cumulative achievement. In J. W. Atkinson & J. O. Raynor (Eds.), *Personality, motivation, and achievement* (pp. 221-242). New York: Wiley.

Baker, J. A. (1996). Everyday stressors of academically gifted adolescents. *Journal of Secondary Gifted Education, 7,* 356-368.

Baldwin, A. Y. (1985). *Baldwin identification matrix 2.* New York: Trillium.

Barell, J. (1991). *Teaching for thoughtfulness.* White Plains, NY: Longman.

Benbow, C. P., & Lubinski, D. (1997). Intellectually talented children: How can we best meet their needs? In N. Colangelo & G. A. Davis (Eds.), *Handbook of gifted education* (2nd ed., pp. 155-169). Boston: Allyn & Bacon.

Betts, G. T. (2004, November). *The social and emotional development of gifted children: What do we know?* Paper presented at the meeting of the National Association for Gifted Children, Salt Lake City, UT.

Betts, G. T., & Kercher, J. K. (1999). *Autonomous learner model: Optimizing ability.* Greeley, CO: Alps Publishing.

Binet, A., & Simon, T. (1905a). Methodes nouvelles pour le diagnostic du niveau intellectuel des anormaux. [New methods for the diagnosis of the intellectual levels of subnormals]. *L'Année Psychologique, 11,* 191-244.

Binet, A., & Simon, T. (1905b). Sur la necessité d'établir un diagnostic scientific des états inférieurs de l'intelligence. [The necessity for establishing diagnostic criteria for subnormal intelligence]. *L'Année Psychologique, 11,* 163-190.

Bloom, B. S., Englehart, M. D., Furst, E. J., Hill, W. H., & Krathwohl, D. R. (1956). *Taxonomy of educational objectives, handbook I: Cognitive domain.* New York: Longmans Green.

Bohnenberger, J., & Terry, A. (2004, November). *Service learning: Inspiring gifted minds through social action.* Paper presented at the meeting of the National Association for Gifted Children, Salt Lake City, UT.

Brennan, R. (2004, May). *The current revolution in testing.* Keynote presentation at the Seventh Biennial Henry B. & Jocelyn Wallace National Research Symposium on Talent Development, Iowa City, IA.

Brody, L. E., & Benbow, C. P. (1987). Accelerative strategies: How effective are they for the gifted? *Gifted Child Quarterly, 31,* 105-110.

Callard-Szulgit, R. (2003). *Parenting and teaching the gifted child.* Lanham, MD: Scarecrow Press.

Callard-Szulgit, R. (2004, November). *Parenting and teaching the gifted.* Paper presented at the meeting of the National Association for Gifted Children, Salt Lake City, UT.

Chae, P. K., Kim, J. H., & Noh, K. S. (2003). Diagnosis of ADHD among gifted children in Relation to DEKI-WISC and T.O.V.A. performance. *Gifted Child Quarterly, 47,* 192-201.

Cohn, S. J. (2002). Gifted students who are gay, lesbian, or bisexual. In M. Neihart, S. M. Reis, N. M. Robinson, & S. M. Moon (Eds.), *Social and emotional development of gifted children: What do we know?* (pp. 145-153). Washington, DC: National Association for Gifted Children.

Cohn, S. J., Carson, E. S., & Adams, D. (2004, November). *How homophobia hurts gifted kids.* Paper presented at the meeting of the National Association for Gifted Children, Salt Lake City, UT.

Cohn, S. J., Kerr, B. A., Carson, E. S., & Adams, D. (2004, November). *Gifted gone wrong: Brilliant sociopaths and bad girls.* Paper presented at the meeting of the National Association for Gifted Children, Salt Lake City, UT.

Colangelo, N. (2003). Counseling gifted students. In N. Colangelo & G. A. Davis (Eds.), *Handbook of gifted education* (3rd ed., pp. 373-387). Boston: Allyn & Bacon.

Colangelo, N. (2004, May). *The Templeton national report on acceleration.* Keynote presentation at the Seventh Biennial Henry B. & Jocelyn Wallace National Research Symposium on Talent Development, Iowa City, IA.

Colangelo, N., & Assouline, S. G. (2000). Counseling gifted students. In K. A. Heller, F. J. Mönks, R. J. Sternberg, & R. F. Subotnik (Eds.), *International handbook of giftedness and talent* (2nd ed., pp. 595-607). New York: Elsevier.

Colangelo, N., & Davis, G. A. (Eds.). (2003). *Handbook of gifted education* (3rd ed.). Boston: Allyn & Bacon.

Colangelo, N., & Kerr, B. A. (1990). Extreme academic talent: Profiles of perfect scorers. *Journal of Educational Psychology, 82,* 404-409.

Coleman, L. J., & Cross, T. L. (2000). Social-emotional development and the personal experience of giftedness. In K. A. Heller, F. J. Mönks, R. J. Sternberg, & R. F. Subotnik (Eds.), *International handbook of giftedness and talent* (2nd ed., pp. 203-212). New York: Elsevier.

Connor, E. W. (1991). Gifted all the time. *Gifted Child Today, 14*(5), 14-17.

Costa, A. L. (2003). In the habit of skillful thinking. In N. Colangelo & G. A. Davis (Eds.), *Handbook of gifted education* (3rd ed., pp. 325-334). Boston: Allyn & Bacon.

Cox, J. N., Daniel, N., & Boston, B. O. (1985). *Educating able learners: Programs and promising practices.* Austin, TX: University of Texas Press.

Cramond, B. (1994). Attention-deficit hyperactivity disorder and creativity—What is the connection? *Journal of Creative Behavior, 28,* 193-210.

Crawford, R. P. (1954). *Techniques of creative thinking.* New York: Hawthorne Books.

Croft, L. J. (2003). Teachers of the gifted: Gifted teachers. In N. Colangelo & G. A. Davis (Eds.), *Handbook of gifted education* (3rd ed., pp. 558-571). Boston: Allyn & Bacon.

Cropley, A. J., & Urban, K. K. (2000). Programs and strategies for nurturing creativity. In K. A. Heller, F. J. Mönks, R. J. Sternberg, & R. F. Subotnik (Eds.), *International handbook of giftedness and talent* (2nd ed., pp. 485-498). New York: Elsevier.

Cross, T. L., Hernandez, N. R., & Coleman, L. J. (1991). Governor's schools: An idea whose time has come. *Gifted Child Today, 14*(3), 29-30.

Dabrowski, K. (1967). *Personality shaping through positive disintegration.* Boston: Little, Brown.

Davidson, J., Davidson, B., & Vanderkam, L. (2004). *Genius denied: How to stop wasting our brightest young minds.* New York: Simon & Schuster.

Davis, G. A. (1975). In frumious pursuit of the creative person. *Journal of Creative Behavior, 9,* 75-87.

Davis, G. A. (1989). Testing for creative potential. *Contemporary Educational Psychology, 14,* 257-274.

Davis, G. A. (2004). *Creativity is forever* (5th ed.). Dubuque, IA: Kendall/Hunt.

Davis, G. A., & Rimm, S. B. (2004). *Education of the gifted and talented* (5th ed.). Boston: Allyn & Bacon.

de Bono, E. (1983). The direct teaching of thinking as a skill. *Phi Delta Kappan, 64,* 703-708.

de Bono, E. (1985, September). Partnerships of the mind: Teaching society to think. *ProEducation,* 56-58.

de Bono, E. (1986). *CoRT thinking skills program.* Oxford, England: Pergamon Press.

de Bono, E. (1992). *Serious creativity.* HarperCollins.

Dixon, F. A., Lapsley, D. K., & Hanchon, T. A. (2004). An empirical typology of perfectionism in gifted adolescents. *Gifted Child Quarterly, 48*, 95-106.

Duff, C. (2000, October). Online mentoring. *Educational Leadership,* 49-52.

Eisenberg, D., & Epstein, E. (1981, December). *The discovery and development of giftedness in handicapped children.* Paper presented at the meeting of the CEC-TAG National Topical Conference on the Gifted and Talented Child, Orlando, FL.

Elkind, D. (1981). *The hurried child: Growing up too fast too soon.* Reading, MA: Addison-Wesley.

Ellingson, M., Haeger, W., & Feldhusen, J. F. (1986, March/April). The Purdue mentor program. *G/C/T,* 2-53.

Evans, R. P. (2004, November). *Welcome to Salt Lake City.* Keynote address presented at the meeting of the National Association for Gifted Children, Salt Lake City, UT.

Feldhusen, J. F. (1991). Saturday and summer programs. In N. Colangelo & G. A. Davis (Eds.), *Handbook of gifted education* (pp. 197-208). Boston: Allyn & Bacon.

Feldhusen, J. F. (1992). Talent identification and development in education. *Gifted Child Quarterly, 36*, 123.

Feldhusen, J. F. (1997). Educating teachers for work with talented youth. In N. Colangelo & G. A. Davis (Eds.), *Handbook of gifted education* (2nd ed., pp. 547-552). Boston: Allyn & Bacon.

Feldhusen, J. F., & Jarwan, F. A. (2000). Identification of gifted and talented youth for educational programs. In K. A. Heller, F. J. Mönks, R. J. Sternberg, & R. F. Subotnik (Eds.), *International handbook of giftedness and talent* (2nd ed., pp. 271-282). New York: Elsevier.

Feldhusen, J. F., & Kolloff, P. B. (1986). The Purdue three-stage enrichment model for gifted education at the elementary level. In J. S. Renzulli (Ed.), *Systems and models for developing programs for the gifted and talented* (pp. 126-151). Mansfield Center, CT: Creative Learning Press.

Feldhusen, J. F., & Sayler, M. F. (1990). Special classes for academically gifted youth. *Roeper Review, 12*, 244-249.

Feuerstein, R. (1980). *Instrumental enrichment: An intervention program for cognitive modifiability.* Baltimore, MD: University Park Press.

Fiedler, E. D. (2004, November). *Career counseling for globally gifted kids.* Paper presented at the meeting of the National Association for Gifted Children, Salt Lake City, UT.

Fleith, D. (2001, Spring). Suicide among gifted adolescents: How to prevent it. *National Research Center on the Gifted and Talented Newsletter*, 6-8.

Flower, L., & Hayes, J. R. (1984). Images, plans, and prose. *Written Communication, 1*(1), 120-160.

Ford, D. Y. (2004, November). *Should the field of gifted education use traditional or nontraditional tools for identifying students for program services?* Presentation at Great Debate #1 at the meeting of the National Association for Gifted Children, Salt Lake City, UT.

Fox, L. H. (1979). Programs for the gifted and talented: An overview. In A. H. Passow (Ed.), *The gifted and talented* (pp. 104-126). Chicago: National Society for the Study of Education.

Frasier, M. M. (1994). *A manual for implementing the Frasier Talent Assessment Profile (F-TAP)*. Athens, GA. Georgia Southern Press.

Freeman, J. M., & Williams, M. T. (2004, November). *Inspiring global citizens.* Paper presented at the meeting of the National Association for Gifted Children, Salt Lake City, UT.

Friedman, R. C., & Shore, B. (Eds.). (2000). *Talents unfolding: Cognition and development*. Washington, DC: American Psychological Association.

Frost, D. (1981, December). *The great debates: For enrichment.* Paper presented at the meeting of the CEC-TAG National Topical Conference on the Gifted and Talented Child, Orlando, FL.

Gagné, F. (2003). Transforming gifts into talents: The DMGT as a developmental theory. In N. Colangelo & G. A. Davis (Eds.), *Handbook of gifted education* (3rd ed., pp. 60-74). Boston: Allyn & Bacon.

Gallagher, J. J. (2000). Changing paradigms for gifted education in the United States. In K. A. Heller, F. J. Mönks, R. J. Sternberg, & R. F. Subotnik (Eds.), *International handbook of giftedness and talent* (2nd ed., pp. 681-693). New York: Elsevier.

Gallagher, J. J. (2004, November). *Should gifted programs and curricula focus more on cognitive or affective development?* Presentation at Great Debate #2 at the meeting of the National Association for Gifted Children, Salt Lake City, UT.

Gardner, H. (1983). *Frames of mind: The theory of multiple intelligences*. New York: Basic Books.

Gardner, H. (1999). *Intelligence reframed: Multiple intelligences for the 21st century*. New York: Basic Books.

Gentry, M. L., & Ferriss, S. (1999). A model of collaboration to develop science talent among rural middle school students. *Roeper Review, 21*, 316-320.

Gifted Child Society. (1990). *The Saturday workshop: Activities for gifted children and their parents*. Glen Rock, NJ: Author.

Goleman, D. G. (1995). *Emotional intelligence: Why it can matter more than IQ.* New York: Bantam Books.

Goodlad, J., & Oakes, J. (1988). We must offer equal access to knowledge. *Educational Leadership, 45,* 16-22.

Greenspon, T. S. (2000). "Healthy perfectionism" is an oxymoron!: Reflections on the psychology of perfectionism and the sociology of science. *Journal of Secondary Gifted Education, 12,* 197-208.

Gross, M. U. M. (1992). The early development of three profoundly gifted children of IQ 200. In P. Klein & A. J. Tannenbaum (Eds.), *To be young and gifted* (pp. 94-140). Norwood, NJ: Ablex.

Gross, M. U. M. (1993a). *Exceptionally gifted children.* New York: Routledge.

Gross, M. U. M. (1993b). The use of radical acceleration in cases of extreme intellectual precocity. *Gifted Child Quarterly, 36,* 91-99.

Gross, M. U. M. (2000). Issues in the cognitive development of exceptionally and profoundly gifted individuals. In K. A. Heller, F. J. Mönks, R. J. Sternberg, & R. F. Subotnik (Eds.), *International handbook of giftedness and talent* (2nd ed., pp. 179-192). New York: Elsevier.

Gross, M. U. M. (2004, May). *Exceptionally gifted children grown up: Findings from the second decade of a longitudinal study.* Keynote presentation at the Seventh Biennial Henry B. & Jocelyn Wallace National Research Symposium on Talent Development, Iowa City, IA.

Halsted, J. W. (2002). *Some of my best friends are books: Guiding gifted readers from preschool to high school* (2nd ed.). Scottsdale, AZ: Great Potential Press, Inc.

Han, K. S., & Marvin, C. (2000). A five year follow-up study of the Nebraska Project: Still a long way to go. *Roeper Review, 23,* 25-33.

Helms, J. E. (1992). Why is there no study of cultural equivalence in standardized cognitive ability testing? *American Psychologist, 47,* 1083-1101.

Henry, A. (2004, May 2). How low will Hollywood go in search of stories? *Wisconsin State Journal,* G4, G11.

Hickey, M. G. (1990). Classroom teachers' concerns and recommendations for improvement of gifted programs. *Roeper Review, 12,* 265-267.

Hollinger, C. L., & Kosek, S. (1986). Beyond the use of full scale IQ scores. *Gifted Child Quarterly, 30,* 74-77.

Hollingworth, L. S. (1942). *Children above 180 IQ Stanford-Binet: Origin and development.* New York: World Book.

Hollingsworth, P. L. (1991). Parts of the whole: Private schools, public schools, and the community. *Gifted Child Today, 14*(5), 54-56.

Hsu, L. (2003). Measuring the effectiveness of summer intensive physics courses for gifted students. *Gifted Child Quarterly, 47,* 212-218.

Hunkins, F. P. (1976). *Involving students in questioning.* Boston: Allyn & Bacon.

Isaacson, K. L. J. (2002). *Raisin' brains: Surviving my smart family*. Scottsdale, AZ: Great Potential Press, Inc.

Isaksen, S. G., & De Schryver, L. (2000). Making a difference with CPS: A summary of the evidence. In S. G. Isaksen (Ed.), *Facilitative leadership: Making a difference with creative problem solving* (pp. 187-248). Dubuque, IA: Kendall/Hunt.

Jacobsen, M. (2004, May). *Perfectionism vs. the urge to perfect in gifted adults: Research and reality*. Presentation at the Seventh Biennial Henry B. & Jocelyn Wallace National Research Symposium on Talent Development, Iowa City, IA.

Jenkins, R. C. (1979). *The identification of gifted and talented students through peer nomination*. Unpublished doctoral dissertation, University of Connecticut, Storrs, CT. *Dissertation Abstracts International, 40*, 167A.

Jensen, A. W. (2004, May). *The fallacies of research on mental ability*. Presentation at the Seventh Biennial Henry B. & Jocelyn Wallace National Research Symposium on Talent Development, Iowa City, IA.

Johnson, S. K., Haensley, P. A., Ryser, G. R., & Ford, R. F. (2002). Changing general education classroom practices to adapt for gifted students. *Gifted Child Quarterly, 46*, 45-63.

Juntune, J. E. (1981). *Successful programs for the gifted and talented*. Washington, DC: National Association for the Gifted and Talented.

Kane, M., & Roeper, A. (2004, November). *The road from dependence to interdependence*. Paper presented at the meeting of the National Association for Gifted Children, Salt Lake City, UT.

Kaplan, S. N. (1974). *Providing programs for the gifted and talented*. Ventura, CA: Office of the Ventura County Superintendent of Schools.

Kaplan, S. N. (2004a, November). *The achievement gap among the gifted and its relationship to differentiation of curriculum and instruction*. Presentation at Great Debate #2 at the meeting of the National Association for Gifted Children, Salt Lake City, UT.

Kaplan, S. N. (2004b, November). *Should gifted programs and curricula focus more on cognitive or affective development?* Paper presented at the meeting of the National Association for Gifted Children, Salt Lake City, UT.

Kardaras, K. (2004, November). *Embedding international experience in interdisciplinary curriculum*. Paper presented at the meeting of the National Association for Gifted Children, Salt Lake City, UT.

Karnes, F. A., & Marquardt, R. G. (2000). *Gifted children and legal issues: An update*. Scottsdale, AZ: Great Potential Press, Inc.

Karnes, F. A., & Marquardt, R. G. (2003). Gifted education and legal issues: Procedures and recent decisions. In N. Colangelo & G. A. Davis (Eds.), *Handbook of gifted education* (3rd ed., pp. 590-603). Boston: Allyn & Bacon.

Karnes, F. A., & Riley, T. L. (1996). *Competitions: Maximizing your abilities.* Waco, TX: Prufrock Press.

Kaufmann, F., Kalbfleisch, M. L., & Castellanos, F. X. (2000). *Attention deficit disorders and gifted students: What do we really know?* Storrs, CT: National Research Center on the Gifted and Talented, University of Connecticut.

Kelble, E. S. (1991). Overview of private schools for the gifted. *Gifted Child Today, 14*(5), 2-4.

Kerr, B. A. (1991). *A handbook for counseling the gifted and talented.* Alexandria, VA: American Association for Counseling and Development.

Kerr, B. A. (1994). *Smart girls* (rev. ed.) Scottsdale, AZ: Great Potential Press, Inc.

Kerr, B. A., & Cohn, S. J. (2001). *Smart boys.* Scottsdale, AZ: Great Potential Press, Inc.

Kerr, B. A., & Colangelo, N. (1988). The college plans of academically talented students. *Journal of Counseling and Development, 67*(1), 42-49.

Kerr, B. A., Kurpius, S. E. R., & Harkins, A. (Eds.). (2005). *Handbook for counseling girls and women: Ten years of gender equity research at Arizona State University, Vol. 2. Talent Development.* Mesa, AZ: Nueva Science Press.

Kirschenbaum, H., & Henderson, V. L. (Eds.). (1989). *The Carl Rogers reader.* New York: Houghton Mifflin.

Klein, A. G. (2002). *A forgotten voice: A biography of Leta Stetter Hollingworth.* Scottsdale, AZ: Great Potential Press, Inc.

Kolloff, P. B. (2003). State-supported residential high schools. In N. Colangelo & G. A. Davis (Eds.), *Handbook of gifted education* (3rd ed., pp. 238-246). Boston: Allyn & Bacon.

Kottke, C. (2003, July 20). Students learn to solve problems creatively at Camp Invention. *Wisconsin State Journal,* D11.

Kulik, J. A. (2003). Grouping and tracking. In N. Colangelo & G. A. Davis (Eds.), *Handbook of gifted education* (3rd ed., pp. 268-281). Boston: Allyn & Bacon.

Kurpius, S. E. R., Kerr, B. A., & Harkins, A. (Eds.). (2005). *Handbook for counseling girls and women: Ten years of gender equity research at Arizona State University, Vol. 2. Talent, Risk and Resiliency.* Mesa, AZ: Nueva Science Press.

Landrum, M. S. (1987). Guidelines for implementing a guidance/counseling program for gifted and talented students. *Roeper Review, 10,* 103-107.

Leader, W. (1995, November). *How and why to encourage metacognition in learners.* Paper presented at the meeting of the National Association for Gifted Children, Tampa, FL.

Leroux, J. A., & Levitt-Perlman, M. (2000). The gifted child with attention deficit disorder: An identification and intervention challenge. *Roeper Review, 22,* 171-176.

Link, F. R. (1985). *Essays on the intellect*. Alexandria, VA: Association for Supervision and Curriculum Development.

Lipman, M. (1988). *Philosophy goes to school*. Philadelphia: Temple University Press.

Lipman, M. (1991). *Thinking in education*. New York: Cambridge University Press.

Lohman, D. (2004, May). *An aptitude perspective on talent development*. Keynote presentation at the Seventh Biennial Henry B. & Jocelyn Wallace National Research Symposium on Talent Development, Iowa City, IA.

Lombroso, C. (1895). *The man of genius*. London: Scribners.

Lupkowski-Shoplik, A., Benbow, C. P., Assouline, S. G., & Brody, L. E. (2003). Talent searches: Meeting the needs of academically talented youth. In N. Colangelo & G. A. Davis (Eds.), *Handbook of gifted education* (3rd ed., pp. 204-218). Boston: Allyn & Bacon.

Maker, S. J. (1980). On instrumental enrichment: A conversation with Frances Link. *Educational Leadership, 38*, 569-571, 582.

Marland, S. (1972). *Education of the gifted and talented*. U.S. Commission on Education, 92nd Congress, 2nd Session. Washington, DC: U.S.C.P.O.

Marshall, B. C. (1981). Career decision-making patterns of gifted and talented adolescents. *Journal of Career Education, 7*, 305-310.

Maslow, A. H. (1970). *Motivation and personality* (2nd ed.). New York: Harper & Row.

Matarazzo, J. D. (1972). *Wechsler's measurement and appraisal of adult intelligence*. London: Oxford University Press.

Mathews, J. (2001, August 7). IB or not IB?: Many colleges decline credit for some advanced courses. *Washington Post*.

McCarney, S. B., & Anderson, P. D. (1998). *Gifted evaluation scale* (2nd ed.). Columbus, MO: Hawthorne Educational Services.

McClusky, K. W., Baker, P. A., & Massey, K. J. (1996). A twenty-four year longitudinal look at early entrance to kindergarten. *Gifted and Talented International, 11*, 72-75

McCoach, D. B., & Siegle, D. (2003). Factors that differentiate underachieving gifted students from high-achieving gifted students. *Gifted Child Quarterly, 47*, 144-154.

Millar, G. W. (1995). *E. Paul Torrance: "The creativity man."* Norwood, NJ: Ablex.

Mills, C. J. (2003). Characteristics of effective teachers of gifted students: Teacher background and personality styles of students. *Gifted Child Quarterly, 47*, 272-281.

Morelock, M. J. (1995). *The profoundly gifted child in family context*. Unpublished doctoral dissertation, Tufts University, Medford, MA.

Morelock, M. J. (2000). A sociohistorical perspective on exceptionally high-IQ children. In R. C. Friedman & B. Shore (Eds.), *Talents unfolding: Cognition and development* (pp. 55-75). Washington, DC: American Psychological Association.

Morelock, M. J., & Feldman, D. H. (2000). Prodigies, savants and Williams syndrome: Windows into talent and cognition. In K. A. Heller, F. J. Monks, R. J. Sternberg, & R. F. Subotnik (Eds.), *International handbook of giftedness and talent* (2nd ed., pp. 227-241). New York: Elsevier.

Morelock, M. J., & Feldman, D. H. (2003). Extreme precocity: Prodigies, savants, and children of extraordinarily high IQ. In N. Colangelo & G. A. Davis (Eds.), *Handbook of gifted education* (3rd ed., pp. 455-469). Boston: Allyn & Bacon.

Mosley, J. H. (1982, November/December). Ten suggestions to insure the brevity of your gifted program. *G/C/T*, 46.

Muratori, M., Colangelo, N., & Assouline, S. (2003). Early-entrance students: Impressions of their first semester of college. *Gifted Child Quarterly, 47,* 219-237.

Naglieri, J. (2004, November). *Should the field of gifted education use traditional or nontraditional tools for identifying students for program services?* Presentation at Great Debate #1 at the meeting of the National Association for Gifted Children, Salt Lake City, UT.

National Association for Gifted Children. (1998). *Pre-K–grade 12 gifted program standards.* Washington, DC: Author.

National Association for Gifted Children. (2000). Web sites to help teachers create more challenging curriculum for gifted students. *Teaching for High Potential, 2*(2), 1-4.

Navan, J. L. (2004, November). *Developing self-actualizing behaviors through the exploration of global education principles.* Paper presented at the meeting of the National Association for Gifted Children, Salt Lake City, UT.

Neihart, M. (1999). Systematic risk-taking. *Roeper Review, 21,* 289-292.

Neihart, M., Reis, S. M., Robinson, N. M., & Moon, S. M. (Eds.). (2002). *Social and emotional development of gifted children: What do we know?* Washington, DC: National Association for Gifted Children.

Oakes, J. (1985). *Keeping track.* New Haven, CT: Yale University Press.

Olszewski-Kubilius, P. (2003). Special summer and Saturday programs. In N. Colangelo & G. A. Davis (Eds.), *Handbook of gifted education* (3rd ed., pp. 219-228). Boston: Allyn & Bacon.

Orange County Department of Education. (1981). *Project IMPACT.* Costa Mesa, CA: Author.

Osborn, A. F. (1963). *Applied imagination* (3rd ed.). New York: Scribners.

Parnes, S. J. (1981). *Magic of your mind*. Buffalo, NY: Creative Education Foundation.

Peterson, J. S. (2004, November). *The social and emotional development of gifted children: What do we know?* Paper presented at the meeting of the National Association for Gifted Children, Salt Lake City, UT.

Peterson, J. S., & Rischar, H. (2000). Gifted and gay: A study of the adolescent experience. *Gifted Child Quarterly, 44*, 231-246.

Piechowski, M. M. (1997). Emotional giftedness: The measure of intrapersonal intelligence. In N. Colangelo & G. A. Davis (Eds.), *Handbook of gifted education* (2nd ed., pp. 366-381). Boston: Allyn & Bacon.

Piirto, J. (2004). *Understanding creativity*. Scottsdale, AZ: Great Potential Press, Inc.

Plucker, J. A. (2004, November). *Should gifted programs and curricula focus more on cognitive or affective development?* Presentation at Great Debate #2 at the meeting of the National Association for Gifted Children, Salt Lake City, UT.

Pollock, W. (1998). *Real boys: Rescuing your sons from the myths of boyhood*. New York: Holt.

Prillaman, D., & Richardson, R. (1989). The William and Mary mentorship model: College students as a resource for the gifted. *Roeper Review, 12*, 114-118.

Purcell, J. H. (1995). Gifted education at a crossroads: The program status study. *Gifted Child Quarterly, 39*, 57-65.

Reis, S. M., & Burns, D. E. (1987). A schoolwide enrichment team invites you to read about methods for promoting community and faculty involvement in a gifted education program. *Gifted Child Today, 49*(2), 27-32.

Reis, S. M., Gentry, M. L., & Maxfield, L. R. (1998). The application of enrichment clusters to teachers' classroom practices. *Journal for the Education of the Gifted, 21*, 310-334.

Reis, S. M., & McCoach, D. B. (2003). The underachievement of gifted students: What do we know and where do we go? *Gifted Child Quarterly, 44*, 152-170.

Renzulli, J. S. (1977). *Enrichment triad model: A guide for developing defensible programs for the gifted and talented*. Mansfield, CT: Creative Learning Press.

Renzulli, J. S. (1986). (Ed.). *Systems and models for developing programs for the gifted and talented*. Mansfield Center, CT: Creative Learning Press.

Renzulli, J. S. (1994). *Schools for talent development: A practical plan for total school improvement*. Mansfield Center, CT: Creative Learning Press.

Renzulli, J. S. (1995, November). *Past reflections—Future directions*. Address presented at the meeting of the National Association for Gifted Children, Tampa, FL.

Renzulli, J. S. (2003). A conception of giftedness and its relationship to the development of social capital. In N. Colangelo & G. A. Davis (Eds.), *Handbook of gifted education* (3rd ed., pp. 75-87). Boston: Allyn & Bacon.

Renzulli, J. S. (2004, November). *Should the field of gifted education use traditional or nontraditional tools for identifying students for program services?* Presentation at Great Debate #1 at the meeting of the National Association for Gifted Children, Salt Lake City, UT.

Renzulli, J. S., & Park, S. (2000). Gifted dropouts: The who and the why. *Gifted Child Quarterly, 44*, 261-271.

Renzulli, J. S., & Reis, S. M. (1985). *The schoolwide enrichment model: A comprehensive plan for educational excellence.* Mansfield Center, CT: Creative Learning Press.

Renzulli, J. S., & Reis, S. M. (1991). The reform movement and the quiet crisis in gifted education. *Gifted Child Quarterly, 35*, 26-35.

Renzulli, J. S., & Reis, S. M. (1997). *The schoolwide enrichment model: A how-to-guide for educational excellence* (2nd ed.). Mansfield Center, CT: Creative Learning Press.

Renzulli, J. S., & Reis, S. M. (2003). Schoolwide enrichment model: Developing creative and productive giftedness. In N. Colangelo & G. A. Davis (Eds.), *Handbook of gifted education* (3rd ed., pp. 184-203). Boston: Allyn & Bacon.

Renzulli, J. S., Smith, L., White, A., Callahan, C., & Hartman, R. (2001). *Scales for rating the behavioral characteristics of superior students* (rev. ed.). Manual and nine rating scales. Mansfield Center, CT: Creative Learning Press.

Richards, R. L. (1999). Affective disorders. In M. A. Runco & S. R. Pritzker (Eds.), *Encyclopedia of creativity* (Vol. 1, pp. 31-43). New York: Academic Press.

Richert, E. S. (1997). Excellence with equity in identification and programming. In N. Colangelo & G. A. Davis (Eds.), *Handbook of gifted education* (2nd ed., pp. 75-88). Boston: Allyn & Bacon.

Richert, E. S. (2003). Excellence with justice in identification and programming. In N. Colangelo & G. A. Davis (Eds.), *Handbook of gifted education* (3rd ed., pp. 146-158). Boston: Allyn & Bacon.

Richert, E. S., Alvino, J., & McDonnel, R. (1982). *National report on identification: Assessment and recommendations for comprehensive identification of gifted and talented youth.* Sewell, NJ: Educational Information and Resource Center.

Rimm, S. B. (2003). *See Jane win for girls: a smart girl's guide to success.* Minneapolis, MN: Free Spirit Publishing.

Rimm, S. B. (2004, November). *Should the field of gifted education use traditional or nontraditional tools for identifying students for program services?* Presentation at Great Debate #1 at the meeting of the National Association for Gifted Children, Salt Lake City, UT.

Rimm, S. B. (2005). Winning girls, winning women. *Gifted Education International,* Vol. 19, No. 3.

Rimm, S. B., & Rimm-Kaufman, S. (2001). *How Jane won: fifty-five successful women share how they grew from ordinary girls to extraordinary women.* New York: Crown.

Rimm, S. B., & Rimm-Kaufman, S. (1999). *See Jane win: The Rimm report on how 1000 girls became successful women.* New York: Crown.

Rivero, L. (2002). *Creative home schooling for gifted children: A resource guide.* Scottsdale, AZ: Great Potential Press, Inc.

Robinson, A. E., Anthony, T. S., Ross, P. O., & Baldus, C. (2004, November). *Appropriateness of AP and IB for secondary gifted students.* Paper presented at the meeting of the National Association for Gifted Children, Salt Lake City, UT.

Robinson, N. M. (2004, November). *Should the field of gifted education use traditional or nontraditional tools for identifying students for program services?* Presentation at Great Debate #1 at the meeting of the National Association for Gifted Children, Salt Lake City, UT.

Roeper, A. (1995). *Annemarie Roeper: Selecting writings and speeches.* Minneapolis, MN: Free Spirit.

Roeper, A. (2004a, November). *The gifted self in joy and grief.* Paper presented at the meeting of the National Association for Gifted Children, Salt Lake City, UT.

Roeper, A. (2004b). *Learning about an expanded reality from the spiritually gifted.* Unpublished report, Roeper Consultation Services, El Cerrito, California.

Rogers, K. B. (1991). *The relationship of grouping practices to the education of the gifted and talented learner.* Storrs, CT: National Research Center on the Gifted and Talented, University of Connecticut.

Rogers, K. B. (2002). *Re-forming gifted education: How parents and teachers can match the program to the child.* Scottsdale, AZ: Great Potential Press, Inc.

Rogers, K. B. (2004, November). *Should gifted programs and curricula focus more on cognitive or affective development?* Presentation at Great Debate #2 at the meeting of the National Association for Gifted Children, Salt Lake City, UT.

Ross, P. O. (1993). *National excellence: A case for developing America's talent.* Washington, DC: U.S. Department of Education.

Ruf, D. L. (2005). *Losing our minds: Gifted children left behind.* Scottsdale, AZ: Great Potential Press.

Russo, C., Harris, J., & Ford, D. Y. (1996). Gifted education and the law: A right, privilege, or superfluous. *Roeper Review, 18,* 179-182.

Sapon-Shevin, M. (1994). *Playing favorites: Gifted education and the disruption of community.* Albany, NY: State University of New York Press.

Schiever, S. W., & Maker, C. J. (2003). New directions in enrichment and acceleration. In N. Colangelo & G. A. Davis (Eds.), *Handbook of gifted education* (2nd ed., pp. 163-173). Boston: Allyn & Bacon.

Schlichter, C. L. (1986). Talents unlimited: An inservice educational model for teaching thinking skills. *Gifted Child Quarterly, 30,* 119, 123.

Schlichter, C. L. (1997). Talents unlimited model in programs for gifted students. In N. Colangelo & G. A. Davis (Eds.), *Handbook of gifted education* (2ⁿᵈ ed., pp. 318-327). Boston: Allyn & Bacon.

Schuler, P. A. (1999). *Voices of perfectionism: Perfectionistic gifted adolescents in a rural middle school.* Storrs, CT: National Research Center on the Gifted and Talented.

Seligman, M. E. P. (1975). *Helplessness: On depression, development and death.* San Francisco: Freeman.

Seligman, M. E. P. (1995). *The optimistic child: A proven program to safeguard children against depression and build lifelong resilience.* New York: HarperCollins.

Shivvers, M. D. (2004, November). *Adventure in creativity, architecture, and design—and the shapes of mathematics.* Paper presented at the meeting of the National Association for Gifted Children, Salt Lake City, UT.

Siegle, D., & Powell, T. (2004). Exploring teacher biases when nominating students for gifted programs. *Gifted Child Quarterly, 48,* 21-29.

Siegle, D., & Schuler, P. A. (2000). Perfectionism differences in gifted middle school students. *Roeper Review, 23,* 39-44.

Silverman, L. K. (1994). The moral sensitivity of gifted children and the evolution of society. *Roeper Review, 17,* 110-116.

Silverman, L. K. (1997). Family counseling with the gifted. In N. Colangelo & G. A. Davis (Eds.), *Handbook of gifted education* (2ⁿᵈ ed., pp. 382-397). Boston: Allyn & Bacon.

Silverman, L. K. (2002a). Asynchronous development. In M. Neihart, S. M. Reis, N. M. Robinson, & S. M. Moon (Eds.), *Social and emotional development of gifted children: What do we know?* (pp. 145-153). Washington, DC: National Association for Gifted Children.

Silverman, L. K. (2002b). *Upside-down brilliance: The visual-spatial learner.* Denver, CO: DeLeon Publishing.

Simonton, D. K. (2000). Genius and giftedness: Same or different? In K. A. Heller, F. J. Mönks, R. J. Sternberg, & R. F. Subotnik (Eds.), *International handbook of giftedness and talent* (2ⁿᵈ ed., pp. 111-121). New York: Elsevier.

Simonton, D. K. (2003). When does giftedness become genius? And when not? In N. Colangelo & G. A. Davis (Eds.), *Handbook of gifted education* (3ʳᵈ ed., pp. 358-370). Boston: Allyn & Bacon.

Slavin, R. E., Madden, N. A., & Stevens, J. R. (1990). Cooperative learning models for the 3 R's. *Educational Leadership, 47*(4), 22-28.

Solorzano, L. (1983, August). Now, gifted children get some breaks. *U.S. News & World Report, 8,* 32.

Spearman, C. E. (1904). "General intelligence" objectively determined and measured. *American Journal of Psychology, 15*(2), 201-293.

Stanish, B. (1977). *Sunflowering.* Carthage, IL: Good Apple.

Stanish, B. (1979). *I believe in unicorns.* Carthage, IL: Good Apple.

Stanish, B. (1981). *Hippogriff feathers.* Carthage, IL: Good Apple.

Stanish, B. (1986). *Mindglow.* Carthage, IL: Good Apple.

Stanish, B. (1988). *Lessons from the hearthstone traveler.* Carthage, IL: Good Apple.

Stanley, J. C. (1991). An academic model for educating the mathematically talented. *Gifted Child Quarterly, 35,* 36-42.

Stanley, J. C., & Benbow, C. P. (1986). Youths who reason exceptionally well mathematically. In R. J. Sternberg & J. E. Davidson (Eds.), *Conceptions of giftedness* (pp. 361-387). New York: Cambridge University Press.

Starko, A. J. (1990). Life and death of a gifted program: Lessons not yet learned. *Roeper Review, 13,* 33-38.

Sternberg, R. J. (1983). Criteria for intellectual skills training. *Educational Researcher, 12*(1), 6-13.

Sternberg, R. J. (1997). *Successful intelligence.* New York: Plume.

Sternberg, R. J. (2000a). Giftedness as developing expertise. In K. A. Heller, F. J. Mönks, R. J. Sternberg, & R. F. Subotnik (Eds.), *International handbook of giftedness and talent* (2nd ed., pp. 55-66). New York: Elsevier.

Sternberg, R. J. (2000b). Wisdom as a form of giftedness. *Gifted Child Quarterly, 44,* 252-260.

Sternberg, R. J. (2003). Giftedness according to the theory of successful intelligence. In N. Colangelo & G. A. Davis (Eds.), *Handbook of gifted education* (3rd ed., pp. 88-99). Boston: Allyn & Bacon.

Strip, C. A., & Hirsch, G. (2000). *Helping gifted children soar: A practical guide for parents and teachers.* Scottsdale, AZ: Great Potential Press, Inc.

Subotnik, R. (1988). Factors from the structure of intellect model associated with gifted adolescents' problem finding in science: Research with Westinghouse science talent search winners. *Journal of Creative Behavior, 22,* 42-54.

Subotnik, R. (1998). The academic road to Capitol Hill: Personal experiences of schooling and the making of educational policy. In N. Colangelo & S. G. Assouline (Eds.), *Talent development IV: Proceedings from the 1998 Henry B. and Jocelyn Wallace National Research Symposium on Talent Development* (pp. 301-316). Scottsdale, AZ: Great Potential Press, Inc.

Tannenbaum, A. J. (1983). *Gifted children: Psychological and educational perspectives.* New York: McMillan.

Tannenbaum, A. J. (2003). Nature and nurture of giftedness. In N. Colangelo & G. A. Davis (Eds.), *Handbook of gifted education* (3rd ed., pp. 45-59). Boston: Allyn & Bacon.

Taylor, C. W. (1986). Cultivating simultaneous student growth in both multiple creative talents and knowledge. In J. S. Renzulli (Ed.), *Systems and models for developing programs for the gifted and talented* (pp. 306-350). Mansfield Center, CT: Creative Learning Press.

Teiso, C. L. (2002). *Effects of grouping and curricular practices on intermediate students' math achievement.* Storrs, CT: National Research Center on the Gifted and Talented, University of Connecticut.

Terman, L. M. (1925). *Genetic studies of genius: Vol. 1. Mental and physical traits of a thousand gifted children.* Stanford, CA: Stanford University Press.

Terman, L. M., & Oden, M. H. (1947). *Genetic studies of genius: Vol. 4. The gifted child grows up.* Stanford, CA: Stanford University Press.

Terry, A. (2003). Effects of service learning on young, gifted adolescents and their community. *Gifted Child Quarterly, 47,* 295-308.

Terry, A., & Bohnenberger, J. (2004, November). *Service learning: Inspiring change, developing potential in gifted learners.* Paper presented at the meeting of the National Association for Gifted Children, Salt Lake City, UT.

Thorndike, R. L., Hagen, E. P., & Sattler, J. M. (1986). *Stanford-Binet intelligence scale* (4th ed.). Chicago: Riverside.

Tolan, S. S. (2004, November). *Saving the world or serving it?* Paper presented at the meeting of the National Association for Gifted Children, Salt Lake City, UT.

Tomlinson, C. A. (2004, November). *Differentiating instruction and the parallel curriculum model.* Paper presented at the meeting of the National Association for Gifted Children, Salt Lake City, UT.

Torrance, E. P. (1962). *Guiding creative talent.* Englewood Cliffs, NJ: Prentice-Hall.

Torrance, E. P. (1966). *Torrance tests of creative thinking.* Bensenville, IL: Scholastic Testing Service.

Torrance, E. P. (1990). *Norms-technical manual: Figural (streamlined) forms A & B.* Bensenville, IL: Scholastic Testing Service.

Torrance, E. P. (1995). *Why fly?: A philosophy of creativity.* Norwood, NJ: Ablex.

Torrance, E. P., & Ball, O. E. (1984). *Torrance tests of creative thinking: Streamlined (revised) manual, figural A and B.* Bensenville, IL: Scholastic Testing Service.

Treffinger, D. J. (1986). Fostering effective, independent learning through individualized programming. In J. S. Renzulli (Ed.), *Systems and models for developing programs for the gifted and talented* (pp. 429-460). Mansfield Center, CT: Creative Learning Press.

Treffinger, D. J. (1995). Creative problem solving: Overview and educational implications. *Educational Psychology Review, 7,* 301-312.

Treffinger, D. J., Isaksen, S. G., & McEwen, P. (1987). *Checklist for preparing for evaluating thinking skills instructional programs*. Sarasota, FL: Center for Creative Learning.

Treffinger, D. J., & Sortore, M. R. (1992). *The programming for giftedness series. Volume I: Programming for giftedness—A contemporary view*. Sarasota, FL: Center for Creative Learning.

VanGundy, A. B. (1983). *108 ways to get a bright idea*. Englewood Cliffs, NJ: Prentice-Hall.

VanTassel-Baska, J. (1983). School counseling needs and successful strategies to meet them. In J. VanTassel-Baska (Ed.), *A practical guide to counseling the gifted in a school setting* (pp. 1-5). Reston, VA: Council for Exceptional Children.

VanTassel-Baska, J. (1986). Acceleration. In C. J. Maker (Ed.), *Critical issues in gifted education* (pp. 179-196). Rockville, MD: Aspen.

VanTassel-Baska, J. (1991). Identification of candidates for acceleration: Issues and concerns. In W. T. Southern & E. D. Jones (Eds.), *The academic acceleration of gifted children* (pp. 148-161). New York: Teachers College Press.

VanTassel-Baska, J. (1993). *Comprehensive curriculum for gifted learners*. Boston: Allyn & Bacon.

Van Tassel-Baska, J. (2003). What matters in curriculum for gifted learners: Reflections on theory, research, and practice. In N. Colangelo & G. A. Davis (Eds.), *Handbook of gifted education* (3rd ed., pp. 174-183). Boston: Allyn & Bacon.

VanTassel-Baska, J. (2004, November). *The social and emotional development of gifted children: What do we know?* Paper presented at the meeting of the National Association for Gifted Children, Salt Lake City, UT.

VanTassel-Baska, J., Avery, L. D., Struck, J., Feng, A., Bracken, B., Drummond, D., & Stambaugh, T. (2004). *William and Mary classroom observation scales* (rev. ed.). Williamsburg, VA: Center for Gifted Education, College of William and Mary.

VanTassel-Baska, J., Zuo, L., Avery, L. D., & Little, C. A. (2002). A curriculum study of gifted student learning in the language arts. *Gifted Child Quarterly, 46*, 30-44.

von Károlyi, C., Ramos-Ford, V., & Gardner, H. (2003). Multiple intelligences: A perspective on giftedness. In N. Colangelo & G. A. Davis (Eds.), *Handbook of gifted education* (3rd ed., pp. 100-112). Boston: Allyn & Bacon.

von Oech, R. (1986). *A kick in the seat of the pants*. New York: Harper & Row.

Walberg, H. J. (1988). Creativity and talent as learning. In R. J. Sternberg (Ed.), *The nature of creativity* (pp. 340-361). New York: Cambridge University Press.

Wallas, G. (1926). *The art of thought*. New York: Harcourt, Brace, & World.

Webb, J. T., Amend, E. R., Webb, N. E., Goerss, J., Beljan, P., & Olenchak, F. R. (2005). *Misdiagnosis and dual diagnoses of gifted children and adults.* Scottsdale, AZ: Great Potential Press, Inc.

Webb, R. M., Lubinski, D., & Benbow, C. P. (2004, May). *Trait constellations in intellectually able adolescents: Distinct preference patterns and educational choices at contrasting levels of spatial ability.* Presentation at the Seventh Biennial Henry B. & Jocelyn Wallace National Research Symposium on Talent Development, Iowa City, IA.

Westberg, K. L. (1996). The effect of teaching students how to invent. *Journal of Creative Behavior, 30,* 249-267.

Westberg, K. L., & Archambault, F. X. (1995). *Profiles of successful practices for high ability students in elementary classrooms.* Storrs, CT: National Research Center on the Gifted and Talented.

Winebrenner, S. (2001). *Teaching gifted kids in the regular classroom.* Minneapolis, MN: Free Spirit.

Winner, E. (1996). *Gifted children: Gifts and realities.* New York: Basic Books.

Winner, E. (2004, May). *Giftedness in the visual arts.* Keynote presentation at the Seventh Biennial Henry B. & Jocelyn Wallace National Research Symposium on Talent Development, Iowa City, IA.

Winner, E., & Martino, G. (2000). Giftedness in non-academic domains: The case of the visual arts and music. In K. A. Heller, F. J. Mönks, R. J. Sternberg, & R. F. Subotnik (Eds.), *International handbook of giftedness and talent* (2nd ed., pp. 95-110). New York: Elsevier.

Winner, E., & Martino, G. (2003). Artistic giftedness. In N. Colangelo & G. A. Davis (Eds.), *Handbook of gifted education* (3rd ed., pp. 335-349). Boston: Allyn & Bacon.

Winocur, S. L., & Maurer, P. A. (1997). Critical thinking and gifted students: Using IMPACT to improve teaching and learning. In N. Colangelo & G. A. Davis (Eds.), *Handbook of gifted education* (2nd ed., pp. 308-317). Boston: Allyn & Bacon.

Ziegler, A., & Heller, K. A. (2000). Conceptions of giftedness from a meta-theoretical perspective. In K. A. Heller, F. J. Mönks, R. J. Sternberg, & R. F. Subotnik (Eds.), *International handbook of giftedness and talent* (2nd ed., pp. 3-22). New York: Elsevier.

Zinner, J. (1985, June). Thinking makes an IMPACT. *Thrust,* 30-32.

Zirkel, P. A. (2003). *The law on gifted education.* Storrs, CT: National Research Center on the Gifted and Talented.

Zirkel, P. A. (2004). The case law on gifted education: A new look. *Gifted Child Quarterly, 48,* 309-314.

Endnotes

Preface

1   P. O. Ross (1993).

2   The author is indebted to Sylvia B. Rimm and Nicholas Colangelo, whose contributions and leadership with *Education of the Gifted and Talented* (5th ed., 2004, by Davis & Rimm) and *Handbook of Gifted Education* (3rd ed., 2003, edited by Colangelo & Davis) supplied much of the content of this book. Both books are available from Allyn & Bacon.

Chapter 1

1   C. A. Strip and G. Hirsch (2000).

2   A. W. Jensen (2004).

3   For your trivia collection, g was first described by Charles Spearman in 1904 and often is referred to as "Spearman's g."

4   A. W. Jensen (2004).

5   Latest editions are the *Stanford-Binet Intelligence Scale-Fourth Edition* and the *Wechsler Intelligence Scale for Children-IV.* That is, S-B-IV and WISC-IV.

6   The normal curve for IQ actually stretches (is *skewed*) further upward than downward. Persons have scored over 200, but never below zero.

7   D. L. Ruf (2005); M. U. M. Gross (1993a).

8   M. J. Morelock and D. H. Feldman (2003).

9   M. J. Morelock (1995, 2000). For many more examples of brilliant and prodigious children, see M. J. Morelock and D. H. Feldman (2000, 2003); M. U. M. Gross (1993a); L. S. Hollingworth (1942); and R. C. Friedman and B. Shore (2000).

10   J. D. Matarazzo (1972).

11   M. J. Morelock and D. H. Feldman (2003).

12   R. M. Webb, D. Lubinski, and C. P. Benbow (2004).

13   E. Winner (2004); E. Winner and G. Martino (2000); E. Winner (1996).

14   L. S. Hollingworth (1942); see also A. G. Klein (2002).

15   L. S. Hollingworth (1942, p. 282).

16   L. M. Terman (1925).

17   A. Binet and T. Simon (1905a, 1905b). Amusing fact: nobody knows "Th." Simon's first name.

18   M. U. M. Gross (2000, 2004).

19   M. U. M. Gross (2004). See also M. U. M. Gross (1993b).

20   J. S. Renzulli and S. M. Reis (2003).

21   Explained further in Chapter 3.

22   D. K. Simonton (2003). See also D. K. Simonton (2000).

23   J. S. Renzulli and S. M. Reis (2003).

24   C. von Károlyi, V. Ramos-Ford, and H. Gardner (2003).

25   R. J. Sternberg (2003); elaborated in Chapter 3.

26   Not many universities offer master's degrees in gifted education.

27   Detailed in Chapter 8. Print a free copy at www.nagc.org.

28   J. Oakes (1985); see also J. Goodlad and J. Oakes (1988).

29   J. A. Kulik (2003); J. S. Renzulli and S. M. Reis (1985).

30   J. S. Renzulli and S. M. Reis (1985, 1997).

31   J. S. Renzulli (1994).

32   See, for example, S. Winebrenner (2001); C. A. Strip and G. Hirsch (2000).

33   R. Brennan (2004).

34   R. E. Slavin, N. A. Madden, and R. J. Stevens (1990).

35   R. Callard-Szulgit (2003, p. 54).

36   R. Callard-Szulgit (2003, p. 54).

Chapter 2

1   L. M. Terman and M. H. Oden (1947).

2   These sources include N. Colangelo and S. G. Assouline (2000); L. J. Coleman and T. L. Cross (2000); M. U. M. Gross (2004); K. S. Han and C. Marvin (2000); L. K. Silverman (1997).

3   Characteristics of creatively gifted students appear in Chapter 11. You may peek ahead, but do not tell anyone.

4   L. K. Silverman (2002a, 2002b).

5   D. Eisenberg and E. Epstein (1981).

6   Based on D. L. Ruf (2005).

7   A. Binet and T. Simon (1905a, 1905b).

8   L. K. Silverman (2002b).

9   See, for example, C. A. Strip and G. Hirsch (2000).

10   M. U. M. Gross (1992).

11   E. Winner and G. Martino (2000, 2003).

12   R. P. Evans (2004).

13 Discussed in Chapter 12.

14 K. Dabrowski (1967); also M. M. Piechowski (1997).

15 B. Cramond (1994); see also F. Kaufmann, M. L. Kalbfleisch, and F. X. Castellanos (2000); J. A. Leroux and M. Levitt-Perlman (2000). ADHD and other problems leading to possible misdiagnoses of gifted students appear in Chapter 12.

16 P. K. Chae, J. H. Kim, and K. S. Noh (2003).

17 C. A. Strip and G. Hirsch (2000).

18 A. Roeper (2004a).

19 L. K. Silverman (1994).

20 J. VanTassel-Baska (1993, 2004).

21 Bibliotherapy essentially is increasing one's self-understanding by reading about others with similar problems.

22 D. G. Goleman (1995, p. ix).

23 J. S. Peterson (2004).

24 A. Roeper (2004a).

25 See, for example, L. K. Silverman (2002b). "Auditory sequential" often is called "verbal linear."

26 Readers' profound reactions to Silverman's book include such comments as: "My stars, I'm glad to finally have a handle for my odd way of perception. I thought I was just loony." "I could not believe my eyes.... There was a description of myself and the answer to why I always felt like an alien. I cried from the sheer relief and profundity!"

27 Partly from L. K. Silverman (2002b). See www.gifteddevelopment.com.

28 K. L. J. Isaacson (2002, pp. 6, 7).

29 K. L. J. Isaacson (2002, p. 156).

30 K. L. J. Isaacson (2002, p. 20).

31 K. L. J. Isaacson (2002, p. 90).

32 A. Roeper (2004b).

33 A. Roeper (2004b, p. 4).

34 A. Roeper (2004a).

35 For example, G. T. Betts (2004); G. T. Betts and J. K. Kercher (1999); J. S. Peterson (2004).

36 D. B. McCoach and D. Siegle (2003). See also S. M. Reis and D. B. McCoach (2003).

37 Adapted from J. F. Feldhusen (1997); L. J. Croft (2003); C. A. Strip and G. Hirsch (2000); J. VanTassel-Baska (1991); and others.

38 C. J. Mills (2003). See also the Chapter 5 discussion of Julian Stanley's (1991; C. P. Benbow and D. Lubinski, 1997) Study of Mathematically Precocious Youth (SMPY), a program that preceded his CTY.

39   C. J. Mills (2003, p. 274).

Chapter 3

1   See, for example, A. Ziegler and K. A. Heller (2000).

2   J. N. Cox, N. Daniel, and B. O. Boston (1985).

3   J. S. Renzulli (1986).

4   This definition was first articulated by S. Marland. The U.S.O.E. is now the U.S. Department of Education.

5   For example, J. S. Renzulli and S. M. Reis (2003).

6   H. Gardner (1983).

7   R. J. Sternberg (1997, 2003).

8   R. J. Sternberg (2000b).

9   R. J. Sternberg (2000a).

10   C. W. Taylor (1986).

11   A. J. Tannenbaum (2003).

12   More information can be found in A. J. Tannenbaum (1983, p. 47).

13   J. W. Atkinson (1978, p. 22).

14   F. Gagné (2003).

15   J. W. Atkinson (1978).

16   From F. A. Karnes and R. G. Marquardt (2000, 2003) and P. A. Zirkel (2003, 2004). This summary is brief and oversimplified. See Karnes and Marquardt and Zirkel for a more thorough summary of legal issues in gifted education. Zirkel (2003) presents state-by-state summaries of policies related to funding, standards, identification, programming, teacher training, and other relevant matters.

17   P. A. Zirkel (2003, p. 3).

18   P. A. Zirkel (2003, p. 4)

19   P. A. Zirkel (2003, p. 9).

20   P. A. Zirkel (2003, p. 7).

21   P. A. Zirkel (2003, p. 3).

22   P. A. Zirkel (2003, p. 3). Don't you hate sentences with three *nots* in them?

23   F. A. Karnes and R. G. Marquardt (2000, pp. 47–48).

24   P. A. Zirkel (2003, p. 7).

25   F. A. Karnes and R. G. Marquardt (2000, 2003).

26   E. S. Richert (2003, p. 82).

27   P. A. Zirkel (2003, p. 16).

28   P. A. Zirkel (2003, p. 17).

29   F. A. Karnes and R. G. Marquardt (2003, p. 595).

30 P. A. Zirkel (2003, p. 13).

31 F. A. Karnes and R. G. Marquardt (2003).

32 F. A. Karnes and R. G. Marquardt (2003).

33 F. A. Karnes and R. G. Marquardt (2000, 2003).

34 P. A. Zirkel (2004).

35 P. A. Zirkel (2003).

36 C. Russo, J. Harris, and D. Ford (1996, p. 182).

Chapter 4

1   Created by S. B. McCarney and P. D. Anderson (1998).

2   C. A. Strip and G. Hirsch (2000).

3   Statistics refresher: *Reliability* means that different tests or different ratings will produce about the same result. *Validity* means that the tests or ratings measure what they are supposed to measure. A test or rating procedure can be reliable (e.g., a yodeling test), but not valid.

4   J. N. Cox, N. Daniel, and B. O. Boston (1985).

5   Response to intervention (RTI) is one approach to identifying specific learning disabilities. It is being proposed as an alternative to the "Discrepancy Model," which waits for the student to demonstrate deficiency before intervention.

6   According to its developers, R. L. Thorndike, E. P. Hagen, and J. M. Sattler (1986).

7   Several ability tests are available in Spanish: *Aprenda: La Prueba de Logros en Expañol, Bateria-R Woodcock-Muñoz*, and *Escala de Intelligencia Wechsler Para Niños, Revisada* (C. A. Strip and G. Hirsch, 2000).

8   The Leiter-R test is available for students with such impairments.

9   D. L. Ruf (2005).

10 D. L. Ruf (2005).

11 E. P. Torrance (1966).

12 Available from Educational Assessment Service, Watertown, WI 53094.

13 Available from Gary A. Davis, 7919 Deer Run Road, Cross Plains, WI 53528.

14 J. Piirto (2004).

15 G. A. Davis (1975, 1989, 2004).

16 Chapter 11 further explores creativity. For still more information, see G. A. Davis (2004).

17 D. Siegle and T. Powell (2004).

18 D. Siegle and T. Powell (2004).

19 S. B. McCarney and P. D. Anderson (1998).

20   The *Gifted Evaluation Scale* is available at www.hes-inc.com.

21   The rating scales may be found in J. S. Renzulli and S. M. Reis (1985); J. S. Renzulli, L. Smith, A. White, C. Callahan, and R. Hartman (2001); and G. A. Davis and S. B. Rimm (2004).

22   Based on R. C. Jenkins (1979).

23   A. Y. Baldwin (1985).

24   E. S. Richert (2003).

25   E. S. Richert, J. Alvino, and R. McDonnel (1982).

26   E. S. Richert (2003).

27   J. S. Renzulli and S. M. Reis (2003).

Chapter 5

1   S. J. Cohn, B. A. Kerr, E. S. Carson, and D. Adams (2004).

2   Administration schedules are determined by each state.

3   Gifted education leader Lynn Fox (1979) originally recommended this helpful distinction.

4   N. Colangelo (2004).

5   K. B. Rogers (2002).

6   K. B. Rogers (1991).

7   S. G. Assouline, N. Colangelo, A. Lupkowski-Shoplik, J. Lipscomb, and L. Forstadt (2003).

8   Gifted education leader Julian Stanley, who himself had been accelerated, graduated from college at age 19, which surprises no one who knew him. His accomplishments on behalf of bright students, especially the mathematically gifted, were legendary, as was his support for acceleration, often over several grades.

9   D. Lohman (2004).

10   S. G. Assouline, N. Colangelo, A. Lupkowski-Shoplik, J. Lipscomb, and L. Forstadt (2003).

11   K. W. McClusky, P. A. Baker, and K. J. Massey (1996).

12   J. F. Feldhusen (1992).

13   K. B. Rogers (2002).

14   For example, N. Colangelo (2003, 2004); N. Colangelo and S. G. Assouline (2000).

15   K. B. Rogers (2002).

16   L. E. Brody and C. P. Benbow (1987); J. VanTassel-Baska (1986).

17   L. Hsu (2003, p. 212).

18   N. Colangelo (2004).

19   A. E. Robinson, T. S. Anthony, P. O. Ross, and C. Baldus (2004).

20   M. Muratori, N. Colangelo, and S. Assouline (2003).

21   M. Muratori, N. Colangelo, and S. Assouline (2003, p. 233).

22   P. B. Kolloff (2003).

23   As described in *Genius Denied*, by J. Davidson, B. Davidson, and L. Vanderkam (2004), pp. 127–132.

24   J. Davidson, B. Davidson, and L. Vanderkam (2004, p. 129).

25   J. Mathews (2001).

26   J. C. Stanley (1991); C. P. Benbow and D. Lubinski (1997). Stanley died on August 12, 2005 at age 87.

27   On the older *Stanford-Binet Intelligence Scale, Form L-M*.

28   Mostly from Lupkowski-Shoplik, Benbow, Assouline, & Brody (2003).

Chapter 6

1   Thinking skills and programs to develop them are the subject of Chapter 10.

2   S. N. Kaplan (2004a, 2004b).

3   For example, J. S. Renzulli (1977).

4   Based mostly on J. S. Renzulli (1977) and S. M. Reis and D. E. Burns (1987).

5   A. Terry (2003).

6   J. Bohnenberger and A. Terry (2004).

7   A. Terry and J. Bohnenberger (2004).

8   A. Terry and J. Bohnenberger (2004).

9   A. Terry (2003).

10   For example, J. S. Renzulli (2003).

11   J. L. Navan (2004).

12   E. D. Fiedler (2004).

13   M. Kane and A. Roeper (2004).

14   S. S. Tolan (2004).

15   J. M. Freeman and M. T. Williams (2004).

16   J. M. Freeman and M. T. Williams (2004). Freeman's enrichment program at her super-high-tech Sherwood Park School in Grand Rapids, MI, also used Odyssey of the Mind, Future Problem Solving, and Junior Great Books, all described later in this chapter.

17   Gifted Child Society (1990).

18   As two age exceptions, Iowa admits 12- to 14-year-olds to their middle school program, and Maryland reaches down to fourth grade.

19   T. L. Cross, N. R. Hernandez, and L. Coleman (1991).

20   Actor Kevin Bacon is an alum.

21 T. L. Cross, N. R. Hernandez, and L. Coleman (1991).

22 C. Kottke (2003).

23 K. Kardaras (2004).

24 Many ideas are from J. F. Feldhusen (1991) and P. Olszewski-Kubilius (2003).

25 J. N. Cox, N. Daniel, and B. O. Boston (1985, p. 74).

26 D. Prillaman and R. Richardson (1989).

27 J. N. Cox, N. Daniel, and B. O. Boston (1985, p. 66).

28 C. A. Kass, personal communication, 1990.

29 M. Ellingson, W. Haeger, and J. F. Feldhusen (1986).

30 C. Duff (2000).

31 The FPS steps are based on the Creative Problems Solving (CPS) steps described in Chapter 11.

32 The program used to be named *Olympics of the Mind*. But the picky International Olympic Committee decided that it owned the word "Olympics." OM creators Ted Gourley and Sam Micklus changed their label.

33 F. A. Karnes and T. L. Riley (1996).

34 National Association for Gifted Children (2000).

35 Adapted from the National Association for Gifted Children (2000).

36 L. Rivero (2002).

37 L. Rivero (2002, p. 5).

38 L. Rivero (2002, p. vii).

Chapter 7

1 SENG is a nonprofit organization that provides information about personal and emotional counseling issues of gifted children and adults and holds national conferences. More information is available at www.sengifted.org. Webb is now in Scottsdale, Arizona, and he remains a leader in SENG. We will look more closely at common psychological problems and counseling measures in Chapter 12.

2 F. A. Karnes and T. L. Riley (1996).

3 J. N. Cox, N. Daniel, and B. O. Boston (1985).

4 J. N. Cox, N. Daniel, and B. O. Boston (1985, pp. 42-43).

5 J. N. Cox, N. Daniel, and B. O. Boston (1985, p. 44).

6 J. N. Cox, N. Daniel, and B. O. Boston (1985, p. 43).

7 J. S. Renzulli and S. M. Reis (1985, 1991).

8 We won't confuse you by mentioning that *district resource programs* also are sometimes called *enrichment centers*.

9   J. E. Juntune (1981).

10   Note that the label *part-time special class* is ambiguously used to describe both the once-or-twice per week pullout strategy *and* spending every afternoon in a special class for the gifted.

11   The name *enrichment clusters* and the procedure were devised by J. S. Renzulli (1994, pp. 64–76). For classroom application information, see S. M. Reis, M. Gentry, and L. R. Maxfield (1998).

12   C. L. Teiso (2002).

13   See P. L. Hollingsworth (1991) and E. S. Kelble (1991) for more information about private schools for gifted students.

14   E. W. Connor (1991).

15   From the school's Internet site: http:\\theloganschool.org.

16   Conserve School is generously funded by the late James R. Lowenstine, former President of the Central Steel and Wire company in Chicago.

17   The school did accept one or two younger children as test cases, but found that there was an increased likelihood of emotional problems due to the young age.

19   Source: www.hoagiesgifted.org/schools (9/1/05).

20   "Yes, Mom, my education was supported by Wichita's Sewer Department!"

21   K. B. Rogers (2002).

22   J. F. Feldhusen and M. F. Sayler (1990).

23   J. Adams-Byers, S. S. Whitsell, and S. M. Moon (2004).

24   For example, J. S. Renzulli and S. M. Reis (1985, 2003) and S. Winebrenner (2001).

25   S. N. Kaplan (1974).

26   A. Roeper (1995, p. 111).

27   K. L. Westberg and F. X. Archambault (1995).

18   J. Davidson, B. Davidson, and L. Vanderkam (2004, p. 133).

Chapter 8

1   Would you like to print a copy for yourself? Go to www.nagc.org.

2   The version of the NAGC standards presented here is slightly rewritten and shortened. For example, in a few cases, the formal NAGC *minimum standard* largely duplicated its *guiding principle*, and so these sometimes were combined in the present interpretation. Also, the *ideal standard* sometimes duplicated the *minimum standard*, and so we eliminated one.

3   NAGC (1998, Table 1).

4   NAGC (1998, Table 2).

5   NAGC (1998, Table 3).

6   Elaborated later in this chapter under "Preparing a Written Program Plan."

7   NAGC (1998, Table 7).

8   NAGC (1998, Table 5).

9   NAGC (1998, Table 6).

10 NAGC (1998, Table 4).

11 J. C. Stanley and C. P. Benbow (1986).

12 D. Frost (1981).

13 M. L. Gentry and S. Ferriss (1999).

14 A few schools for the gifted actually include the word "creative" in their titles—for example, the Logan School for Creative Learning in Denver and the Creative Learning Center in Dallas.

15 D. J. Treffinger (1986).

16 We mentioned earlier that district G/T coordinators normally have either a master's degree in gifted education or college coursework in the area. The coordinators help establish programs, teach pullout G/T classes, and may lead thinking skill activities for entire regular classes.

17 N. Robinson (2004).

18 D. Y. Ford (2004).

19 S. B. Rimm (2004).

20 J. Naglieri (2004).

21 J. S. Renzulli (2004).

22 E. S. Richert (2003, p. 149). We described Richert's Project APOGEE in Chapter 4.

23 E. S. Richert (1997, p. 82).

24 M. M. Frasier (1994); A. Y. Baldwin (1985). The Baldwin Identification Matrix was reviewed briefly in Chapter 4.

25 Counseling and problems of the gifted are the subjects of Chapter 12.

26 J. A. Plucker (2004).

27 K. B. Rogers (2004).

28 S. N. Kaplan (2004b).

29 J. J. Gallagher (2004).

30 As noted in Chapter 5, however, attention to certain criteria—such as intellectual precocity, emotional readiness—helps guarantee the success of early admission and grade acceleration.

31 R. Subotnik (1998).

32 For example, S. K. Johnson, P. A. Haensley, G. R. Ryser, and R. F. Ford (2002).

33 J. N. Cox, N. Daniel, and B. O. Boston (1985).

34 J. H. Purcell (1995).

35   From M. G. Hickey (1990); J. H. Mosley (1982); A. J. Starko (1990); J. S. Renzulli (1995); and M. Sapon-Shevin (1994). Additional program difficulties and benefits appear in G. A. Davis and S. B. Rimm (2004).

Chapter 9

1   See, for example, J. S. Renzulli and S. M. Reis (1997, 2003).

2   Many thinking skill are reviewed in Chapter 10.

3   "Visual communication" is never explained. It is probably reading. Perhaps smiling, nodding, pointing, waving, holding up a sign, or watching TV.

4   J. S. Renzulli and S. M. Reis (2003).

5   J. S. Renzulli (1994); J. S. Renzulli and S. M. Reis (1997).

6   A brief 15-page summary appears in J. S. Renzulli and S. M. Reis (2003).

7   J. S. Renzulli and S. M. Reis (1997, p. 72).

8   J. S. Renzulli and S. M. Reis (2003, p. 186).

9   C. A. Tomlinson (2004).

10   From p. 1 of the 2004 NAGC conference program in Salt Lake City, Utah.

11   G. T. Betts and J. K. Kercher (1999).

12   "Multiple intelligences" often refers to Calvin Taylor's totem pole concept, described later in this chapter.

13   G. T. Betts (2004).

14   G. T. Betts and J. K. Kercher (1999).

15   J. VanTassel-Baska (1993, 2003); J. VanTassel-Baska, L. Zuo, L. D. Avery, and C. A. Little (2002).

16   John Feldhusen and Penny Kollof's (1986) Purdue Three-Stage Enrichment Model—oversimplified in one sentence—includes: (1) developing divergent and convergent thinking abilities, (2) developing creative problem solving abilities, and (3) developing independent study skills. Treffinger and Sortore's Programming at Four Ability Levels appears later in this chapter.

17   For further information and elaboration, see J. VanTassel-Baska (1993, 2003) and J. VanTassel-Baska, L. Zuo, L. D. Avery, and C. A. Little (2002).

18   J. VanTassel-Baska (2003, p. 181).

19   J. N. Cox, N. Daniel, and B. O. Boston (1985).

20   J. N. Cox, N. Daniel, and B. O. Boston (1985, p. 135).

21   Table 7.1 in Chapter 7 lists special schools for the gifted at all age levels.

22   Although two decades old, the 1985 Cox, Daniel, and Boston book *Educating Able Learners* remains extremely informative.

23   D. J. Treffinger and M. R. Sortore (1992).

24   C. Schlichter (1986, 1997).

25   C. W. Taylor (1986, pp. 315-316).

26 J. S. Renzulli and S. M. Reis (1997); G. T. Betts and J. K. Kercher (1999).

27 G. A. Davis and S. B. Rimm (2004); J. S. Renzulli (1986).

Chapter 10

1 A. L. Costa (2003).

2 R. J. Sternberg (1997, 2003).

3 For example, J. S. Renzulli and S. M. Reis (2003).

4 A. L. Costa (2003).

5 W. Leader (1995).

6 J. Barell (1991).

7 E. de Bono (1986).

8 E. de Bono (1985).

9 M. Lipman (1988, 1991).

10 Orange County Department of Education (1981); S. L. Winocur and P. A. Maurer (1997).

11 J. Zinner (1985).

12 R. Feuerstein (1980). Also F. R. Link (1985); S. J. Maker (1980).

13 Personal communication. For information, visit thinkingskillsuk.org/fiep.htm. See also F. R. Link (1985).

14 J. VanTassel-Baska et al. (2004).

15 S. N. Kaplan (2004a).

16 B. S. Bloom, M. D. Engelhart, E. J. Furst, W. H. Hill, and D. R. Krathwohl (1956).

17 Based on F. P. Hunkins (1976).

18 For example, E. de Bono (1983); R. J. Sternberg (1983); D. J. Treffinger, S. G. Isaksen, and P. McEwen (1987).

Chapter 11

1 Chapter 5, on acceleration strategies, is the single exception.

2 J. S. Renzulli and S. M. Reis (2003).

3 E. P. Torrance (1966, 1990); E. P. Torrance and O. E. Ball (1984).

4 See, for example, B. Cramond (1994); F. Kaufmann, M. L. Kalbfleisch, and F. X. Castellanos (2000); J. A. Leroux and M. Levitt-Perlman (2000); and J. T. Webb, et al. (2005).

5 R. L. Richards (1999); H. J. Walberg (1988).

6 R. L. Richards (1999, p. 300).

7 For example, E. P. Torrance (1962, 1966, 1995). See also Garnet W. Millar's (1995) biography, *E. Paul Torrance: "The Creativity Man."*

8 R. Subotnik (1988).

9   L. Flower and J. R. Hayes (1984).

10 A. Henry (2004, pp. G4, G11).

11 E. P. Torrance (1995).

12 A. H. Maslow (1970).

13 R. L. Richards (1999, p. 34). See also J. Piirto (2004).

14 G. Wallas (1926).

15 A. F. Osborn (1963).

16 For example, D. J. Treffinger (1995); S. G. Isaksen and L. De Schryver (2000).

17 S. J. Parnes (1981).

18 S. J. Parnes (1981, p. 131).

19 G. A. Davis (1975, 2004).

20 H. Kirschenbaum and V. L. Henderson (1989).

21 Note that usual brainstorming instructions (think of wild ideas, do not criticize others' ideas) are hardly needed, given the nature of the problems.

22 See, for example, G. A. Davis (2004).

23 G. Wallas (1926); A. F. Osborn (1963); S. J. Parnes (1981).

24 M. D. Shivvers (2004).

25 A. F. Osborn (1963).

26 R. P. Crawford (1954, p. 96).

27 A. F. Osborn (1963).

28 K. L. Westberg (1996); see also G. A. Davis (2004).

29 For example, G. A. Davis (2004); E. de Bono (1992); A. F. Osborn (1963); A. B. VanGundy (1983); R. von Oech (1986).

30 B. Stanish (1977, 1979, 1981, 1986, 1988).

Chapter 12

1   L. S. Hollingworth (1942).

2   N. Colangelo (2003). Colangelo teaches counseling psychology at the University of Iowa and counsels gifted students.

3   L. Solorzano (1983). See also J. S. Renzulli and S. Park (2000).

4   The classic book is *Perfectionism*, by M. R. Adderholdt-Elliot (1987). See also M. R. Adderholdt and J. Goldberg (1999); J. A. Baker (1996); F. A. Dixon, D. K. Lapsley, and T. A. Hanchon (2004); T. S. Greenspon (2000); M. Jacobsen (2004); and P. A. Schuler (1999).

5   R. Callard-Szulgit (2003).

6   P. A. Schuler (1999). See also D. Siegle and P. A. Schuler (2000).

7   R. Callard-Szulgit (2003, 2004).

8   B. A. Kerr (1991).

9   J. T. Webb et al. (2005, p. 37).

10   From J. T. Webb et al. (2005).

11   M. Neihart, S. M. Reis, N. M. Robinson, and S. M. Moon (2002); J. T. Webb et al. (2005).

12   J. T. Webb et al. (2005).

13   J. T. Webb et al. (2005, p. 109).

14   G. A. Davis (2004, p. 10).

15   From J. T. Webb et al. (2005).

16   From J. T. Webb et al. (2005).

17   M. Neihart (1999).

18   J. T. Webb et al. (2005, p. 126).

19   M. E. P. Seligman (1975, 1995).

20   J. T. Webb et al. (2005, p. 134).

21   J. T. Webb et al. (2005, p. 136).

22   S. J. Cohn, E. S. Carson, and D. Adams (2004).

23   S. J. Cohn (2002).

24   J. S. Peterson and H. Rischar (2000, p. 232).

25   From J. S. Peterson and H. Rischar (2000).

26   M. Neihart, S. M. Reis, N. M. Robinson, and S. M. Moon (2002, p. 94).

27   D. Fleith (2001).

28   N. Colangelo (2003).

29   B. C. Marshall (1981); B. A. Kerr (1991).

30   N. Colangelo and B. A. Kerr (1990).

31   B. A. Kerr and S. J. Cohn (2001).

32   Although they may overachieve in an area of high personal interest, such as the physics of skateboarding (Kerr and Cohn's example).

33   W. Pollock (1998).

34   B. A. Kerr and S. J. Cohn (2001).

35   B. A. Kerr and S. J. Cohn (2001, p. 11).

36   B. A. Kerr and S. J. Cohn (2001, p. 6).

37   B. A. Kerr and S. J. Cohn (2001).

38   G. W. Millar (1995).

39   J. E. Helms (1992).

40   B. A. Kerr and S. J. Cohn (2001).

41   B. A. Kerr (1994).

42   B. A. Kerr (1994, p. 103).

43 B. A. Kerr (1994, p. xiv).

44 S. B. Rimm (2003, 2005); also S. B. Rimm & S. Rimm-Kaufman (2001) and S. B. Rimm, S. Rimm-Kaufman, and I. J. Rimm (1999).

45 B. A. Kerr (1994).

46 B. A. Kerr (1991, p. 105).

47 B. A. Kerr and N. Colangelo (1988).

48 A current question in the news, no doubt intended to incite major riots, is: "Are boys smarter than girls?" Now you know the scientific answer: "Yes"—as measured at the ozone level of math ability tests. The *tiny* difference at extremely high test levels is *absolutely inconsequential* in regard to career aspirations and success. And girls are smarter than boys at the very highest levels of the English section of the ACT.

49 B. A. Kerr (1991, p. 111).

50 B. A. Kerr (1994, p. 47).

51 B. A. Kerr (1994, p. xvi).

52 S. E. R. Kurpius, B. A. Kerr, and A. Harkins (2005); B. A. Kerr, S. E. R. Kurpius, and A. Harkins (2005); also S. J. Cohn, B. A. Kerr, E. S. Carson, and D. Adams (2004).

53 J. W. Halsted (2002).

54 Halsted reproduced this catchy quote: "Some [gifted] people aren't so good at being children. But they will be good adults" (2002, p. xix).

55 Noted Halsted, this is why it is important for preschoolers to develop strong confidence in their own worth.

56 M. S. Landrum (1987).

57 J. VanTassel-Baska (1983).

58 N. Colangelo (2003, p. 377).

59 N. Colangelo (2003).

60 B. A. Kerr (1991, p. xxi).

Index of Names

Index of Subjects

Girls
    at-risk, 276
    counseling, 275
    cultural effects, 276
    gifted, 273-277, 283
    math and science abilities, 274-275
    problems of, 276-277
Global awareness, 119, 121, 140
Golda Meier School, 150-151, 159, 165
Governor's School programs, 18, 22,
    105, 123-124, 141, 159, 209, 287
Grade skipping, 10, 99, 100-101, 111,
    170, 172, 178, 183, 275
Grouping
    benefits and problems, 146-148
    cross-grade, 150, 165, 209
    gifted students, 145-166
    options, 178-179
    recommendations for teaching, 164
    temporary grouping for reading and
        math, 150
    within-class, 150, 165, 178, 209

H

Home schooling, 62, 138-140, 143, 296
Homogeneous grouping, 88, 161, 166, 285
Horton's Helpers, 121
Houston High School for the Perform-
    ing and Visual Arts, 210
How Do You Think? (HDYT), 80
Humor, 39-40, 47, 79-80, 83, 84, 90, 92,
    133, 200, 239, 249, 254, 260-263
Hurried Child, The, 18, 288

I

Idea checklists, 253, 256, 300
Idea squelchers, 248-249, 255
Identification and admission, 11, 16,
    69-94
    considerations, 11, 13, 50
    criteria, 15, 151
    recommendations and issues, 22
    restrictive, 195
Independent projects, 12, 70, 90,
    116-117, 140, 164, 168, 178, 181,
    201-203, 206, 211, 251, 253
Individualized Identification Plan (IEP),
    60
Individualized Programming Planning
    Model, 207

Individuals with Disabilities Education
    Act (IDEA), 61, 64
Instructional strategies, 115, 169, 170, 175
Instrumental Enrichment, 225, 227, 233,
    288, 298
Integrated Curriculum Model (ICM),
    207, 213-214
Intellectual excitability, x
Intellectually gifted, 27-28, 184, 262
Intelligence
    analytic, 15
    benefits of, 6-7
    creative, 15
    crystallized, 4, 20
    defined, 3
    extraordinary, 3, 6
    fluid, 4, 20
    general, 3-4, 13, 20, 51, 57, 298
    practical, 15-16
Intelligence tests, 73-76, 91
    group, 75-76
    individual, 3, 10-11, 20, 187
    weaknesses, 75-76
Internal control, 32-33, 46
International Baccalaureate (IB) pro-
    grams, 107-108, 111, 208, 210
Internet research, 115, 140, 147, 162, 179
Invent America program, 116
Iowa Acceleration Scale, 99, 285
Iowa Test of Basic Skills, 15, 78, 92, 239,
    254, 285, 293
IQ scores, 3-6, 7, 10-15, 20-21, 51, 55,
    71-77, 81, 87, 91, 186, 290

J

*Jacob K. Javits Gifted and Talented Students
    Education Act*, 64
Junior Great Books, 134, 142, 147, 211, 309

K

Keeping Track, 17, 294

L

Language
    camps, 127
    precocious, 31, 46
Leadership Characteristics Scale, 83, 87
Learned helplessness, 265, 282
Learning centers, 118-119, 140, 149,
    178, 209

About the Author

Gary A. Davis earned his Ph.D. in the Department of Psychology at the University of Wisconsin, Madison, in 1965 and served with the UW Department of Educational Psychology from 1965 until his retirement in 1994. He has authored numerous books and journal articles, mainly on problem solving, creativity, and gifted education. He created the college-level *How Do You Think?* test and the secondary school *Group Inventory for Finding Interests* (with S. Rimm).

Dr. Davis has made numerous presentations at psychology and educational psychology conferences. In 1990, he was invited to organize and chair a paper session on creative problem solving for the International Congress of Psychology meeting in Leipzig, East Germany. In 1996, he was invited to present at the Arabian Gulf University in Bahrain. Three years later, in 1999, he received an E. Paul Torrance Creativity Award from the Creativity Division of the National Association for Gifted Children. The next year, in March, 2000, he was again invited to participate in a conference at the Arabian Gulf University. His books include *Psychology of Problem Solving*, *Educational Psychology*, *Creativity Is Forever*, *Training Creative Thinking* (with J. Scott), *Teaching Values*, *Values Are Forever*, *Education of the Gifted and Talented* (with S. Rimm), and the *Handbook of Gifted Education* (with N. Colangelo).